POSITIVE HUMAN FUNCTIONING FROM A MULTIDIMENSIONAL PERSPECTIVE

VOLUME 3

PROMOTING HIGH PERFORMANCE

PSYCHOLOGY OF EMOTIONS, MOTIVATIONS AND ACTIONS

Additional books in this series can be found on Nova's website under the Series tab.

Additional E-books in this series can be found on Nova's website under the E-book tab.

PSYCHOLOGY OF EMOTIONS, MOTIVATIONS AND ACTIONS

POSITIVE HUMAN FUNCTIONING FROM A MULTIDIMENSIONAL PERSPECTIVE

VOLUME 3

PROMOTING HIGH PERFORMANCE

A. RUI GOMES
RUI RESENDE
AND
ALBERTO ALBUQUERQUE
EDITORS

nova
publishers
New York

NOTICE TO THE READER

Additional color graphics may be available in the e-book version of this book.

Library of Congress Cataloging-in-Publication Data

ISBN: 978-1-62948-974-2

ISSN: 2332-5542

Published by Nova Science Publishers, Inc. † New York

This book is dedicated to…

… all my family, especially my parents who were persistent in giving me the best life and educational opportunities, and to my wife Ana and daughters Joana and Tiago who give me the best opportunities to be a happy person every day. And I would like to recognize the six years of working together with our research group, "Adaptation, Performance and Human Development", because the insights and constant encouragement of all the members were critical for the success of this book.

A. Rui Gomes

… Inês and Artur for the meaning they bring to our existence (mine and of Ana, my wife) and the hope they carry to the future.

Rui Resende

… my parents who, if they were alive, would love to know that this book was finished. This book happened because of them; I owe almost everything to them.

To my wife, Suzana, who has always been the great supporter of my personal and professional life.

To my children (Marta, Tiago, Diana, and João) and grandchildren (Zé, Clara, and Francisco), who are the most important people in my life. The success of this book is also their own success.

I also thank my companions on this journey, Rui Gomes and Rui Resende.

Alberto Albuquerque

CONTENTS

EDITOR'S NOTE

THE BOOK

"Positive human functioning from a multidimensional perspective" tries to understand factors involved in the human adaptation to stressful situations, the human adoption of healthy life styles, and the human training for high performance. Considering these main goals, the book is edited in three volumes related to human adaptation, human development, and human training.

For all volumes, the opening chapter is written by Mihaly Csikszentmihalyi. This chapter addresses the fascinating topic titled "Towards a fully functioning humanity", serving as an introduction to how positive psychology can contribute to the flourishing of humanity in the future.

VOLUME 1

Positive human functioning from a multidimensional perspective: Promoting stress adaptation

The main goal of this volume is to analyze human adaptation to life situations. Using examples of work and sport contexts, topics related to stress, emotions, and burnout, both from a theoretical and an empirical point of view, are discussed. How to promote positive adaptation to adaptational contexts is addressed by authors Cary Cooper, Michael P. Leiter, Ronald J. Burke, Marc Jones, Thomas Raedeke, Peter Crocker, and many others.

VOLUME 2

Positive human functioning from a multidimensional perspective: Promoting healthy life styles

The main goal of this volume is to analyze human development through the life cycle. Using examples of life skills and exercise practice, topics related to how to organize life skills programs for children, youth, and adults and how to assume healthy life styles by doing regular exercise are discussed. How to promote positive development across the life cycle is addressed by authors Martin I. Jones, Daniel Gould, Tanya Forneris, James E. Maddux, Kimberley L. Gammage, Ali A. Weinstein, and many others.

VOLUME 3

Positive human functioning from a multidimensional perspective: Promoting high performance

The main goal of this volume is to analyze human training to achievement contexts. Using examples of developmental and high performance contexts, topics related to talent development, athletes and teams' training for high performance situations, and leaders' training to maximum professional efficacy (including mainly the cases of sports coaches) are discussed. How to coach individuals, teams, and leaders to high performance is addressed by authors Jean Côté, Eduardo Salas, Robert S. Weinberg, Wade Gilbert, Gordon Bloom, Harold Riemer, and many others.

This is the journey through the complexity of human functioning being assumed in this book; it is a broad and deep perspective of the factors involved in human adaptation, human development, and human training. In sum, this book addresses the fundamental challenge referred to by Kennon M. Sheldon in the Preface of this book, namely, how to make things go right in our lives.

PREFACE

It is with great pleasure that I write this preface, in part because it takes me back to some "golden days" of my professional youth. In 1999 I was fortunate enough to be invited to the Akumal conference, which was held on the Yucatan peninsula, in Mexico. This was the conference which formally hatched the positive psychology movement. It was an exciting time, as eminent researchers (such as Martin Seligman, Mihaly Csikszentmihalyi, and Alice Isen) and "promising young scholars" (such as me, Barbara Fredrickson, and Sonja Lyubomirsky) debated how to proceed. We considered topics such as whether "positive psychology" was the right name for the movement; whether positive psychology was just about people, or whether it should also about relationships, organizations, and institutions; whether positive psychology should have a manifesto, and if so, what should be in it; whether positive psychology was just humanism in a different guise; whether our group itself was too elitist, as we enjoyed our luxury accommodations in a tropical paradise; and much more. Although in subsequent years there were two further conferences held at Akumal, none matched the first for intensity and novelty.

Today, 15 years later, I am very pleased that the positive psychology movement has continued to expand and develop. The robustness of the movement is a testament to people's desire for, and even hunger for, positive psychological perspectives. Twentieth century psychology focused overmuch on human problems, difficulties, errors, and pathologies. It produced manuals for fixing what can go wrong in life, which of course is a depressingly long list. But what about a 21st century "owner's manual" for making things go right in life, for doing what we want? The owner's manuals of our cars do not mainly tell us how to fix problems; instead, they tell us how to operate the car, to do what we want (e.g., how to use the variable-intermittent windshield wiper function, how to check and change the oil). Typically, there is a much shorter problem-solving section at the end of such manuals.

Similarly, the owner's manual for operating human beings could potentially be much longer, or at least more important, than the manual for fixing human beings. This might occur in part because when humans function well, many so-called "problems" evaporate or fix themselves of their own accord. Human misery is in part a function of maladaptive forms of interpreting, construing, and coping with ongoing experience. One enduring premise of positive psychology is that the right sort of "mental tune-up" can sometimes get people to simply replace their maladaptive ways of experiencing, with much more adaptive and proactive ways of experiencing. As one example, a fairly short training in mindfulness meditation can turn a person's experience from feelings of stress, anxiety, and dread of being overwhelmed and unmasked, to a recognition that these feelings are possibilities only -- possibilities that one now has the tools to avoid or sidestep. This new and more adaptive way of encountering stress, rather quickly learned, can sometimes quickly transform an anxious, flustered approach to a much more confident approach to the tasks at hand. Maybe it is better to let problems resolve naturally, rather than try to apply a band-aid to each problem – better to find a single global solution, rather than a host of patches and stop-gaps.

In short, positive psychology is dedicated to balancing the psychological research equation by focusing on human strengths, virtues, health, and happiness in addition to human weaknesses, failings, sicknesses, and unhappiness. And it is working: a recent search found more than 3500 "hits" in PsychInfo for the topic "positive psychology," a number which does not even include the thousands of articles and chapters that address positive psychology themes and topics (happiness, strengths, virtues, skills, capacities) without explicitly referencing the term positive psychology. In addition, dozens of books have been published on positive psychology, including my own "Optimal Human Being: An integrated multilevel perspective" (Sheldon, 2004), "Self-determination theory in the clinic: Motivating mental and physical health" (Sheldon, Williams, & Joiner, 2001) and "Designing positive psychology: Taking stock and moving forward" (Sheldon, Kashdan, & Steger, 2011).

This brings me to the special pleasure of introducing this book with three volumes. As a researcher I have long been interested in what promotes optimal functioning and the highest degree of happiness in individuals. I have mostly taken a personality perspective on this question, focusing on peoples' goals, values, identities, traits, motives, psychological needs, narratives, and more. Typical research studies of mine attempt to predict change in some positive individual outcome (i.e., well-being, happiness, resilience, need-satisfaction) from prior changes in some positive personality characteristic (i.e. goal-attainment, value change, identity development) or from some other positive experience (i.e., a mindfulness intervention, a goal planning procedure, a positive activity induction). Interested readers might see my book "Optimal human being: A integrated multi-level perspective" (Sheldon, 2004) for a summary of conclusions regarding what personality, social, and cultural characteristics are most conducive to promoting human health and wellness.

The authors in the current book, *Positive human functioning from a multidimensional perspective*, have addressed the very same types of question, while taking a somewhat different route. The book has three volumes, each of which addresses optimal human functioning in a particular way. In the first section the book addresses positive human adaptation, in an abstract sense. This includes personality processes but also a variety of other processes, from biological to social. However, there is a twist: the authors focus on adaptation primarily in work and sport contexts, two very important achievement settings for human beings. Thus, there is very tangible, applied angle taken throughout the book, meaning that the book is not just a set of airy abstractions. The second volume of the book addresses positive development, as derived from the positive processes discussed in the first section. Especially at work and in sport, how can people be helped to develop a healthy style of life, one which maximizes their achievement potential and also maximizes their physical and psychological health? The third volume is the most concrete of all, addressing specific training techniques to human performance: how to teach and train individuals, teams, and leaders to best adapt to the present, and best develop in the future. Thus the book leads the reader through the entire process of understanding the nature of positive adaptation, understanding the ways in which positive development occurs given this nature, and understanding the specific ways that this information may be applied for the benefit of real individuals. I commend the editors for settling on this framework, and expect that the book will be popular with a wide spectrum of audiences ranging from theorists to researchers to clinicians to practitioners to teachers, coaches, and even parents. In fact, I can't wait to get my own copy!

Kennon M. Sheldon
Department of Psychology
University of Missouri
Columbia. USA

REFERENCES

Sheldon, K. M. (2004). *Optimal human being: An integrated multi-level perspective.* New Jersey: Erlbaum.

Sheldon, K. M., Kashdan, T., & Steger, M. (Eds) (2011). *Designing the future of positive psychology: Taking stock and moving forward.* Oxford University Press.

Sheldon, K. M., Williams, G., & Joiner, T. (2003). *Self-Determination Theory in the Clinic: Motivating physical and mental health.* Yale University Press.

OPENING CHAPTER

In: Positive Human Functioning …   ISBN: 978-1-62948-974-2
Editors: A. R. Gomes, R. Resende & A. Albuquerque   © 2014 Nova Science Publishers, Inc.

Chapter 1

TOWARDS A FULLY FUNCTIONING HUMANITY

Mihaly Csikszentmihalyi

School of Behavioral and Organizational Sciences, Claremont Graduate University, US

ABSTRACT

The chapter reviews briefly the emergence of Positive Psychology in the context of the evolution of psychology as a science, and it suggests how it might contribute to the flourishing of humanity in the future. Focusing on the recently evolved human capacities for self-reflective consciousness and agency, we are now in the position of playing a crucial role in the survival and further evolution of the human species. Whatever decisions we shall collectively take should be informed by a scientific knowledge of the human capacity for creative, constructive – as well as destructive – action, and of the ways these positive capacities can best be applied to shaping a desirable future.

ON THE DEFINITION OF A FUNCTIONING HUMAN

The study of human beings conducted by human beings has adopted the conceptual models and the methods that have served the physical and biological sciences so well in the last few centuries. The followers of the sociology of Auguste Comte or the psychology of B.F. Skinner considered people as organisms that followed behavior patterns established by external stimuli. Men and women had little or no choice over their destiny. The discoveries of Darwin and later those of genetics added even more weight to a reductionist determinism in the study of humanity. The quip attributed to an eminent life scientist: "Molecules are real. All the rest is sociology" is symptomatic of how too many "hard" scientists dismiss explanations of what men and women do that are not based on the most elementary units of organic matter.

Yet, just as biology cannot be reduced to chemistry without losing sight of what makes life different from inorganic processes, so we cannot reduce human life to the simplest organic processes without losing sight of the unique properties of human existence. These properties must include the development of the frontal and pre-frontal cortices – a result of slow biological evolution – which in turn made possible the emergence of *consciousness*, which is an attribute not yet found outside our species. In many ways it is more accurate to say about humans that: "Consciousness is real. All the rest is biology".

Of course, trying to define consciousness is a controversial matter – not surprisingly, since it is such a late gift of evolution. In this context I want to focus on a minimalist definition; by consciousness I mean the information in the mind that is available to our attention. So it includes early genetic instructions like hunger, fear, and sexual attraction. But it also includes our earliest individual memories, the instructions of our parents and our tribe. And it includes learned responses to beauty, to values like generosity or courage. And above all else, consciousness includes the ability to choose from the information it contains a course of action that would not be always predictable even if we had perfect knowledge of the individual's genetic instructions or previous experience (Csikszentmihalyi, 1993).

For a long time, however, the social sciences, and psychology in particular, have tried to ignore the inconvenience that consciousness introduced into the familiar mechanistic conception of the universe that Galileo, Newton, and Leibnitz had so elegantly developed to account for the movements of planets and of molecules. And of course the social sciences have discovered many interesting and important things about the human species. For instance, that most of the time we act as if we were simple robots programmed for self-aggrandizement, for getting the most pleasure available, for using violence and deceit to reach predictable, selfish goals.

Impressed by its own sagacity, the social sciences have then drawn the conclusion that people, like billiard balls, were simply pushed one way or another by outside forces. Of course the forces acting on humans were much more varied and conflicting than those typically propelling billiard balls; but the general idea was by and large the same. So to make matters simple, many of our colleagues concluded that consciousness and its derivatives were merely epiphenomena they could safely dismiss. Ignoring the last few tens of thousands of years of evolution, they found the keys to human action in the behavior of rats and monkeys, while forgetting the wise words attributed to Albert Einstein; "Make things as simple as possible, but not simpler."

The first psychological laboratory, founded by Wilhelm Wundt in Leipzig about a hundred years ago, tried to make the measurement of human behavior as simple as possible concentrating on neurological and muscular response-times; his followers on both sides of the Atlantic followed in his footsteps – arguably reducing the study humankind to something that is too simple to reveal the range of human possibilities.

Of course, there have been many eminent psychologists, ranging from Carl Jung to Abraham Maslow and Karl Rogers, who felt that in pursuing simple rigor psychology had made a bad bargain. Nevertheless, almost all the young people entering graduate programs in psychology were taught that the future of the discipline required that they become more and more reductionist, until they reached the blessed state of technicians dressed in white gowns, who work surrounded by microscopes, computers, and the latest paraphernalia of high technology.

Yet as time passed it became increasingly obvious that there were many questions the 20th century paradigm of psychology had a hard time resolving. For instance Roy Baumeister, a noted social psychologist, asked himself how it was possible for so many new ideas, lifestyles, technologies to appear in human history if everything we did was a product of the past. Clearly the intervention of human consciousness must be a game changer, creating novelties that arose from imagination as well as from the past. He and Marty Seligman (a staunch behaviorist in his youth) developed the notion of *prospection* to account for that part of human action that was determined not only by the past, but also by future goals anticipated in the mind (Seligman, Railton, Baumeister, & Sripada, 2013). Behaviors such as generosity, filial piety, patriotism, altruism might be built on inheritance and learning, but become actual influences on conduct when they are named, defined, and taught.

Baumeister (2008) went so far as resuscitating the long discredited concept of *free will*, arguing that the belief in conscious choice was by itself a recently evolved causal factor in human action. If you believed you had a choice, this belief allowed you to choose between the various options – overriding, if necessary, both the genetic and the social instructions programmed in consciousness.

In fact, ignoring this new development in the functioning of the brain – the ability to make choices among alternatives – leads to untenable results. If people have no other options than to simply act out the instructions contained in their genes or their environment, it would make no sense to hold them responsible for their actions. Instead of relatively autonomous agents, people would be seen as complex robots. Then a well-functioning human being would be one that went through life satisfying his biologically programmed needs as much as possible, while interfering as little as possible with the needs of other human beings. In many ways this would not be such a bad definition, yet it seems to fall far short of the image of man that we are used to. Not to mention that the logic of this simple definition allows individuals who are convinced of their genetic superiority to dominate and exploit the rest of the population in order to satisfy their own requirements for wellbeing. Recent history has shown what can happen when the megalomania of a Hitler or a Stalin becomes translated into public policy.

The view of what a well-functioning person is like is quite different in the emerging perspective of positive psychology. Human beings are seen as a work in progress; tied by strong bonds to the past, but acquiring new powers due to both biological and to cultural evolution. Of course there is no guarantee that this process will have a positive outcome. It will depend in large part on our own decisions whether the future will be flourishing or dismal. But the first step towards a better future is to realize that we can choose, and that it is our choices that will make the difference. So a fully functioning human being, according to this perspective, is a person who accepts his or her unique position in history, with all the bio-social facticity attached, and accepts the responsibility to work for a future in synchrony with the arc of evolutionary movement towards higher levels of complexity. In other words, a fully functioning human being accepts responsibility for piloting spaceship earth.

MY PERSONAL JOURNEY TO POSITIVE PSYCHOLOGY

The considerations described in the previous sections, important as they are, were not the main reasons that I became dissatisfied with the psychology of the past century. The reasons were much less rational and more experiential. As a child during World War II, I saw some people act with honesty and dignity, others with craven selfishness. I knew that my father, who was the Hungarian consul in the Italian city of Fiume (now Rijeka, in Croatia), was issuing visas and passports to fugitives trying to escape from the Fascist authorities, even though we knew that his superiors in the State Department might fire or even have him imprisoned for flaunting the official policy. He did not ask for payment for this service, in fact he sometime had to lend his own money to people who had not the means to make an escape. By the time I was ten years old, the entire social, cultural, economic, and political system collapsed; relatives (including my older brother Károly) were killed; people lost their jobs, property – and all too often, their reason for living. It seemed to me that some of the adults I knew made choices that kept them sane, efficient, and helpful to others – while others made choices that left them bitter and useless to themselves and everyone else.

In the midst of all the shooting, the fires, the fear and the hunger I made an unexpected discovery. An older cousin taught me how to play chess. After learning the basic moves, I found that the game had such a power over my mind that I hardly noticed a building collapse across the street, or a burst of machine-gun bullets miss the window by inches. I learned something that 30 years later I found out philosophers from Heraclitus to Plato and down to Nietzsche and Sartre had remarked on for many centuries: play provides an alternative reality where we can feel in harmony with the world, and feel more free than at any time in "real" life.

Later on, I had the same experience while mountain climbing, or playing soccer and basketball. All these "games" were able to limit reality to a playing field and a set of rules for action, providing a small world sheltered from the larger world; a small world where one could act with clear purpose and full engagement. A few years later I discovered that the same experience of full concentration could be had from activities where you made up your own purpose, determined your own goals: for instance painting, writing short stories, or even when reading a good novel that forced you to imagine how it would be to be the character in the story, in a place and a time different from the one your body happened to be in.

By the time I was 20 years old, I had decided to become a psychologist, to understand better why some people could live relatively happy lives, while others were just marking time in misery. This was not easy to do in post-war Europe, especially for someone like me who had dropped out of high school at age 14 in order to work and survive. After a long wait for a visa, I entered the USA at age 22, with $1,25 in my pocket, found a nighttime job as a cashier in a large Chicago hotel, while during the day I worked on a BA in psychology at the University of Illinois, where I was admitted after taking an equivalency exam.

But the psychology being taught in the mid-50s was not what I had expected after having read the works of Carl Jung in Europe. It was a discipline that prided itself on its objectivity, seeing human behavior as no different from the behavior of the great apes, or even rats. It indulged in what the social philosopher Hannah Arendt has called the "debunking perspective" of the social sciences emerging out of the older natural sciences, eager to demonstrate their own scientific rigor. Many times over the next ten years I was tempted to leave the study of psychology, and do something less fanciful: like become a forest ranger, or a fiction writer (I had been able to place two short autobiographical stories that I wrote for an English language class in the elite literary magazine *The New Yorker*). For better or for worse, with the help of some wise and understanding teachers at the University of Chicago where I transferred, I went on to finish my doctorate – after which I was hired to teach sociology and anthropology (two subjects that interested me, but had taken just one course in each during my academic career) at a small but vibrant liberal arts college. I taught there for five years, then was invited back to the faculty of the prestigious University of Chicago, where I slowly developed the concept of *flow* and the systems model of creativity, in an effort to move psychology in a direction that was closer to what I thought it should be.

THE PUBLIC STORY OF THE FIRST TEN YEARS OF POSITIVE PSYCHOLOGY

In the winter of 1998, my wife and I booked a week's vacation at a resort on the Kona Coast of Hawaii. By a rare coincidence, the second day of our stay Martin Seligman and I almost literally ran into each other at a nearby beach. We had met before at psychology meetings, but never had a chance to really talk. Now it turned out that he and his family were staying at the same resort we were. So for the next few days, from breakfast to after dinner, we exchanged ideas about our profession. This was the year before Marty became President of the APA, and he was aware that a once-in-a-lifetime opportunity to leave a legacy was about to open for him.

Even though our training and life experiences were quite different, we soon felt that our views of where psychology should be moving were very similar. We both felt that the reductionist model of man that psychologists, in their desire to appear hard-nosed scientists, had been following for the past few generations, was missing the point. After they discovered behind the veil of Victorian pieties that human beings were obeying instincts inherited from ancestors indistinguishable from apes, psychologists were left with the conclusion that human behavior was *nothing but* animal behavior. The accomplishments that we are so proud of, like the use of language that resulted in the works of Homer, Dante, Shakespeare, or Goethe, are simple side-effects of an evolutionary pattern based on complex thought processes that were selected because they gave our species an advantage in the struggle for survival. Similarly love, gratitude, courage, spirituality, are not things we cherish for their own sake, but because they help us endure, survive, and reproduce.

Neither Marty nor I were comfortable with this. Somewhere the baby had been thrown out with the bathwater. The development of the pre-frontal cortex in humans had been a game-changer; people have developed internal representations of goals they hope for, things they desire and love – and these have become real and important in determining their behavior. It was time, we felt, for psychologists to take seriously the whole spectrum of human functioning, not just the part of it we share with our simian ancestry.

Of course, by then many people outside of psychology and some within it had come to the same conclusion. The teachings of Maslow and Rogers, which spawned Humanistic Psychology, are eloquent examples. However, we felt that the critique of scientism usually falls into the opposite extreme, ignoring the insights of science while rejecting its misapplied reductionism. So where did that leave us? We decided to try formulating our views in a way that our colleagues in the profession would feel compelling. But the effects of whatever we wrote would take years to bring fruit, and by then Marty's presidency would long be over. How could we implement what we thought was an important enrichment of the science of psychology within a shorter span of time?

It was at this point that my PhD thesis and subsequent publications on creativity began to suggest some choices – even though, at the time, I was not consciously aware of it (Csikszentmihalyi, 1996; Getzels & Csikszentmihalyi, 1976). What I knew – based on

8

Mihaly Csikszentmihalyi

Thomas Kuhn's work with the rise of new paradigms in science, and Pierre Bourdieu's analysis of cultural change – was that it is easier to influence the future course of a science by appealing to the curiosity and energy of younger scientists than by trying to influence the already established practitioners, who had much to lose and little to gain from a new perspective that could replace the one in which they had prospered. So instead of appealing to our peers, we decided to invite a small group of young psychologists for a week of meetings, to discuss what these ideas might contribute to the future of psychology.

A few key decisions we made at this point turned out to be inspired. Marty, because of his recent campaigning for the APA Presidency, knew most of the leading psychologists in the country. We decided to write to 50 of these individuals, asking them to nominate a former student less than 30 years of age, who might be sympathetic to our ideas, *and who had a chance to become chairpersons of their psychology departments before they reached the age of 50*. We would then write to the nominated individuals, ask them for their c.v.'s, and invite about twenty to spend a week in a sleepy fishing village Marty knew in Quintana Roo – on the "Mayan Riviera" of Mexico.

This way, we thought, we might kick-start the formation of a *field*. As to the *domain*, -- or the specific content and rules that distinguish one discipline from others -- we thought that there were enough books and articles at the margins of the psychological literature to get things started; the newly constituted field would then take over with the contribution of their own work. If the domain and field turned out to have credibility, it would then attract *persons* to the new sub-domain, which after long deliberations we came to call *Positive Psychology* (Seligman & Csikszentmihalyi, 2000).

The week we spent in the village of Akumal with the twenty young colleagues went by very rapidly, but left an enduring mark on the profession. Of these participants, several (e.g. Barbara Fredrikson, Jonathan Haidt, Corey Keyes, Sonja Ljiubomirski, Ken Sheldon) have written their own book (or books) on various aspects of positive psychology. Practically all of them are still very actively shaping the emerging sub-domain. And they are not alone: the Third World Congress of positive psychology took place in Los Angeles in 2013, with the attendance of about 1500 psychologists form all over the world. It was an unqualified success both in scientific and humane terms. Earlier world congresses have taken place in the United Kingdom and in Philadelphia; European Congresses were held in Stresa, (Italy); Opatija, near Rijeka, the town I was born in, (Croatia); Copenhagen (Denmark), and in the summer of 2012 in Moscow, Russia.

This astonishing growth was made possible in large part because so many young people felt that psychology needed to expand in new directions. Thus our ideas resonated with the spirit of the times. But they needed the exertions of the emerging sub-field to become actualized. Here Marty played an indispensible role. For instance, he was able to secure the financial support of the Templeton Foundation to establish a series of prizes for young scholars in positive psychology, including a yearly $100,000 first prize, which was (and still is) one of the largest monetary recognition for breakthrough research done in psychology. The symbolic significance of such support sent the message that the new sub-domain was not a fleeting affair, but was taken seriously by the world at large. The Meyerson Foundation then helped funding the VIA *Dictionary of Strengths* (intended as the Positive Psychology counterpart to the DSM IV dictionary of psychopathology), spearheaded by Chris Petersen (2006).

Marty also started the highly successful and influential MA program in positive psychology at the University of Pennsylvania, which has inspired similar programs in Denmark, Italy, South Korea, and elsewhere. In 2006 the first PhD program in Positive Psychology was started at the Claremont Graduate University in California. The *Journal of Positive Psychology* also started publishing a few years ago, and is gaining momentum and reputation.

WHAT POSITIVE PSYCHOLOGY CONTRIBUTES TO THE UNDERSTANDING OF HUMAN BEHAVIOR

At this point in its development, Positive Psychology claims to have three main goals. The first is to understand and learn how to improve the momentary affective states of individuals. The second is to study more permanent traits (or "strengths") that some individuals possess, and learn how those who lack them can acquire them. The third addresses the question of how institutions, from families to nation states, might help develop such strengths.

Peterson and Seligman's classification of strengths and virtues (2004) has become one of the main planks of positive psychology. Based on an extensive review of what "virtues" are universal to mankind, it consists of 24 "strengths" grouped in 6 higher-order virtues. Anyone can measure his or her strengths against established norms, and establish their *signature strengths*.

This attempt to single out some traits and calling them *strengths* has caused many lifted eyebrows in the psychological community. Positive psychology has been accused of introducing value judgments in what should be an objective science. But of course psychology, like medicine or even biology, has never been value-free. It has always tried to avoid disease and considered pathology a condition to be changed. What positive psychology has done is simply develop the other end of the continuum from pathology to flourishing, by identifying various kinds of traits and conditions that lead to good physical and mental health. Psychiatrists and psychologists have been turning the pages of the thick tomes of the *Diagnostic and Statistical Manual*, or DSM, which lists the symptoms and possible cures of all that can go awry in the human mind. What Peterson and Seligman did was to try to develop the opposite, which they subtitled *A Dictionary of the Sanities*.

THE FUTURE OF POSITIVE PSYCHOLOGY

The amount of research, publications, meetings and organizations that have been inspired by positive psychology has indeed been incredibly widespread. A simple linear projection into the future would suggest that this "movement" will have hundreds of thousand members in just a few years, and that its influence will permeate institutions around the world, from schools to families, from businesses to governments. History, however, rarely proceeds in a linear direction. Even the history of science is not quite linear: physicists at the beginning of the 20th century thought that their science had exhausted all the mysteries of matter; then in the first quarter of the century the advent of subatomic physics expanded the horizons of the science in unimaginable directions; and by the end of the century physicists had acquired the mantle of the magi of knowledge. Yet only a few decades later new horizons beacon: microbiology, astrophysics, nanotechnologies – to name just a few domains on the ascendant – promise to answer the mysteries of creation.

So whether positive psychology will keep its momentum going is by no means certain. One thing to remember that the higher and swifter a new idea raises, the faster and farther it can fall. The danger with positive psychology is that if too many people expect quick and easy solutions to their lives, and these don't happen, then they turn against the idea and ruin its reputation. Yet many self-styled "life coaches" believe that positive psychology provides a panacea they can promote to clients who are unhappy with their lives. It is important to remember that positive psychology is not a miracle cure. It is simply a perspective that can help scientists advance knowledge in ways that in the fullness of time will allow individuals to improve the quality of their lives. It will not be an easy journey, or a quick one. But it is absolutely necessary that we start on it.

As for what direction Positive Psychology is likely to go in the foreseeable future I must confess ignorance. The problem is that no future course of events is really "foreseeable", especially when it depends on human action. The variables are too many, and too complexly interrelated. I think speculating about what will happen in the future is a worthless exercise.

I do, however, have very strong opinions about what Positive Psychology *should* be trying to accomplish. In fact, my ambitions in that respect are rather extravagant. It seems to me that three main tasks will determine whether humankind will prosper in the future, or cease to exist. I don't know if we will have the vision, and the resolution, to take on these tasks and bring them to a positive resolution. But we have come to a point in the evolution of the species where we can, and we must, take control of our own lives. If we do not, or if we make the wrong choices, we will have only ourselves to blame for our demise.

The first task is to decide *Who We Want To Be*. Each human group that has survived in the past had an idea of what a person should be like, and tried – never with complete success – to educate, train, inspire and force people to come close to that ideal. Cultures changed rather slowly in the past, adjusting their notion of desirable personhood over generations as technologies, political and economic realities changed. The changes that cultures have undergone in the past two generations are more rapid and more radical than they had ever been. On the other hand, the image of what constitutes a good person has not caught up with the new realities. Yet human genetics and biotechnology have now reached the point that we can imagine ordering "designer babies" from illustrated catalogs, with genes tweaked to facilitate learning, or domineering, or nurturing – as well, of course, as hair and eye color. What choices will we make? And who will make them? In a few years, these questions will have to be faced. And Positive Psychology should be in a position to help inform the public discourse on these issues, pointing out the long-term as well as the short-term results of various actions to the self and to the community.

The second task we will have to decide is, *Where do We Want To Live*? On a planet that increasingly resembles a Garden of Eden, or a planet that has become an orbiting garbage can? Which of these outcomes will come true, depends exclusively on us. And again, Positive Psychology should help the other social sciences involved in policies of sustainability and conservation, to show people how their lifestyle habits, and the policies of their elected officials, can create a better world for our grandchildren to live in.

Finally, the last question is, *What Shall We Do*? The cultural changes of the past century have affected every aspect of our lives: What kind of families our children are born into, what education they receive, what opportunities to express themselves they have, what jobs are open for them... and so on and on, until the ever prolonged period of late life, where people feel increasingly useless and abandoned...

In many parts of the world, the normal development of teenagers, and even children, is interrupted and twisted forever by narcotics dealers, diamond smugglers, or sweatshops. In Africa alone, the number of children who are given weapons and taught to kill is estimated at a minimum of 100,000. In the richer and more stable countries of the world, millions of young people, deprived of a context of development and with nothing to do, become prey of illusory chemical solutions. Similarly, untold millions of adults are left without a job, without a role in society. Those fortunate enough to find employment often work at jobs that were not designed to improve the life of workers, but to generate the maximum profit to wealthy investors.

Positive psychology will deserve its place among the great achievements of mankind to the extent that it takes seriously its responsibility to contribute the accumulating knowledge it produces to the solution of these three challenges facing us: To decide who we will be, where will we live, and what will we do.

REFERENCES

Baumeister, R. (2008). *Are we free? Psychology and free will*. New York: Oxford University Press.

Csikszentmihalyi, M. (1993). *The evolving self: A psychology for the third millennium*. New York: Harper/Collins.

Csikszentmihalyi, M. (1996). *Creativity: Flow and the psychology of discovery and invention*. New York: Harper/Collins.

Getzels, J. W. & Csikszentmihalyi, M. (1976). *The creative vision*. New York: Wiley.

Peterson, C. (2006). *A primer in positive psychology*. New York: Oxford University Press.

Peterson, C. & Seligman E. M. (2004*) Character strengths and virtues: A handbook of classification*. New York: Oxford University Press.

Seligman, M. E. & Csikszentmihalyi, M. (2000). Positive psychology: An introduction. *American Psychologist, 55*, 1, 5-14.

Seligman, M. E., Railton, P., Baumeister, R. & Sripada, C. (2013). Navigating into the future or driven by the past. *Perspectives on Psychological Science, 8*(2), 119-141.

INDIVIDUALS AND TEAMS

In: Positive Human Functioning …   ISBN: 978-1-62948-974-2
Editors: A. R. Gomes, R. Resende & A. Albuquerque   © 2014 Nova Science Publishers, Inc.

Chapter 2

BIRTH ADVANTAGES, SOCIAL AGENTS, AND TALENT DEVELOPMENT IN YOUTH SPORT

David J. Hancock[1,2] and Jean Côté[2]
[1]Division of Allied Health Sciences
Indiana University Kokomo. Kokomo, Indiana, US
[2]School of Kinesiology and Health Studies
Queen's University. Kingston, Ontario, Canada

ABSTRACT

Several factors might impact youth talent development in sport. Among the many variables are two influences: dynamic (e.g., practice hours, coaching) and static (e.g., socioeconomic status, birth order). In this chapter, we focus on two static influences, relative age and birthplace, which we term *birth advantages*. We consider birth advantages to be static influences, as you cannot change your birthdate or birthplace; however, these advantages can be regulated by parents, coaches, and athletes. This chapter details the ways in which birth advantages can be reduced, making sport more equitable for all participants. By reducing birth advantages, youth talent development (such as training outcomes and elite sport participation) would not be dictated by arbitrary factors such as when an athlete is born; rather, they would be determined by talent and skill.

INTRODUCTION

Imagine being born on January 1, 2005. On your first day of school, you realize you are taller than most of your peers. During your first soccer tryouts, the coach admires your taller stature, and you are selected as a starting player on the competitive team. Throughout childhood, adolescence, and even adulthood, you notice these physical advantages. Now imagine you were born December 31, 2005 and you are shorter than all your peers, never get selected to a competitive team, and feel disadvantaged throughout your life. This hypothetical tale encapsulates how advantages at birth can impact an individual's life. In this chapter, we will discuss similar advantages in the context of youth sport.

Youth sport is arguably the most important stage of sport development, as the experiences children gain during this period are related to eventual sport participation patterns. For instance, children with negative youth sport experiences are more likely to drop out of sport later in life (Fraser-Thomas, Côté, & Deakin, 2008), while children with positive youth sport experiences are more likely to continue recreational sport participation as adults – and for a select few, elite sport participation (Côté, Lidor, & Hackfort, 2009). As such, understanding the training environment in youth sport is paramount.

Youth sport training can be affected in several ways. Many of these influences are dynamic, meaning it can be changed or altered throughout development; for example, the balance between deliberate practice and deliberate play in sport. Deliberate practice is training with the main purpose of skill development rather than enjoyment (Ericsson, Krampe, & Tesch-Römer, 1993), such as taking 50 free throws in a basketball practice to improve shooting technique. Deliberate play, on the other hand, is a game-based activity done amongst peers for inherent enjoyment, rather than skill development (Côté, 1999). At younger ages (e.g., 6 to 12 years), high amounts of deliberate play promote sport enjoyment and sport participation, while preventing sport dropout. During early adolescence, (e.g., 13-15 years), a balance between deliberate practice and deliberate play can be a precursor to elite sport participation. Finally, in late adolescence and adulthood (e.g., 16 years and older), an intense focus on deliberate practice is suggested for elite athletes (Côté & Fraser-Thomas, 2008). Thus, the balance between deliberate practice and deliberate play is a dynamic influence that impacts the frequency and intensity of youth sport training.

Researchers in sport performance and talent development often focus on dynamic influences such as deliberate practice (Helsen, Starkes, & Hodges, 1998), developmental activities (Côté, Erickson, & Abernethy, 2013), commitment (Scanlan, Carpenter, Schmidt, Simons, & Keeler, 1993), and motivation (Duda, 2005). Less studied in the context of training outcomes are static influences – those variables that generally cannot be altered. One important static influence, and the focus of this chapter, is *birth advantages*. Birth advantages is an encompassing term that we use to explain variables present at birth that have long-lasting influences throughout development. Examples include birth order (Hopwood, Baker, MacMahon, & Farrow, 2012), socioeconomic status (Statistics Canada, 2008), relative age (Musch & Grondin, 2001), and birthplace (Curtis & Birch, 1987). It is important to clarify our term "static influences". While static influences generally cannot be altered, we do believe that these influences create an environment that becomes malleable through the social relationships that occur in sport. For instance, a child cannot change his or her birthdate; hence, we term this a static influence. However, a parent or coach can have a significant positive or negative influence on the child's resultant outcomes in sport based on the child's birthdate. Thus, an individual's birth advantages are positively and negative influenced by social agents. Recently, Hancock, Adler, and Côté (2013) used a social agent model to explain relative age effects in sport. In the following sections, we adapt this model (see Figure 1) and illustrate how it can be applied to help understand two birth advantages: relative age and birthplace.

CONCEPTS AND EMPIRICAL FINDINGS

As mentioned, the two birth advantages discussed herein are relative age and birthplace, each of which has been shown to impact youth sport development and outcomes through the influence of coaches, parents, and peers. In this section we will provide a conceptual understanding of each birth advantage, and then finish the section by integrating the two variables using a social agent model (Hancock et al., 2013).

Relative Age

Relative age can be divided into two components. First, relative age simply refers to the small age differences that exist between people born in the same calendar year. Pertaining to the sport context, relative age is defined as age differences between athletes participating in the same annual age-band. In European soccer, for instance, players born from January 1 to December 31 in 2005 would all participate in the same age-band. In American baseball, however, players born from May 1, 2005 until April 30, 2006 constitute a single annual age-band. Thus, in sport, we disregard the label "calendar year" and instead refer to this as the *selection year*. The second component of relative age is participation and performance (dis)advantages. A participation disadvantage would be if a group of athletes, based on relative age, have a higher frequency of dropout from sport. For performance advantages, we most often conceptualize this as a group of athletes who are selected to elite sport teams and share a similar (and often older) relative age. Therefore, in sport, when relative age differences in a selection year lead to discrepancies in participation or performance outcomes, it is termed the *relative age effect* (Musch & Grondin, 2001).

There are numerous examples of relative age effects in sports; however, it is beyond the scope of this chapter to detail the findings of this literature – essentially, the effect is mostly found in male, team sports, with relatively older athletes having participation or performance advantages (for a review, see Cobley, Baker, Wattie, & McKenna, 2009). While this tells us that the relative age effect exists, continued replication does not further our comprehension of these effects. Therefore, studies that aim to understand the mechanisms that underpin relative age effects are of utmost importance (e.g., Hancock et al., 2013).

Birthplace

An individual's birth location can also have an impact in youth sport. Using a broad example, children born in northern Canada are much more likely to play ice hockey compared to children born in southern United States. When discussing *birthplace effects*, however, researchers are referring to advantages or disadvantages that are associated with the city in which an individual is born (Côté, MacDonald, Baker, & Abernethy, 2006). The theory underpinning birthplace effects is that cities of different sizes offer individuals different sporting opportunities. In smaller cities, it is typical to witness sport as less organized with more opportunities for play (Balish & Côté, 2013; Kytta, 2002), whereas in larger cities, often there is increased competition and high-level coaches, leading to highly-organized and structured sport systems (Kristjansdottir & Vilhjalmsson, 2001). While conventional wisdom might have us conclude that increased competition and access to better coaching during childhood would lead to better sport outcomes, the opposite appears to be true. A tangible example from the United States is Aliquippa, Pennsylvania (population since 1980 less than 20,000), which has produced 11 professional athletes, including notable athletes such as Mike Ditka and Tony Dorsett (both National Football League Hall of Fame players). It is likely that the physical and social environment of Aliquippa offers something unique that leads to such sporting success.

The birthplace effect has mostly been studied in North American contexts, with fairly consistent results. In the United States, for example, athletes born in cities with populations greater than 500,000 are less likely to make professional leagues than those born in cities with fewer than 500,000 people (Côté et al., 2006). Furthermore, in Canada, athletes born in smaller cities are more likely to participate in sport (cities < 100,000; Turnnidge, Hancock, & Côté, 2012) and remain engaged in sport (cities < 250,000; Imtiaz, Hancock, & Côté, in press). Again, a full analysis of the literature is beyond the purview of this chapter, but an excellent review can be found from MacDonald and Baker (2013). A recent methodological shift has led researchers to examine city of development or city of initial registration, rather than birthplace (Schorer, Baker, Lotz, & Büsch, 2010). Though this is a more accurate method to understanding the youth sport environment (e.g., someone could be born in a city of 2,000,000, but move at three years old to a city of 10,000), the results of these studies show the same patterns: youth from smaller cities appear to be advantaged in sport compared to youth from larger cities (Schorer et al., 2010). Rather than focus our attention on the methodological nuances, we instead aim to offer plausible explanations of birthplace effects. Similar to relative age, we believe that the birthplace effect is explained and altered by social agents in the youth sport environment. Thus, the following section describes how social agents can impact birth advantages in youth sport.

Birth Advantages: A Social Agent Perspective

To realize the full potential of youth athletes, it is crucial that they participate in an equitable sport system. This will lead to long periods of sport engagement, maximizing participation rates, and eventually, maximizing the resultant talent pool. Our contention is that relative age and birthplace can significantly contribute to youth development in sport (they can either facilitate or restrict sport development), but that birth advantages can be amplified or mitigated by the social agents involved in youth sport – specifically, parents, coaches, and athletes. This has been proposed by Hancock et al. (2013), but will be expanded upon herein. Before detailing the contribution of each social agent on birth advantages, it is important to understand three main theoretical principles used to explain social agents' influences on athlete development: Matthew effects, Pygmalion effects, and Galatea effects.

Matthew effects (Merton, 1968) describe situations where individuals with initial advantages maintain those advantages, while those who are disadvantaged continue to be disadvantaged. This is often referred to as "the rich get richer, and the poor get poorer" (e.g., Rigney, 2010). Pygmalion and Galatea effects fall within the realm of the self-fulfilling prophecy (Merton, 1948). Merton (1948) outlined the self-fulfilling prophecy as a phenomenon whereby a false belief (e.g., real-estate prices in North America will increase

10% in 2014), leads to new behaviors (e.g., realtors in North American overvalue homes by 10%) that result in the original false belief becoming true. Derived from the self-fulfilling prophecy, Pygmalion (Rosenthal & Jacobson, 1968) and Galatea effects (Merton, 1957) refer to the notion that eventual outcomes reflect initial expectations. Using a sport example, when a coach expects a particular player to excel, that player will excel, but when a coach anticipates a player will fail, that player indeed fails. The difference between the two effects is that Pygmalion effects refer to an outside party placing an expectation on an individual (i.e., the coach in the above situation), while Galatea effects refer to individuals placing expectations on themselves (i.e., the player in the above situation). Using these theories, we propose that parents, coaches, and athletes influence birth advantages in sport through Matthew effects, Pygmalion effects, and Galatea effects, respectively (see Figure 1).

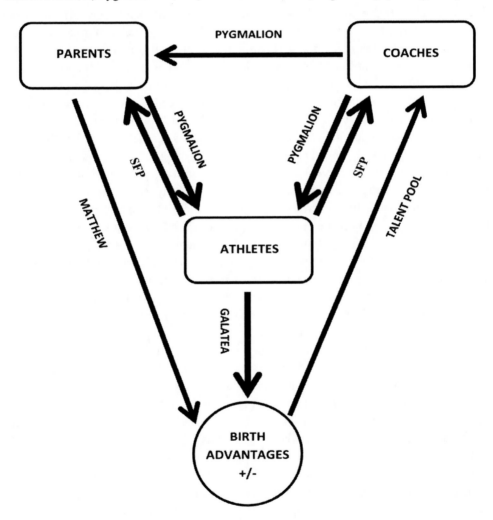

Figure 1. A social agent model explaining birth advantages in youth sport. Adapted from "A proposed theoretical model to explain relative age effects in sport", by D. J. Hancock, A. L. Adler, and J. Côté, 2013, *European Journal of Sport Science*, p. 6. Taylor & Francis Ltd., Reprinted by permission from Taylor & Francis Ltd., http://www.tandf.co.uk/journals.

Parents. Sport offers children several benefits including physical, health, skill development, and psychosocial (e.g., Debate, Gabriel, Zwald, Huberty, & Zhang, 2009); thus, it would seem obvious that all parents should encourage their children to be active in unorganized and/or organized sport. Yet the current decline in sport participation rates (Statistics Canada, 2008) and the increase in childhood diseases such as obesity (World Health Organization, 2013) suggest that parents are failing their children. Being involved in sport from an early age seems advantageous to children, while not being involved in sport seems disadvantageous; thus, it is not surprising that we propose that parents' actions can have a significant impact on birth advantages, which can be explained through Matthew effects (a system of advantages), as demonstrated on the left-hand side of our adapted model (see Figure 1).

Hancock et al. (2013) proposed that relative age effects begin due to parental enrollment decisions in sport (initial enrollment bias) – specifically, that parents of relatively older children enroll their children in sport at early ages, but parents of relatively younger children withhold their children from sport. We postulate that parents contribute to the birthplace effect as well. In particular, we believe that due to the environment of smaller cities (e.g., open space and safety), parents might be encouraging their children to participate in sport (e.g., "Go outside and play soccer with your friends") more often than parents in larger cities. Through this encouragement, children in smaller cities would be developing healthy active lifestyles that are continued for years, but are also engaging in sport and having more opportunities for informal learning. As such, children with advantageous birth dates and birth locations might gain initial advantages in sport due to early enrollment and increased opportunities for play that continue throughout life. This is a result of the Matthew effect.

Though much research must be done, this proposal has, at the very least, face validity. Consider the example of Terri, a girl born in January in a small city (< 20,000 people). At age 6, Terri's parents decide to enroll her in soccer for the summer and basketball for the winter. Furthermore, after school and on weekends, Terri is frequently provided with opportunities to play sports outside with her neighborhood friends. Thus, for the year she is 6 years old, Terri engages in organized sport for 80 total hours (2 seasons, 20 weeks per season, and 2 hours per week) and unorganized sport for 150 hours (approximately 3 hours per week), giving Terri 230 hours of sport exposure. Meanwhile, another girl, Stacey, is born in December in a large city (> 1,000,000 people). While Terri is playing soccer and basketball, Stacey's parents believe she is too physically and cognitively immature for sports, so they withhold her from sport until the following year. Furthermore, the park nearest to their house in the city can be, at times, unsafe. Therefore, Stacey only plays sports at the park once a week under adult supervision. In the same calendar year where Terri amassed 230 sport hours, Stacey merely totals 50 hours (approximately 1 hour per week), which likely leads to sizeable differences in sport skill due to the disparity in formal and informal sport learning. Demonstrated this way, the initial advantage that Terri has received is quite large, and speaks to Matthew effects created by parents that can lead to long-term discrepancies in skill development.

In our adapted model (see Figure 1), we indicate that parents can have a positive or negative impact on birth advantages through Matthew effects. To counteract Matthew effects that lead to birth advantages, we believe that parents simply need to provide their children with sporting opportunities. Côté and colleagues (Côté, 1999; Côté et al., 2013; Côté et al., 2009) state that children should be given opportunities to sample sports and engage in deliberate play. Following this suggestion, we believe birth advantages could be minimized.

Regardless of relative age, children can enroll in organized sports. While some parents might be concerned about the safety of their children in certain sports (e.g., ice hockey and gridiron football), many associations have systems in place that make initial entry divisions safer for all participants (e.g., Initiation program in Hockey Canada and flag football). These programs allow children to gain a modicum of sport-specific skills, while limiting their chances of physical and emotional harm. Similarly, regardless of one's birthplace, children need to be encouraged to play unorganized sports. In such settings children have valuable learning experiences, gain competence/confidence, and develop creativity and initiative (Côté et al., 2013). It is of the upmost importance, therefore, that parents in all cities seek methods to provide their children with playful sport opportunities. In cities with safety concerns, this could involve a neighborhood group where parents rotate through supervisory duties. For cities with limited access to green spaces, parents can be creative and suggest that their children play ball hockey or stick-ball on quiet streets, or they could organize weekly carpools to nearby parks. This would also teach children about the value of unstructured sport. While sport opportunities for relatively older children born in smaller cities might be facilitated more easily, there are solutions for all parents to offer their children initial opportunities in sport, thereby reducing, or possibly eliminating, Matthew effects that contribute to birth advantages in sport. This reduction in the Matthew effect might also rebalance the talent pool that coaches are currently provided (the right-hand side of Figure 1). Presently, the talent pool in sport appears relatively older (Delorme, Boiché, & Raspaud, 2010; Hancock, Ste-Marie, & Young, 2013), but by reducing Matthew effects, coaches would then have a more heterogeneous talent pool, which might lead to more equitable team selections and increasing the number of talented athletes.

Coaches. Coaches are vital to the success of sport programs and for facilitating positive outcomes in young athletes (Fraser-Thomas, Côté, & Deakin, 2005). The most effective coaches are those that integrate professional, interpersonal, and intrapersonal knowledge in order to meet the needs of all youth athletes (Côté & Gilbert, 2009). For the purpose of this chapter, we reiterate that effective coaches serve the needs of *all* athletes. Thus, any coaching style or philosophy that advantages some athletes while disadvantaging others is an example of ineffective coaching. One way in which this manifests in sport is through coach expectations (Rejeski, Darracott, & Hutslar, 1979), and therefore, when discussing coaches, we refer to Pygmalion effects (where expectations lead to outcomes).

In their original model, Hancock et al.; (2013) intimated that Pygmalion effects contribute to the relative age effect. The postulated theory was that coaches view relatively older athletes as more talented (expectation), possibly due to increased physical size, and select those athletes to elite teams. After additional training and coaching, the relatively older athletes indeed become better athletes, thus the initial expectations lead to the subsequent outcomes. Herein, we agree with this theory and apply it to birthplace effects as well. For the adapted model (see Figure 1), we propose that coaches do not directly influence birth advantages; instead, they have a self-fulfilling prophecy (Pygmalion effect) with athletes, which in turn creates birth advantages.

For the first discussed birth advantage, relative age, it seems obvious that coaches would have higher expectations of talent from relatively older athletes, who would then develop into better athletes (thus, outcomes match expectations)[1]. Essentially, it is believed that coaches view physical prowess, which is associated with relatively older athletes, as talent. Accordingly, coaches then select relatively older athletes to their teams, placing high expectations upon them. This has been discussed in this chapter and by other authors (Hancock et al., 2013; Sherar, Baxter-Jones, Faulkner, & Russell, 2007; Till et al., 2011), so we will not expound on it here.

When considering birthplace advantages, researchers often speculate that the structure of sport differentiates large and small cities (Balish & Côté, 2013; Kristjansdottir & Vilhjalmsson, 2001; Kytta, 2002). In large cities, it is suggested that sports are highly stratified, have state-of-the-art facilities, and recruit highly-specialized coaches (Kristjansdottir & Vilhjalmsson, 2001). Oppositely, in small cities, it is believed that sports tend to group a diverse number of children, have fewer chances for deselection, offer older facilities, and retain coaches that might coach several sports (Balish & Côté, 2013). While the above description seems like it would create high expectations for athletes in larger cities, the birthplace effect actually favors children born in smaller cities (Côté et al., 2006; MacDonald & Baker, 2013). In the following paragraphs we will use some examples to explain this, mostly related to expectations of efficient and effective sport programs (Côté, Coakley, & Bruner, 2012).

Regarding birthplace, the explanation of the effect and integration of Pygmalion effects through coaching are less obvious. As adults, we are inclined to believe that specialized coaches and facilities are requisite components in the journey toward expert sport participation – and we are likely correct. Children, however, ought not to be treated as adults. If children had the same physical, cognitive, mental, and psychosocial abilities as adults, there would be no need for the term "children" in our lexicon. Yet we know this is not the case, and as such, it is important that sport programs – and our expectations of what sport programs provide – be geared toward what is developmentally appropriate for children.

In large cities, sport programs seem to be designed for *effective* talent development (Côté et al., 2012). Specifically, world-class facilities, specialized coaches, and multiple competitive levels lead many invested parties to believe that the primary focus of the sport program is performance. Thus, when coaches select teams in this system, they expect performance related results (Pygmalion effects). To be clear, we believe this is often – not always – the case. Coaches also deselect athletes and it is likely that deselected athletes subsequently have low expectations of their abilities. While this sport program design might attain short-term goals that are expected from the coach, and possibly even produce a handful of elite athletes, it is a system that relies heavily on extrinsic motivation and excludes many athletes. Therefore, it does not have the sustainability of sport programs designed to maximize the efficiency of talent development. While Pygmalion effects are present in an efficient system (coaches have high expectations of athletes, and those expectations are met), these expectations focus on long-term sport participation, explaining why smaller cities produce significantly more elite athletes than larger cities.

Contrary to larger cities, smaller cities appear to possess many characteristics that are beneficial for *efficient* talent development (Côté et al., 2012). Often in small-city environments, facilities might be of poorer quality, but are more accessible to youth (Balish &

---

[1] These coach expectations might also lead to parents having higher expectations of their children (see the top of Figure 1), thus amplifying the effect (Hancock et al 2013).

Côté, 2013). Furthermore, coaches might not be highly-specialized, and instead focus on facilitating participation and positive outcomes for youth (Balish & Côté, 2013). There are fewer selections/deselections, meaning that sport is more inclusive for participants (Côté et al., 2012). In this system, we believe that coaches expect (Pygmalion effects) their athletes to have prolonged engagement in sport, be representatives of their small city, and learn skills at a developmentally appropriate pace. While this program design will not likely lead to elite performance at young ages, it is a system that is ripe for cultivating intrinsic motivation and initiative (Larson, 2000) in the sampling years (Côté, 1999; Côté et al., 2013). Once children from smaller cities reach the specializing or investment years (Côté, 1999; Côté et al., 2013), they would then be equipped to invest in more skill-based learning, which will be fueled by their intrinsic motivation. As such, coaches' expectations of participation would in fact lead to elite performance outcomes in smaller cities, explaining the birthplace effect.

We have used previous literature and reasoning to formulate this hypothesis, but it still must be researched and studied extensively. For now, we wish to provide a detailed hypothetical example to illustrate our point. Consider Larry and Sylvain, both baseball players who are 9 years old. Larry is from a large city and plays AAA (highest competitive level) baseball. His team is coached by a former Major League Baseball player, and they play at a beautiful new baseball diamond. Sometimes, they play their games at their local professional team's baseball diamond in the city. Larry's coach often tells the athletes that they beat out several players to make this team, so they are expected to maintain a high performance standard. Moreover, because they have such a talented team and specialized coach, they are expected to win their regional playoffs at the end of each season. At first Larry is excited to be part of such a talented team, and the expectations of winning do not cause him duress; however, as the years go on, the message from the coach becomes old and tiring. Larry is only extrinsically motivated to practice hard in order to meet the coach's expectation of winning, and eventually, with no intrinsic motivation to practice, Larry discontinues baseball. Sylvain, on the other hand, is from a small city and plays recreational baseball this year – there are not enough quality players to form a competitive team, so the young boys form three recreational teams to compete against each other for the summer. Sylvain's coach was a high school baseball player, but did not progress beyond this. Furthermore, the town's only baseball diamond was built over 30 years ago, and while it is still an effective diamond, it does not have any outstanding features. Sylvain's coach preaches to the team to have fun and enjoy baseball, just as he did when he was younger. Where possible, the coach provides advanced skill instructions, but mostly teaches the children about the fundamental skills, strategies, and rules. At the end of the season, Sylvain tells his parents he wants to keep playing and becoming a better baseball player – his motivation is not to win or make a team; rather, he is motivated by enjoyment of the sport. As the years progress, Sylvain, and many of his teammates, spend more time practicing and playing baseball, a self-initiated activity. By age 14, there are 15 baseball players that have enough talent to form a competitive team, thus testing their skills at a higher level. Our example ends here, but we can foresee that some of these players might develop enough talent to continue playing baseball in university, or possibly even professionally.

In no way are we stating that this is exactly what happens in large and small cities around the world. We simply believe that this is a sound theory, grounded in talent development frameworks (e.g., Côté, 1999; Côté et al., 2009; Vaeyens, Lenoir, Williams, & Philippaerts, 2008), and that it might explain a good portion of the birth advantages witnessed in sport. The question remains, however, how do we change this imbalance? Should we remove all expectations? Our answer to that is no. First, we believe that is it vital that expectations of youth sport programs are shifted to align with the efficient talent development perspective (Côté et al., 2012). We should expect that children enjoy sport, have fun with their friends, and learn fundamental skills. These are long-term expectations with long-terms rewards. We should not be short-sighted and expect children to respond to extrinsic motivators such as winning. It is excellent to have highly-specialized coaches and state-of-the-art facilities available for children, but these should only be used once the children are developmentally prepared for them.

This addresses birthplace effects, but we have not yet spoken of how to adapt relative age effects. Recall that the general premise of Pygmalion effects and relative age effects is that coaches select relatively older players to their teams as they expect them to be more talented (Hancock et al., 2013). The reason for selection, therefore, is related to the short-term goal of winning. Under our proposed system, by removing short-term expectations, we might also remove relative age effects. Simply put, if coaches are expecting children to have fun, enjoy sport, and learn fundamental skills, there is less emphasis on selection to teams and overt talent development. Thus, we can use Pygmalion effects to our advantage. If coaches are taught to set their expectations based on the notion of efficient talent development, birth advantages might start to be assuaged.

Athletes. Our final social agent group is athletes, the beneficiaries of positive or negative Matthew and Pygmalion effects. The way in which athletes interpret these effects likely impacts their perceptions of talent and ability. As such, here we link athletes with Galatea effects, which describe self-expectations and resultant outcomes. In our adapted model (see Figure 1), parents and coaches influence athletes through their expectations, which in turn leads to birth advantages based on athletes' resultant expectations.

Hancock et al. (2013) suggested that relative age effects and Galatea effects are a natural fit. Their explanation was that relatively older athletes are selected to elite teams, which in turn, increases athletes' expectations of talent and ability. Thus, these athletes might believe that they are more talented than is actually the case. This perception, however, will lead to increased training and commitment, which will make them more talented, thus completing the Galatea effect.

The Galatea effect seems to explain relative age effects, but the explanation of birthplace effects is less obvious. For that, we still consider Galatea effects, but propose that they are instigated through the big-fish-little-pond-effect (BFLPE; Marsh, Chessor, Craven, & Roche, 1995; Marsh & Parker, 1984). Before continuing, it is important to note that we do not condone or suggest that we seek ways to reduce athletes' self-expectations in order to create a fair sport system. Instead, it is important to explore methods for increasing self-expectations of low-expectancy athletes.

The BFLPE was originally noted in educational settings, and showed that students of equal academic ability had different academic self-concepts depending on their environment (Marsh et al., 1995; Marsh & Parker, 1984). That is, if the school they attended had a very high academic ability, their academic self-concept would be low, while the opposite was true if the school had a very low academic ability. This concept has pervaded into sport and has been previously used to describe birthplace effects (Fraser-Thomas, Côté, & MacDonald, 2010). Our conceptualization of the birthplace effect is that when athletes come from smaller cities, their self-concept of ability is greater due to a less talented reference group, whereas when athletes come from larger cities, their self-concept of ability is lower due to a more talented reference group. The first author was an ice hockey referee in Ontario for 18 years, and using his anecdotal experience, the BFLPE can be explained further.

The first author refereed in many small and large cities across Ontario, but two cities in particular demonstrate the point. The first is Ottawa (population approximately 1,000,000). Amongst the many ice hockey teams, Ottawa has a Junior A team[2]. On a typical night, the Junior A team would draw 25 to 50 fans. Being in Ottawa, the Junior A team had to compete with the Ottawa 67's (Ontario Hockey League) and the Ottawa Senators (National Hockey League) for fans. Needless to say, the players on the Junior A team were small fish in a big pond, with higher-caliber teams providing a stronger reference group. The second city is Westport (population less than 1,000). Westport has a Junior B team, which is not as good as Junior A, but it is the top level of ice hockey available in Westport. In fact, the nearest Junior A team is 45 minutes away, while the nearest Ontario Hockey League team is 60 minutes away, and the closest National Hockey League team is 90 minutes away. The Westport players are treated incredibly well by the community, and games become a community event, with most games having 300 to 500 fans in attendance. These players are truly big fish in a little pond and this creates a strong sense of community sport culture (Carlson, 1988). Though Junior A players are typically 16 to 20 years old, the sport culture likely filters down to youth sport participants who are watching these games and partaking in this environment.

We add to the BFLPE by suggesting that it integrates with Galatea effects as well. The BFLPE states that being in such an environment will increase an individual's self-concept (Marsh & Parker, 1984). We believe that an increased self-concept might also heighten one's self-expectations. In the little pond environment, athletes might receive more attention, are given recognition, and can become the focal point of the community. This might raise one's self-expectations, leading to increased training and subsequent performance outcomes. Thus, the Galatea effect is completed. Again, under no circumstances do we believe that youth athletes should have their high self-expectations arbitrarily reduced; rather, we seek to provide all children with high self-expectations.

The question then is if the BFLPE is beneficial for self-concept, how can we structure environments to provide all children with this feeling? Two possibilities involve team identity and community support. Feeling a sense of team identity might help improve one's self-concept. Having team track suits or warm-up attire can increase team identity (Gruneau & Whitson, 1993). Also, having a unique team name might be helpful. Many team names simply involve colors (Team Red/Team Blue) or are off-shoots of professional teams (e.g., Ottawa Junior Senators, in our above Junior A example). Being more unique might also provide a distinct team identity. For community support, having a number of fans is important, but also having media coverage (e.g., newspaper or television stories) might help athletes to feel important within their community. This is a more difficult avenue to pursue, but could be fruitful for creating environments whereby athletes share an increased self-

---

[2] There are many levels of ice hockey in Canada. There is the National Hockey League (the most elite ice hockey league in the world), and immediately below it is the American Hockey League (a professional league). Providing players for these leagues is the Canadian Hockey League (an amateur league), comprised of the Western Hockey League, Ontario Hockey League, and Quebec Major Junior Hockey League. Below this level are three junior ice hockey leagues, from most to least elite: Junior A, Junior B, and Junior C. Finally, there are several levels of youth ice hockey below Junior.

concept, and subsequently have higher athletic self-expectations. Regardless, methods to improve team identity and community support ought to be explored.

Unlike parental and coach influences, we are not suggesting that athletes are doing anything "incorrectly" that lead to birth advantages. In fact, this section is on self-expectations, and we believe it would be counter-productive to the talent development process to reduce athlete self-expectations (not to mention the ethical issues associated with such an approach). Rather than correct a situation, we simply argue that governing bodies should provide all children with methods to increase self-expectations. This might be achieved through fewer selections/deselections at young ages, or arming deselected children with the proper coping mechanisms to maintain high self-expectation standards (e.g., increasing intrinsic motivation). Essentially, we must adapt what we know from the BFLPE to enable young athletes from larger cities to maintain high expectations. In doing so, we do not eliminate Galatea effects; instead we strengthen the effect, but strengthen it for all athletes. In turn, we should witness better talent development for all athletes due to equally high self-expectations.

PRACTICAL IMPLICATIONS

We have spent the majority of this chapter providing evidence for the existence of birth advantages in youth sport, and offering a comprehensive explanation for why they exist (social agents, Matthew effects, Pygmalion effects, and Galatea effects). This hypothesis provides a solid theoretical foundation for future researchers to use when testing birth advantages at all levels of sport. Yet it is also important to discuss how to implement our theory into a practical setting; that is, how can youth sport participants incorporate this chapter into their sporting realm? The goal of such changes would be to keep more children involved in sport for longer periods of time, thereby increasing the odds of grooming talented athletes. We believe that this can be done by reducing Matthew effects, adapting Pygmalion effects, and increasing Galatea effects.

From the evidence presented in this chapter, it seems that birth advantages are limiting the talent pool through the attitudes and behaviors of parents, coaches, and athletes. The prevalence of birth advantages has increased over the past three decades, which also happens to correspond with increases in the professionalization of youth sport (Weinberg & Gould, 2011). That is, youth sport tends to be more specialized, has extensive training, encourages team selections, and involves higher costs (e.g., financial, travel, and time) than in the past. Interestingly, the professionalization of youth sport is counter-productive to the development of expertise. In fact, the professionalization of youth sport promotes behaviors in adults (parents and coaches) and young athletes that are sometimes conflicting with long-term participation and talent development in sport. Thus, sport programs ought to be developed in a manner that truly facilitates talent development, while also alleviating birth advantages. As a sport policy maker, parent, or coach, the questions is, "What specifically can I do to better implement or serve such a program?"

The genesis of such programs is with sport policy makers. When governing bodies mandate certain criteria from their constituents, the mandate is generally followed. As such, it is vital that sport policy makers review the structure of their sports. Once this structure is set, parents and coaches can play an active role in talent development. Here we make several practical recommendations to consider.

The first step to rebalancing birth advantages is to reduce Matthew effects. Having children begin sport (organized or unorganized) at young ages is a great way to begin the talent development process. Our goal as sport scientists, however, should be to seek methods whereby all children can begin sport at young ages. For this, our main recommendation is to have sport policy makers create and advertise a sporting structure that facilitates early participation. An excellent policy is to offer organized sport to young children (e.g., 5-7 years old), but in an unstructured way. At such a young age, there is no need for formal teams, stratified competitive levels, or high amounts of deliberate practice. Instead, sport policy makers should simply be providing a venue to encourage participation, which will facilitate sport enjoyment and social connections.

Supplementing this sport system, it would be beneficial for parents to encourage their children to engage in significant amounts of play and unorganized sport. Play will allow children to implicitly learn sport fundamentals while enjoying the social aspect of sport. Further, it has low costs (e.g., time and money) to parents. Finally, coaches who buy-in to this sport system would focus on teaching fundamental skills, but through less traditional pedagogical approaches such as play practice and teaching games for understanding, rather than focusing on deliberate practice. In such a system, all children (regardless of birthdate and birthplace) would gain benefits from early sport experiences, which would minimize initial advantages and young ages, thus reducing the Matthew effect. As a result, the potential to retain talented children in sport increases.

Our second practical implication for birth advantages is to adapt the Pygmalion effect. We believe that children should be given expectations in sport by social agents, especially at young ages. However, a more inclusive system (and one that subsequently increases the talent pool through increasing participation) would shift expectations from short-term goals such as winning, to long-term goals such as talent development. This paradigm shift likely needs to be instigated by sport policy makers to be properly implemented. To truly accomplish this paradigm shift, sport policy makers need to have a thorough, introspective look at the values of their current sport system. Tough questions need to be asked such as, "Should we keep score?", "How many competitive levels ought to be offered?" (e.g., in Hockey Canada, a 12-year-old player can currently register in AAA, AA, A, B, or recreational, amongst others), and "Can we monitor coaches' and parents' attitudes toward winning and talent development?" One recommendation is to reduce team selections (e.g., offer no more than one competitive level at young ages), and keep smaller teams that allow for more playing time for all athletes. In doing so, athletes are more likely to receive increased personalized training, build social connections, and concentrate on training and playing. It will still be important for parents and coaches to maintain high expectations of youth athletes; however, their expectations should focus on effort, participation, remaining engaged, having fun, and learning skills. The expectations of the athletes ought to remain high, thereby keeping Pygmalion effects, but these expectations should be equal across all athletes, irrespective of birthdate and birthplace. Again the result of this would be a system with additional athletes, and more potential for talented athletes.

The final implication revolving around birth advantages is to increase Galatea effects. Once again, sport policy makers have the ability to structure sport in a way that will increase children's expectations, regardless of birth date or birthplace. Specifically, sport policy makers should seek ways to make young athletes feel special and unique within their communities. By feeling like part of a community (e.g., being a member of a small team or having opportunities on less competitive teams to represent your community), athletes are more likely to remain engaged in sport for many years, and along the way can begin to specialize their training to increase their talent. Thus, the long-term effect of increasing sport participation contributes to talent development; however, the focus of sport for children should be on the short-term effects of participation. Parents and coaches also play a critical role in athletes' self-expectations. If parents and coaches continue to demonstrate to youth that sampling, play, and being creative are more important than specializing, deliberate practice, and mastering a specific skill, then youth are more likely to accept this as the sport culture. Subsequently, athletes' self-expectations would focus on effort, participation, and enjoyment – constructs not likely effected by birth advantages.

In this section, we have focused mostly on young children, and adaptations to the system must be made as children grow older. Based on guidelines from Côté (1999), Côté and Fraser-Thomas (2008), and our recommendations above, we suggest that sport policy makers, parents, and coaches consider three stages of development: sampling, specializing, and investment. During the sampling years (approximately age 6 to 12), social agents should encourage play (e.g., 80:20 ratio of deliberate play-like activities and deliberate practice), allow children to sample many sports, reduce team selections, and create smaller teams with increased playing time. Once entering the specializing years (approximately age 12 to 16), social agents should facilitate a balance of play and practice (e.g., 50:50 ratio of deliberate play-like activities and deliberate practice), start reducing the number of sports to two or three, and begin some stratification of competitive levels. Finally, in the investment years (approximately age 16 and older), social agents can offer more deliberate practice (e.g., 20:80 ratio of deliberate play-like activities and deliberate practice), reducing the number of sports to one or two, have highly stratified competitive levels, and adjust playing time based on skill. Implementing a system such as this is likely to reduce birth advantages, but also allow for talent development and expertise.

The birth advantages discussed in this chapter shed light on the important roles that sport policy makers, parents, and coaches play in youth sport. The adults involved in youth sport are the primary determinants of the Matthew, Pygmalion, and Galatea effects and ultimately affect sport participation in youth sport. It is important for adults to keep in mind the joyful and enjoyable short-term aspects of youth sport when investing in the long-term goal of developing talented athletes.

KEY POINTS TO PROMOTE POSITIVE HUMAN FUNCTIONING

We began this chapter by discussing dynamic and static influences in sport. Birthdate and birthplace were labeled as static influences, but as we have explained in above sections, these static influences are indeed quite malleable through all the people and relationships that constitute organized youth sport. While one cannot change one's December birthdate, the impact of that birthdate will be dictated by the actions and beliefs of parents, coaches, and athletes. Hence, there are likely very few influences in sport that are truly static. In fact, setting up an ideal sport system can likely change static influences, such as birth advantages, to non-factors in sport participation. It simply requires a change of focus from sport policy makers, parents, coaches, and athletes to think about enjoyment and all youths' well-being in the long-term pathway of talent development in sport. There are a few key points to consider in terms of promoting positive human function, which in this case would be the healthy development of talent:

1. Mathew, Pygmalion, and Galatea effects are determined by the interactions between parents, coaches, and youth in the sport environment.
2. Social agents play a key role in optimizing the sport environment, with sport policy makers likely leading the process, while parents and coaches supplement and support the sport system.
3. It is important to follow developmentally appropriate stages of talent development, such as the sampling, specializing, and investment years.
4. Reducing team selections and stratification of competitive levels will likely reduce relative age effects.
5. Increasing play activities and having smaller teams will likely reduce birthplace effects.

From a holistic approach, these guidelines seek to increase social opportunities, learning, athlete development, and talent in a fun, enjoyable, and depressurized setting.

CONCLUSION

By reading this chapter, we hope that you have been engaged in the discussion of birth advantages and the social interactions that affect talent development in youth sport. There are many aspects to consider when designing youth sport program aimed at developing talent, but we believe we have presented a strong case here for why relative age and birthplace should not impact talent. It is imperative now that parents, coaches, and athletes seek ways to reduce Matthew effects, adapt Pygmalion effects, and increase Galatea effects in order to rebalance the talent development process and enhance the positive experience of all young people involved in sport.

REFERENCES

Balish, S., & Côté, J. (2013). The influence of community on athletic development: An integrated case study. *Qualitative Research in Sport, Exercise and Health.* doi: 10.1080/2159676X.2013.766815.

Carlson, R. (1988). The socialization of elite tennis players: An analysis of the players' backgrounds and development. *Sociology of Sport Journal, 5,* 241-256.

Cobley, S., Baker, J., Wattie, N., & McKenna, J. (2009). Annual age-grouping and athlete development: A meta-analytical review of relative age effects in sport. *Sports Medicine, 39,* 235-256.

Côté, J. (1999). The influence of the family in the development of talent in sport. *The Sport Psychologist, 13*, 395-417.

Côté, J., Coakley, C., & Bruner, M. (2012). Children's talent development in sport. Effectiveness or efficiency? In S. Dagkas, & K. Armour (Eds.), *Inclusion and exclusion through youth sport* (pp. 172-185). New York, NY: Routledge.

Côté, J., Erickson, K., & Abernethy, B. (2013). Play and practice during childhood. In J. Côté, & R. Lidor (Eds.), *Conditions of children's talent development in sport* (pp. 9-20). Morgantown, WV: Fitness Information Technology.

Côté, J., & Fraser-Thomas, J. (2008). Play, practice, and athlete development. In D. Farrow, J. Baker, & C. MacMahon (Eds.), *Developing elite sport performance: Lessons from theory and practice* (pp. 17-28). New York, NY: Routledge.

Côté, J., & Gilbert, W. (2009). An integrative definition of coaching effectiveness and expertise. *International Journal of Sports Science and Coaching, 4*, 307-323.

Côté, J., Lidor, R., & Hackfort, D. (2009). ISSP position stand: To sample or to specialize? Seven postulates about youth sport activities that lead to continued participation and elite performance. *International Journal of Sport and Exercise Psychology, 9*, 7-17.

Côté, J., MacDonald, D. J., Baker, J., & Abernethy, B. (2006). When "where" is more important than "when": Birthplace and birthdate effects on the achievement of sporting expertise. *Journal of Sports Sciences, 24*, 1065-1073.

Curtis, J. E., & Birch, J. S. (1987). Size of community of origin and recruitment to professional and Olympic hockey in North America. *Sociology of Sport Journal, 4,* 229-244.

Debate, R. D., Gabriel, K. P., Zwald, M., Huberty, J., & Zhang, Y. (2009). Changes in psychosocial factors and physical activity frequency among third- to eighth-grade girls who participated in a developmentally focused youth sport program: A preliminary study. *Journal of School Health, 79*, 474-485.

Delorme, N., Boiché, J., & Raspaud, M. (2010). Relative age effect in elite sports: Methodological bias or real discrimination? *European Journal of Sport Science, 10*, 91-96.

Duda, J. L. (2005). Motivation in sport. The relevance of competence and achievement goals. In A. J. Elliot & C. S. Dweck (Eds.), *Handbook of competence and motivation* (pp. 318-335). New York, NY: The Guilford Press.

Ericsson, K. A., Krampe, R. T., & Tesch-Römer, C. (1993). The role of deliberate practice in the acquisition of expert performance. *Psychological Review, 100*, 363-406.

Fraser-Thomas, J., Côté, J., & Deakin, J. (2005). Youth sport programs: An avenue to foster positive youth development. *Physical Education & Sport Pedagogy, 10*, 19-41.

Fraser-Thomas, J., Côté, J., & Deakin, J. (2008). Examining adolescent sport dropout and prolonged engagement from a developmental perspective. *Journal of Applied Sport Psychology, 20*, 318-333.

Fraser-Thomas, J., Côté, J., & MacDonald, D. J. (2010). Community size in youth sport settings: Examining developmental assets and sport withdrawal. *PHENex Journal, 2*, 1-9.

Gruneau, R., & Whitson, D. (1993). Communities, civic boosterism, and fans. In R. Gruneau & D. Whitson (Eds.), *Hockey night in Canada* (pp. 199-221). Toronto, ON: Garamond Press.

Hancock, D. J., Adler, A. L., & Côté, J. (2013). A proposed theoretical model to explain relative age effects in sport. *European Journal of Sport Science. doi*:10.1080/17461391.2013.775352.

Hancock, D. J., Ste-Marie, D. M., & Young, B. W. (2013). Coach selections and the relative age effect in male youth ice hockey. *Research Quarterly for Exercise and Sport, 84*, 126-130.

Helsen, W. F., Starkes, J. L., & Hodges, N. J. (1998). Team sports and the theory of deliberate practice. *Journal of Sport & Exercise Psychology, 20*, 12-34.

Hopwood, M. J., Baker, J., MacMahon, C., & Farrow, D. (2012, June). *Faster, higher, stronger, and younger? Birth order, sibling sport participation and sport expertise.* Paper presented at the North American Society for the Psychology of Sport and Physical Activity. Honolulu, HI, USA.

Imtiaz, F., Hancock, D. J., & Côté, J. (in press). Place of development and dropout in youth ice hockey. *International Journal of Sport and Exercise Psychology.*

Kristjansdottir, G., & Vilhjalmsson, R. (2001). Sociodemographic differences in patterns of sedentary and physically active behaviour in older children and adolescents. *Acta Paediatrica, 90*, 429-435.

Kytta, M. (2002). Affordances of children's environments in the context of cities, small towns, suburbs, and rural villages in Finland and Belarus. *Journal of Environmental Psychology, 22*, 109-123.

Larson, R. W. (2000). Toward a psychology of positive youth development. *American Psychologist, 55*, 170-183.

MacDonald, D. J., & Baker, J. (2013). Circumstantial development: Birthdate and birthplace effects on athlete development. In J. Côté, & R. Lidor (Eds.), *Conditions of children's talent development in sport* (pp. 197-208). Morgantown, WV: Fitness Information Technology.

Marsh, H. W., Chessor, D., Craven, R., & Roche, L. (1995). The effects of gifted and talented programs on academic self-concept: The big fish strikes again. *American Educational Research Journal, 32*, 285-319.

Marsh, H. W., & Parker, J. W. (1984). Determinants of student self-concept: Is it better to be a relatively large fish in a small pond even if you don't learn to swim as well? *Journal of Personality and Social Psychology, 47*, 213-231.

Merton, R. K. (1948). The self-fulfilling prophecy. *The Antioch Review, 8*, 193-210.

Merton, R. K. (1957). *Social theory and social structure.* Glencoe, IL: The Free Press.

Merton, R. K. (1968). The Matthew effect in science. *Science, 159*, 56-63.

Musch, J., & Grondin, S. (2001). Unequal competition as an impediment to personal development: A review of the relative age effect in sport. *Developmental Review, 21*, 147-167.

Rejeski, W., Darracott, C., & Hutslar, S. (1979). Pygmalion in youth sport: A field study. *Journal of Sport Psychology, 1*, 311-319.

Rigney, D. (2010). *The Matthew effect: How advantage begets further advantage.* New York, NY: Columbia University Press.

Rosenthal, R., & Jacobson, L. (1968). *Pygmalion in the classroom.* New York, NY: Holt, Rinehart & Winston.

Scanlan, T. K., Carpenter, P. J., Schmidt, G. W., Simons, J. P., & Keeler, B. (1993). An introduction to the Sport Commitment Model. *Journal of Sport & Exercise Psychology, 15*, 1-15.

Schorer, J., Baker, J., Lotz, S., & Büsch, D. (2010). Influences of early environmental constraints on achievement motivation in talented young handball players. *International Journal of Sport Psychology, 41*, 42-58.

Sherar, L., B., Baxter-Jones, A. D. G., Faulkner, R. A., & Russell, K. W. (2007). Do physical maturity and birth date predict talent in male youth ice hockey players? *Journal of Sports Sciences, 25*, 879-886.

Statistics Canada (2008). *Sport participation in Canada, 2005* (81-595-MIE- No.060). Ottawa, ON: Statistics Canada. Retrieved from: http://www.statcan.gc.ca/pub/81-595-m/81-595-m2008060-eng.pdf.

Till, K., Cobley, S., O'Hara, J., Brightmore, A., Cooke, C., & Chapman, C. (2011). Using anthropometric and performance characteristic to predict selection in junior UK Rugby League players. *Journal of Science and Medicine in Sport, 14*, 264-269.

Turnnidge, J., Hancock, D. J., & Côté, J. (2012). The influence of birth date and place of development on youth sport participation. *Scandinavian Journal of Medicine & Science in Sports*. doi: 10.1111/sms.12002.

Vaeyens, R., Lenoir, M., Williams, A. M., & Philippaerts, R. M. (2008). Talent identification and development programmes in sport. Current models and future directions. *Sports Medicine, 38*, 703-714.

Weinberg, R.S., & Gould, D. (2011). *Foundations of sport and exercise psychology* (5th edition). Champaign, IL: Human Kinetics.

World Health Organization (2013). *Global strategy on diet, physical activity and health. Childhood overweight and obesity*. Retrieved from http://www.who.int/dietphysicalactivity/childhood/en.

In: Positive Human Functioning …   ISBN: 978-1-62948-974-2
Editors: A. R. Gomes, R. Resende & A. Albuquerque   © 2014 Nova Science Publishers, Inc.

Chapter 3

TRAINING TEAMS TO HIGH PERFORMANCE: EFFICACY AND IMPLICATIONS FOR PRACTICE

Tripp Driskell and Eduardo Salas

Institute for Simulation and Training, University of Central Florida, US

ABSTRACT

The aim of this chapter is to present the reader with a theoretically- and empirically-based discussion of how to train teams to high performance. This discussion is organized around the tenets of team training. We begin by providing the reader with a foundation concerning the science of teams and team training. We follow this discussion by offering our approach to training teams to high performance. Our approach reflects before, during, and after team training considerations. In order bolster comprehension, we illustrate, where appropriate, key concepts by providing examples from sport, specifically soccer. We conclude the chapter by advancing a list of tips for training teams to high performance.

INTRODUCTION

I am a member of a team, and I rely on the team, I defer to it and sacrifice for it, because the team, not the individual, is the ultimate champion.
— Mia Hamm (U.S. Women's Soccer)

We begin this chapter with a simple exercise demonstrating the universality of teams. We ask you to list, in your head, as many definitively individual sports (i.e., non-team sports) as possible. For us, the first sports that come to mind are tennis, golf, boxing, and auto racing. However upon further examination, each of these sports requires a high-functioning team in order to attain high performance. The professional tennis player spends countless hours training with his/her coach(es) and hitting partner(s); the golfer trains with his/her coach(es), caddy, and often times a sports psychologist; the boxer has trainers and sparring partners; and the auto racer has an entire pit crew. In short, "the team, not the individual, is the ultimate champion," or borrowing an Aristotelian outlook, the whole is greater than the sum of its parts.

According to estimates, nearly half (48%) of organizations leverage teams to achieve organizational goals (Devine, Clayton, Philips, Dunford, & Melner, 1999). More recently, a survey of 185 professionals representing 185 different organizations found that 94% of the professionals surveyed indicated that their organizations employ teams (DiazGranados et al., 2008). Moreover, data on collaboration in research publications show an unprecedented use of teams. The National Science Foundation (National Science Board, 2012), for example, reports that over 90% of published science and engineering articles with at least one U.S. academician had two or more authors, with an overall average across sciences of 5.6 authors. If you are still not convinced of the pervasiveness of teams, a search of the PsycINFO database using the search term "teams" produces over 48,000 results with 61% of these results published within the last decade. The point we are trying to get across is that teams are all around us, often helping ordinary individuals attain extraordinary outcomes.

CHAPTER ORGANIZATION

The aim of this chapter is to answer the following overarching question: How do we best train teams to achieve high performance? Although this is a formidable task, we purpose to provide the reader with a theoretically- and empirically- driven discussion framed chronologically from team formation to team performance, while maintaining an emphasis on team training. The chapter is outlined as follows.

First, as is necessary in any scholarly discussion, we will present an overview of key terminology and attempt to provide the reader with a foundation regarding the science of teams and team training. Specifically, we will delimit how teams are defined in the literature and discuss the fundamental characteristics of teams. Following, we discuss team training and its role in enhancing team performance.

The second section of this chapter outlines how we propose to best train teams to high performance. In order to accomplish this objective, we adopt what we believe to be a unique and informative approach. Specifically, we answer the question of how to train teams to high performance as if we were given the unfettered opportunity to create and train a championship contending team. This approach will allow us to couple our scientific opinions with the science of teams and team training. Furthermore, we illustrate, where appropriate, key concepts by providing examples from the beautiful game, soccer (or football to our European readers). We use soccer to provide examples because it is an archetypical example of a team sport and because it is the most popular and most played sport worldwide. This section will begin with a discussion on team formation and selection, followed by a step-by-step presentation of how to turn high-performing team members into a high-performing team.

We conclude this chapter by advancing a list of tips and considerations that can be used to guide efforts to train high-performance teams.

TEAMS, TEAMWORK, AND TEAM TRAINING

Teams vs. Groups

The terms "teams" and "groups" are often used interchangeably in the literature (Kozlowski & Bell, 2003). Although we agree with Kozlowski and Bell's (2003) choice to use the terms interchangeably, we believe, at least upfront, that it is useful to distinguish between the two terms. A *team* is defined as "a distinguishable set of two or more people who interact, dynamically, interdependently, and adaptively toward a common and valued goal/objective/mission, who have been assigned specific roles or functions to perform, and who have a limited life-span of membership" (Salas, Dickinson, Converse, & Tannenbaum, 1992, p. 4). In comparison, a *group* can be defined as set of two or more people who "share information, perspectives, and insights; to make decisions that help each person do his or her job better; and to reinforce individual performance standards" (Katzenbach & Smith, 1993, p. 3). Although some would argue that all teams are groups, but not all groups are teams, we use the terms interchangeably, and instead point to perhaps the most important characteristic of teams: interdependency. In interdependent tasks, team members cannot complete their individual tasks without input from other team members.

Integrating the works of Thompson (1967) and Van de Ven, Delbecq, and Koenig (1979), researchers have identified four types of task interdependence: pooled, sequential, reciprocal, and team (Saavedra, Early, & Van Dyne, 1993). The types of task interdependencies range from independent work flow (e.g., work groups) to simultaneous interactions. *Pooled interdependence* reflects tasks that require individual output without the need for team member interactions. An example might be girl scouts selling Girl Scout cookies where each scout contributes individually to the total number of cookies sold. *Sequential interdependence* resembles an assembly line in which work flows from person A to person B and so forth. *Reciprocal interdependence* necessitates two-way interactions between team members (e.g., A↔B, B↔C). Lastly, *team interdependence* represents the most integrated level of interdependence marked by simultaneous or mutual interactions required for task performance. For the current chapter, we are most concerned with reciprocal and team interdependence.

Taskwork vs. Teamwork

Teams that execute interdependent tasks do so by carrying out both taskwork and teamwork responsibilities (Bowers, Braun, & Morgan, 1997). *Taskwork* pertains to the activities conducted at the individual level by team members that are necessary for successful team task completion. In other words, these activities do not require input or actions from other team members. *Teamwork*, on the other hand, involves actions that require the interaction of two or more team member to complete. Marks, Mathieu, and Zaccaro (2001) provide a good distinction between taskwork and teamwork. Specifically, taskwork describes *what* teams are doing and the teamwork describes *how* they do it.

Teamwork, the central focus of this chapter, consists of three core categories of competencies, labeled the ABCs of teamwork (Shuffler, DiazGranados, & Salas, 2011). The

ABCs refer to the attitudes (e.g., collective efficacy, cohesion) behaviors (e.g., mutual performance monitoring, backup behaviors), and cognitions (e.g., shared mental models, shared situation awareness) of teams. *Attitudes* can be described as the internal state of teams that allow team members to interact effectively as a unit. *Behaviors* are the processes and skills that enable team members to execute team goals. And *cognitions* are the knowledge and experiences of the team that facilitate teamwork. Salas and Cannon-Bowers (2000) provide a useful distinction for the ABCs of teamwork. Specifically, these competencies reflect what team members *feel*, *do*, and *think*, respectively. The ABCs of teamwork represent a wide-ranging set of processes and emergent states that have been identified as drivers of team performance. Recently, Salas, Shuffler, Thayer, Bedwell, and Lazzara (in press) have recognized six core process and emergent states from the myriad of team constructs represented in the literature. These include cooperation, coordination, communication, cognition, coaching, and conflict and are defined in Table 1.

Table 1. Six C's of teamwork

Competency	Definition	References
Cooperation	A willingness for team members to work together towards task completion	Kozlowski & Bell, 2003; Wagner, 1995;
Coordination	Activities (e.g., organize team resources, activities and response) performed by team members to manage interdependencies during task performance	Cannon-Bowers et al., 1995; Kozlowski & Bell, 2003;
Communication	The exchange(s) of information between teammates regardless of communication medium	McIntyre & Salas, 1995; Salas, Sims, & Burke, 2005;
Cognition	Cognitive activity that transpire within teams including emergent knowledge structures and "between-the-heads" processes	Wildman et al., 2012; Klimoski & Mohammed, 1994;
Coaching	Establishing goals and planning a course to achieve these goals in order to help teams perform effectively	Fleishman et al., 1991; Hackman & Wageman, 2005;
Conflict	Real or perceived discrepancies or incompatibilities among team members	De Dreu, & Weingart, 2003; Jehn & Bendersky, 2003.

Training vs. Team Training

Training is a pedagogical approach aimed at facilitating the systematic acquisition of knowledge, skills, and attitudes (KSAs) via instructional delivery methods (i.e., information, demonstration, practice) with the purpose of improving performance. *Team training* is defined as "a set of instructional strategies and tools aimed at enhancing teamwork knowledge, skills, processes, and performance," (Tannenbaum, Salas, & Cannon-Bowers, 1996, p. 516). The critical distinction between training and team training is the central focus of training. The specific focus of team training is teamwork competencies, as opposed to taskwork competencies.

Research on enhancing team effectiveness has traditionally adopted an input-process-output (IPO) perspective (Marks, Sabella, Burke, & Zaccaro, 2002), whereby team training is intended to enhance team process. However, recently researchers have expanded upon this model in order to broaden the interpretation of team process. For example, Ilgen, Hollenbeck, Johnson, and Jundt (2005) advance an input-mediator-output-input (IMOI) model, where they argue "Substituting 'M' for 'P' [in the IPO model] reflects the broader range of variables that are important mediational influences" (p. 520). That is, the "M" in this model reflects both team process and team emergent states. *Team process* characterizes "members' interdependent acts that convert inputs to outcomes through cognitive, verbal, and behavioral activities directed toward organizing taskwork to achieve collective goals" (Marks et al., 2001, p. 357). *Team emergent states* are "constructs that characterize properties of the team that are typically dynamic in nature and vary as a function of team context, inputs, processes, and outcomes" (Marks et al., 2001, p. 357). Below is a simplified framework relating team training to team performance (Figure 1).

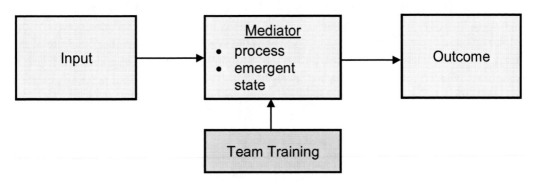

Figure 1. General model of team performance.

The evidence demonstrating the efficacy of team training is robust. In the past decade, meta-analytic integrations have shown team training to be a valuable intervention for enhancing affective, cognitive, process, and performance outcomes (Salas, Nichols, & Driskell, 2007; Salas et al., 2008). Moreover, team training interventions have been shown to be effective across a wide variety of settings, tasks, and team types.

TRAINING TEAMS TO HIGH PERFORMANCE

The following sections progress through the steps we would take in order to create and train a team to high performance. We begin by identifying team member selection criteria, and then delineate how we would prepare for training, followed by what we would train, how training would be delivered, and what we would do after training.

Team Formation and Selection

Like Rome, high-performance teams aren't built in a day. Moreover, at their onset, all teams are not created equal. In this section, we briefly outline our considerations for selecting and forming a high-performance team. Although these considerations do not explain how to train teams to high performance, we believe it is important to first delineate certain desirable team member characteristics, as these characteristics will impact team training and team performance.

The first, and perhaps most obvious, consideration is the skill level and ability of the team members. As previously mentioned, individual task proficiency should be a prerequisite to team training. In other words, before team members are trained to perform as a team they should possess the skills necessary to complete the team tasks. This brings to mind the seminal work of Ivan Steiner (1972) who laid out the following model of team performance: actual productivity of the group equals potential productivity (i.e., the individual contributions of the team members) minus process losses (e.g., motivation losses and coordination losses; see Forsyth, 2009). Clearly, some team members will be more adept than others at task performance. According to Steiner's model, teams with more skilled members have a greater capacity to perform than teams with less skilled members, potentially leading to greater process gain. If we use soccer as an example, most managers would select a player of the caliber of Lionel Messi (four-time world player of the year) as a team member over one of the current authors. Thus, we operate under the assumption that our hypothetical team is comprised of individuals with advanced levels of skills. This is in line with previous research and recommendations to omit low-ability team members for complex tasks (Bowers, Pharmer, & Salas, 2000).

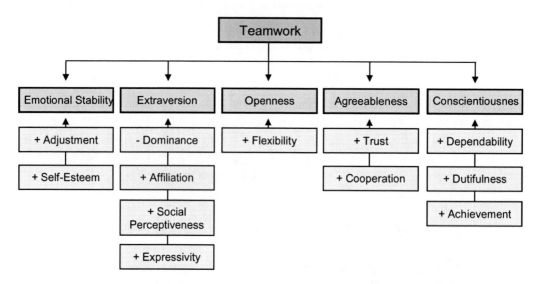

Figure 2. Traits related to teamwork. Adapted with permission from Driskell, J. E., Goodwin, G. F., Salas, E., & O'Shea, P. G. (2006). What makes a good team player? Personality and team effectiveness. Group Dynamics: Theory, Research, and Practice, 10(4), 249-271.

The second, and more relevant, consideration is the traits of individuals that make them good team players. Setting out to answer this question, Driskell, Goodwin, Salas, and O'Shea (2006a) advanced a hierarchical model of personality variables related to teamwork. This model comprises lower-order traits (e.g., trust and flexibility) mapping onto the Big Five model of personality (see Figure 2). The relationship between these traits and team performance is complex; however, research has demonstrated positive relationships between the higher- and lower- order factors and team performance. For example, a meta-analysis conducted by Bell (2007) found a positive relationship between several of the Big Five traits and team performance. However, it is important to note that the relationship between personality variables and team performance is complex and is moderated by factors such as the type of task a team performs, where performance is measured, among others. Moreover, as Driskell et al. (2006a) note, "Whereas the broad higher-level constructs [i.e., the Big Five] offer an efficient and parsimonious way of describing personality, the more specific facets can offer higher fidelity of trait descriptions and greater predictive validity" (p. 250), thus suggesting the comprehensiveness of the Big Five may obfuscate relationships with team performance. For example, the trait agreeableness has been defined in terms of the lower-order facets trust and cooperation (Driskell et al., 2006a). Findings from the team literature demonstrate that both of these facets relate positively to teamwork and team outcomes (De Jong, & Dirks, 2012; Mesmer-Magnus & DeChurch, 2009). Nonetheless, the traits identified above represent a good reference point in determining what traits to consider when selecting team members. Additionally, these traits are similar to traits identified as useful predictors of performance under stress (Driskell, Wadsworth, & Krokos, 2009). This is relevant considering that although teams may train in innocuous environments; they are often expected to perform in stressful, high demand ones.

What, How, and When of Team Training

Once a team is selected and formed, preparations can be taken for designing, developing, and implementing team training. The following section outlines three essential considerations for team training: What should be trained?; How should they be trained?; and When, or how often, should team training occur? Before addressing these questions, we first turn to an often overlooked precursor of team training: the pretraining environment.

Prepare Teams for Training

Salas and Cannon-Bowers (2001) called attention to the importance of the relationship between pretraining contextual factors and learning outcomes. Specifically, they emphasized two contextual factors that have been demonstrated to impact learning: (a) how training is framed, that is how training is represented to trainees, and (b) prior experiences with training. These contextual factors are suggested to moderate trainee self-efficacy and motivation to learn, both of which have been linked to positive attitudes toward training, learning acquisition and retention, and transfer of training (Salas, Tannenbaum, Kraiger, & Smith-Jentsch, 2012). For example, Quiñones (1995) demonstrated that labeling a training intervention as "advanced" enhanced self-efficacy, motivation, and learning outcomes over the same training intervention labeled "remedial." These results have been substantiated (e.g., Tai, 2006) and advanced as a means of improving team training (Burke, Salas, Wilson-Donnelly, & Priest, 2004). In relation to previous experiences with training, for instance, Smith-Jentsch, Jentsch, Payne, and Salas (1996) found a positive relationship between the number of trainee negative events related to the intention of the training intervention and posttraining performance. The authors suggest that this relationship was attributed to an increase in motivation to learn stemming from an increased perceived need for training.

There are several important implications that should be drawn from these findings in respect to training teams to high performance. First, training should be framed to bolster self-efficacy and motivation by explicitly delineating the intervention as "expert" or "advanced." Second, training should be framed to persuade trainees that training is in fact needed and will lead to better sustained performance. Third, these findings highlight the significance of the relationship between self-efficacy, motivation, and performance for training. Thus, additional strides should be taken to augment trainee self-efficacy and motivation prior to training.

A particularly useful strategy for improving motivation in team training interventions is goal-setting (see Locke & Latham, 1990, 2013). Goal-setting for team training is unique in that it is multi-level (i.e., individual and team goals; Kramer, Thayer, & Salas, 2013). Evidence for individual and team performance suggests that goals should be specific and difficult (Locke & Latham, 2002; Kleingeld, van Mierlo, & Arends, 2011). For example, at the team-level Kleingeld et al. (2011) found that specific, difficult goals had a substantial effect ($d = .80$) on group performance. Although Kleingeld et al. (2011) note that individual goals can promote group performance, some research suggests that individual goals may detract from processes driving group performance (e.g., coordination), especially when interdependency is high (van Mierlo & Kleingeld, 2010). Thus, caution should be taken when developing individual level goals.

What Should Be Trained?

In order to train teams to high performance, it is necessary to determine what teamwork competencies (e.g., team processes and states) team training should focus on. The answer to this question is typically derived from a *team-training needs analysis* (Salas & Cannon-Bowers, 2000). A comprehensive needs analysis is comprised of three principal components: organizational, task, and person analysis. These types of analyses examine what, how, and who the training consists of, respectively. Although each of these components is central to team training development and delivery, we focus here on the *team task analysis* and *person analysis* as these processes identify the content and concentration of team training. The general aim of a *team task analysis* is the identification of the critical KSAs and teamwork competencies requisite of team performance. For example, analysis of a soccer team will likely identify coordination as a critical teamwork competency illustrative of task performance. Thus, enhancing team coordination would be an objective of team training. A *person analysis* examines who needs training and what type of training they need. For team training, the team itself may be considered as an "individual unit" (Shuffler, Pavlas, & Salas, 2012). An important outcome of the person analysis is the identification of competency deficiencies, at both the individual and team level, thus identifying what types of KSAs need more or less focus during team training.

Although the specific content of a team training intervention will differ depending on the task to be trained, we can offer several general considerations for training teams to high performance. These considerations are identified below.

Focus on Teamwork Competencies. As previously mentioned, the aim of team training is to facilitate and enhance teamwork skills, or as Salas, Burke, and Cannon-Bowers (2002) describe, "the behavioral, cognitive, and attitude skills needed to communicate, interact, and coordinate tasks effectively with other team members" (p. 240). This is not to say that individual skills should be overlooked. In fact team training should focus on enhancing both individual and team skills. The six team competencies advanced by Salas et al. (in press) represent a good starting point for team-based content. Beyond these six competencies, it is worthwhile to foster a deeper understanding of team cognition and adaptive behaviors, both of which have a definitive impact on team performance.

Promote Team Cognition. Despite being identified as one of the six core team competencies by Salas et al. (in press), it is useful to present a separate discussion of team cognition. Team cognition can be defined as "the observable cognitive processes that occur within the team" (Wildman et al., 2012, p. 85) or the "interplay of the individual cognition of each team member and team process behaviors" (Cooke, Salas, Kiekel, & Bell, 2004, p. 85). Much has been learned about team cognition in the past several decades (e.g., DeChurch & Mesmer-Magnus, 2010a, 2010b; Salas & Fiore, 2004). As a result, there are several constructs with well-established evidence linking them to positive team outcomes. Those we deem to be most germane to team training include transactive memory, shared mental models (SMM), and team situation awareness (team SA).

Transactive Memory Systems. A transactive memory system (TMS) is a property of a group that describes the group as a single information processing system responsible for encoding, storing, and retrieving information (Hollingshead; 1998, Wegner, 1987). At a high-level, transactive memory includes a combination of team member knowledge and awareness of who has what knowledge (Austin, 2003). However, Lewis and Herndon (2011) note that this conceptualization fails to recognize the importance of differentiated knowledge, transactive processes, and the dynamic nature of TMSs. According to Ren and Argote (2011) a team member's memory consists of two components: individual memory (i.e., differentiated and shared) and transactive memory (i.e., understanding of who knows what). In high-functioning teams, members of the team operate as external memory storage facilities for each other, and it is not until these members engage in transactive processes (i.e., encoding, storage, and retrieval processes) that individual knowledge is combined. Thus, for high-functioning teams, and consequently high-functioning TMSs, an understanding of who has what knowledge is critical, as this allows team members to access more information than they would be able to individually. Moreover, TMSs are dynamic which suggests that (a) TMSs may become more fine-tuned and (b) robust across time (Lewis & Herndon, 2011). In other words, teammates may develop a better understanding of who has what knowledge, in addition to developing a larger knowledge repository. Research has demonstrated the efficacy of TMSs for enhancing team process and performance (DeChurch & Mesmer-Magnus, 2010a). As an example, a soccer player may have been recently traded from a rival team. In a well-functioning TMS, the player's new teammates would recognize this and use his or her knowledge of the rival team's players and strategies to their advantage.

Shared Mental Models. Shared mental models are defined as "knowledge structures held by members of a team that enable them to form accurate explanations and expectations for the task, and, in turn, to coordinate their actions and adapt their behavior to demands of the task and other team members"(Cannon-Bowers, Salas, & Converse 1993, p. 229). Shared mental models are central to team performance and have been suggested as an explanatory factor in how teams effectively adapt and perform in complex environments (Cannon-Bowers et al., 1993). Research on SMM generally delineate between two types of mental models: task-based and team-based. The former represents shared knowledge of the technology/equipment team members interact with and the procedures underlying task performance, while the latter describes a shared understanding of how to interact as a team and knowledge about team members (e.g., KSAs, preferences, etc.; Mathieu, Heffner, Goodwin, Salas, & Cannon-Bowers, 2000). Similar to TMSs, SMMs has been shown to improve team process and performance (Mathieu et al., 2000; Smith-Jentsch, Mathieu, & Kraiger, 2005). A good example of a well-functioning SMM is the defensive back four of the late 1980's and early 1990's Arsenal team who became famous for their offside trap and their ability to function as a single unit.

Team Situation Awareness. Team SA represents the degree of SA necessary for each team member to complete taskwork and teamwork responsibilities (Endsley, 1989; Prince, Ellis, Brannick, & Salas, 2007). Overall, SA can be considered as the perception, comprehension, and prediction of elements in one's environment. At the team-level, this comprises both a team member's unique SA and the SA shared between other team members. Team SA has been shown to be an important driver of team performance (e.g., Prince et al., 2007). A good anecdote demonstrating team SA occurred when Dimitar Berbatov was playing at Tottenham Hotspur FC. During practice, teammate Jamie O'Hara was calling for the ball to Berbatov who had his back turned and was 40-yards away. O'Hara notes that "Berba dropped his shoulder and, without looking, he played a pinpoint pass right to my feet. After training, he said to me: 'I know where you are. You don't have to shout.'" (Hytner, 2012).

Facilitate Adaptive Behaviors. Teams must perform in naturalistic settings that are often characterized by dynamic and continually changing conditions, real-time reactions to these changes, ill-defined goals and ill-structured tasks (Klein, Orasanu, Calderwood, & Zsambok, 1993). Subsequently, an important quality of high-performance teams is their ability to adapt to these types of conditions. The cognitive emergent states described above assist in promoting adaptive team performance (Burke, Stagl, Salas, Pierce, & Kendall, 2006). In addition to these cognitive states, team behaviors (i.e., processes) allow teams to adapt to changing conditions. The taxonomy of team process advanced by Marks et al. (2001), currently the most widely acknowledged and validated (see LePine, Piccolo, Jackson, Mathieu, & Saul, 2008), recognizes three superordinate team process dimensions: transition processes, action processes, and interpersonal processes (see Figure 3). *Transition processes* primarily describe team planning and evaluation processes. *Action processes* describe team activities that directly lead to goal attainment. *Interpersonal processes* describe activities that teams engage in to manage interpersonal relations. The following section will discuss transition and action processes as these have been suggested to be most predictive of performance quality and efficiency (Marks et al., 2001).

Transition processes include *mission analysis, goal specification*, and *strategy formulation and planning*. These team activities allow for greater preparation and consequently an increased capability to adapt to changing and/or novel situations. For example, planning is comprised of deliberate planning (e.g., a primary course of action), contingency planning (e.g., conditional propositions), and reactive strategy adjustment (e.g., a what now approach). Employing an *if...then* strategy can allow teams to better adapt to foreseen circumstances and may result in an enhanced perception of control over extraneous factors. For instance, a soccer team may develop the following contingency plan: *if* player X is injured, *then* player Y assumes his or her position and the team transitions to a different formation. Although these types of decisions may be made on the fly, preparation allows for increased efficiency, which in critical or dangerous conditions can prove invaluable.

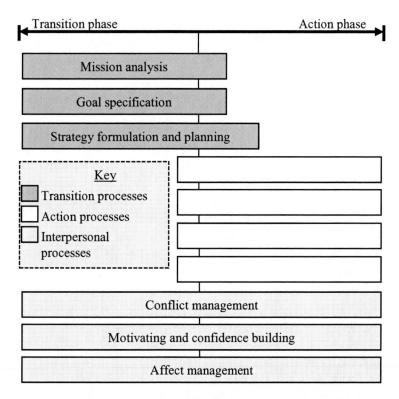

Figure 3. Team processes across transition and action phases. Adapted with permission from Marks, M. A., Mathieu, J. E., & Zaccaro, S. J. (2001). A temporally based framework and taxonomy of team processes. *Academy of Management Review*, *26*(3), 356-376.

In contrast to transition process, action processes describe what teams do during task performance. This process category includes *monitoring progress toward goals*, *monitoring team resources and environmental conditions*, *backup behaviors*, and *coordination* (Marks et al., 2001). Although the processes focused on during team training depend on the type of task performed, team researchers have identified several team behaviors especially relevant to team effectiveness. For example, Salas et al. (2005) proposed a "Big Five" model of teamwork including three types of action processes: *mutual performance monitoring*, *backup behavior*, and *adaptability*. Mutual performance monitoring refers to a team's ability to monitor each other's performance, while carrying out individual tasks (McIntyre & Salas, 1995). The aim of mutual performance monitoring is not to keep tabs on one another, but to ensure that the team is functioning as expected. This may include catching team member mistakes preemptively or after they have occurred. Backup behavior refers to an active shift in work responsibilities by a fellow team member as a result of a perceived workload distribution problem (i.e., an individual's workload has surpassed their capacity to accommodate it). Typical backup behaviors include (a) feedback provision/coaching, (b) task assistance, and (c) task completion (Marks et al., 2001). According to Salas et al. (2005), backup behaviors moderate the relationship between mutual performance monitoring and team effectiveness. Perhaps the most important implication for training teams to high performance is the increased degree of flexibility backup behaviors afford under stress. For instance, during a soccer game a player may find him or herself defending more than one player. A teammate observing this and tracking over to mark the additional player is a good example of a backup behavior. Considered as a team process, adaptability refers to a team's ability to identify changes and accommodate to these changes (e.g., adjust strategies) throughout task performance. Adaptability requires a strong shared understanding of the roles and responsibilities of the team (i.e., SMM), in addition to the application of transition processes (e.g., strategy formulation and planning) and action processes (e.g., mutual performance monitoring and backup behavior).

Promote a Positive Team Functioning Perspective. Positive team functioning is a multilevel concept encompassing both individual- and team-level positive subjective experiences (e.g., motivational and affective states) and positive traits (e.g., adaptability; Seligman & Csikszentmihalhi, 2000). For the reason that this chapters central focus is on teams and training, we will address the concept of positive team functioning by examining team-level states (i.e., motivational and affective states of teams). However, we note that the distinction between individual- and team-level traits and states are not mutually exclusive. For instance, cohesion, a team-level state, has been shown to increase individual member satisfaction (Martens & Peterson, 1971). Moreover, from a positive team functioning perspective it is important to identify the relationships between team processes, positive subjective states, and team performance. For example, effective team communication can cultivate a sense of cohesion among the team members, which in turn may enhance team performance. These relationships are cyclical, meaning that emergent states (e.g., cohesion), for instance, can also be considered inputs in an I-P-O cycle (Marks et al., 2001). Following the previous example, cohesion may also serve to increase communication, thus potentially facilitating team performance by this link. Marks et al. (2001) suggest that interpersonal processes such as conflict management, motivation and confidence building, and affect management serve to "lay the foundation for the effectiveness of other processes" (p. 368) and influence critical emergent states such as cohesion.

In the following section we discuss several motivational and affective states of teams that have been shown to positively affect both team process and performance. These constructs are important for several reasons. First, they represent important constructs that may represent a focus of team training. And most importantly, these constructs highlight the importance of developing positive team functioning not only for individual and team well-being, but for developing high-performance teams. From an organizational buy-in standpoint, this is significant as organizations will appreciate a tangible return (e.g., improved performance) as a result of improving positive team functioning. The specific motivational and attitudinal constructs discussed below include: cohesion, collective efficacy and potency, interpersonal trust, and psychological safety. It is worth noting at the onset that research has established a high degree of correlation between many of the emergent states (Mathieu, Maynard, Rapp, & Gilson, 2008).

Cohesion. Cohesion has been one of the most widely studied, and consequently most widely validated constructs in the team literature. It is generally referred to as the "forces that exist between group members" that generate motivational and social bonds amongst teams (Beal, Cohen, Burke, & McLendon, 2003, p. 989). Over the years, researchers have identified three central components of cohesion based on Festinger's (1950) conceptualization: *interpersonal attraction, task commitment,* and *group pride* (Beal et al., 2003, Kozlowski & Ilgen, 2006; Mullen & Cooper, 1994). Beal et al. (2003) define *interpersonal attraction* as "A shared liking for or attachment to the members of the group;" *task commitment* as "The extent to which the task allows the group to attain important goals or the extent to which a shared commitment to the group's task exists;" and *group pride* as "The extent to which group members exhibit liking for the status or the ideologies that the group supports or represents, or the shared importance of being a member of the group."

In the past 25 years, over half a dozen meta-analyses have been published investigating the moderators and outcomes of cohesion (Beal et al., 2003; Carron, Colman, Wheeler, & Stevens, 2002; Chiocchio & Essiembre, 2009; Evans & Dion, 1991; Gully, Devine, & Whitney, 1995; Mullen & Cooper, 1994; Oliver, Harman, Hoover, Hayes, & Pandhi, 1999). Overall, a positive relationship between cohesion and team performance has been found. Everton FC in the English Premier League is a good example of a team who is often said to have strong character, which can make them difficult to play against due to their high-level of cohesiveness.

Collective Efficacy and Potency. Although unique constructs, collective efficacy and potency are closely related (Stajkovic, Lee, & Nyberg, 2009). Collective efficacy can be defined as "a group's shared belief in its conjoint capabilities to organize and execute the courses of action required to produce given levels of attainments" (Bandura, 1997, p. 477). Similarly, potency has been defined as "the collective belief in a group that it can be effective" (Guzzo, Yost, Campbell, & Shea, 1993, p. 87). Potency can be regarded as a more generalized version of collective efficacy. Specifically, potency refers to a team's belief that they can perform across a range of tasks and circumstances, while collective efficacy refers to a team's belief in their ability to perform a specific task. Meta-analyses on collective efficacy and potency have confirmed a positive relationship between these constructs and team performance (Gully, Incalcaterra, Joshi, & Beaubien, 2002; Stajkovic et al., 2009). It is worth noting that the meta-analysis conducted by Stajkovic et al. (2009) examined the mediating relationship of collective efficacy on potency and team performance demonstrating full mediation. This finding suggests that although a general belief in team capability is important, confidence in task-specific capability is essential for high-performing teams. Kozlowski and Ilgen (2006) suggest that team training interventions are a constructive means of developing collective efficacy and potency.

Interpersonal Trust and Psychological Safety. As Edmondson (2004) argues [and we agree with her], trust and psychological safety are similar yet distinct constructs. We discuss them together here because they represent intrapsychic states related to team member interactions that involve perceptions of vulnerability and risk (Edmondson, 2004). At the team-level, the trust construct has experienced considerable ambiguity in terms of definition, conceptualization, and measurement (De Jong & Dirks, 2012). For example, trust has been defined as "a willingness to rely on an exchange partner in whom one has confidence" (Moorman, Zaltman, & Deshpande, 1992, p. 315) and as "a party's decision to rely on another... under a condition of risk... that allows its fate to be determined by the other party" (Currall & Inkpen, 2002, p. 484). Although research is not clear about how to define trust or how trust affects team performance (e.g., directly via team processes and performance or indirectly through motivation; see Dirks, 1999), there is sufficient evidence to conclude that trust enhances team performance (De Jong & Dirks, 2012; De Jong & Elfring, 2010).

Psychological safety has been described as "a shared belief...that the team is safe for interpersonal risk taking" (Edmondson, 1999, p. 350). Thus a critical distinction between trust and psychological safety is the referent. Specifically, the referent of trust is other team members, while the referent of psychological safety is the self (Edmondson, 2004).

Psychological safety has been shown to improve team performance. Specifically, Edmondson (2004) suggests that psychological safety enhances team performance by promoting six team learning behaviors: (a) help-seeking behaviors, (b) feedback-seeking behaviors, (c) speaking up about errors and concerns, (d) creativity, and (e) boundary spanning behaviors.

How Should Team Training Be Delivered?

Many practitioners fail to recognize that team training is theoretically-based and systematic in delivery. In other words, team training consists of a specific set of instructional strategies and tools that when combined correctly, should enhance team process and performance. That being said, the components of a team training intervention can be delivered in a variety of ways. Three key components that should be considered when training teams to high performance include how training is delivered, what team training strategy should be employed, and how feedback ought to be provided. These components of training delivery are discussed in turn.

Instructional Delivery Methods. A comprehensive team training intervention incorporates three methods of delivering training: information-based, demonstration-based, and practice-based. Although we acknowledge that the application of each of these delivery methods may not be necessary or feasible (e.g., due to organizational constraints) for every team training intervention, given unlimited resources we would undoubtedly utilize all three. The following sections describe each delivery method and provide examples regarding the context of training a soccer team to high performance.

Information. The general aim of this type of instructional delivery is to provide trainees with a baseline of declarative knowledge and knowledge about upcoming events. Information-based methods include slide presentations, information packets, advanced organizers, and lectures. Information-based methods are often used in training for the reason that they are comparatively cheap and easy to administer. Information-based methods can be used to initially develop shared mental models and a shared knowledge of who has what information/skills set. For example, a training packet may contain information about team member roles and responsibilities, while stressing the importance and influence of shared mental models on team performance. One of the chief advantages of information-based methods is its effectiveness on team outcomes when combined with other methods of delivery. For instance, Weaver, Rosen, Salas, Baum, & King (2010) note that independently, information-based methods have a minimal influence on team training effectiveness, thus suggesting that these types of instructional delivery methods should be used in combination with other delivery methods (i.e., demonstration and practice). An example of information-based delivery in a team training program aimed at a soccer team, say Barcelona, is inculcating new players in "the Barcelona way."

Demonstration. Based on social learning theory (Bandura, 1977) and behavior modeling training (Sorcher & Goldstein, 1972), demonstration-based methods entail trainees observing prespecified taskwork and teamwork behaviors modeled by actors (e.g., trainers, actors, etc.). In team training, demonstrations represent good and bad examples of team-based competencies (e.g. coordination). The specific team competencies to be demonstrated depend on the results of the team needs analysis. For example, if communication has been recognized as a critical team competency of team performance and a deficiency has been identified for this competency, then one goal of training would be to provide amble demonstrations of good and bad team communication. Demonstrations offer researchers and practitioners a flexible means of delivering instructional content, as they can be delivered in-person, via video, or through simulations. Moreover, the research demonstrating the efficacy of demonstrations on learning outcomes is well documented (Taylor, Russ-Efts, & Chan, 2005). In general, a successful demonstration for team training is one that accurately depicts how to – and how not to – apply teamwork behaviors. In training a youth soccer team, a demonstration-based method may entail having the youth players watching first team players practice or play.

Practice. Practice is an indispensable component of any team training program that purports to be comprehensive and high-caliber. In respect to training teams to high performance, practice-based methods offer the biggest bang for the buck. Practice-based methods allow teams to apply targeted competencies in safe, secure environments. Practice in and of itself is insufficient for training. Instead an important qualification should be made. Specifically, practice throughout training should be guided. That is, practice should focus on key competencies executed in a systematic fashion. The notion of guided practice is similar to that of deliberate practice (Ericsson, Krampe, & Tesch-Römer, 1993), where practice is focused on specific identified competencies, performing these competencies in increasing difficulty, with the aim of mastering performance. Salas et al. (2002) suggest that guided practice enhances team training effectiveness by ensuring that targeted team competencies are practiced, thereby enabling the most efficient and effective use of practice time. Research demonstrating the efficacy of practice on team outcomes is unequivocal: practice improves performance (Salas et al., 2008). It is also not a coincidence that the top players (e.g., David Beckham, Cristiano Ronaldo) are often the last players to leave the practice pitch. This method of training has been aptly described by Gregory van der Wiel's when describing the Ajax method: "You do things again and again and again, then you repeat it some more times" (quoted in Sokolove, 2010).

Instructional Strategy. Team training strategies come in many shapes and sizes. These instructional strategies vary depending on team training context, focus, and training mission. As Gregory, Feitosa, Driskell, Salas, and Vessey (2013) note, team training strategies are not a "one-size-fits-all" approach and should be tailored to coincide with the results of a team needs analysis. A comprehensive strategy is comprised of team training tools (e.g., team task analysis), methods, (i.e., information, demonstration, and practice), and content (i.e., KSAs). Despite the plethora of existing strategies (see Salas, Burke, & Stagl, 2004; Salas & Priest, 2005), we highlight several strategies we think are of particular value for training high-performance teams: cross-training, guided team self-correction training, and stress exposure training. The efficacy of these strategies has previously been demonstrated in a variety of contexts (Salas et al., 2007; Saunders, Driskell, Johnston, & Salas, 1996). Each strategy is discussed in turn.

Cross-training. Put simply, cross-training allows team members to experience what it is like to be in each other's shoes. According to Volpe, Cannon-Bowers, Salas, and Spector (1996), cross-training is defined as "a strategy in which each team member is trained on the tasks, duties, and responsibilities of his or her fellow team members" (p. 87). The general aim of cross-training is to allow team members to develop interpositional knowledge, which in turn develops accurate shared mental models. Through the development of accurate shared mental models, cross-training is expected to enhance coordination – especially implicit coordination (i.e., coordination without explicit communication) – amongst the team.

Moreover, cross-training has been suggested to aid in the development of a positive team functioning perspective, specifically team moral, cohesion, and confidence (Blickensderfer, Cannon-Bowers, & Salas, 1998).

Cross-training is primarily applied via three methods: positional clarification, positional modeling, and positional rotation. Positional clarification entails providing general knowledge about team member roles and responsibilities. Positional modeling involves an observation approach whereby team members observe each other perform team tasks and responsibilities in a simulated situation. Lastly, positional rotation allows team members to gain hands-on experience performing each other's roles by rotating positions among the team. In respect to training teams to high performance, we suggest that either a positional modeling or positional rotation approach be employed if applying a cross-training strategy. This recommendation is consistent with extant research. For example, Marks et al. (2002) note that both positional modeling and positional rotation served to enhance equivalent shared team-interaction mental models. It is worth noting that although cross-training has demonstrated its effectiveness in a variety of settings, concrete evidence supporting the efficacy of cross-training on team performance is lacking (see Salas et al., 2007).

Guided Team Self-correction Training. Guided team self-correction training is a structured approach that leverages team briefings and debriefings to develop a shared vision (e.g., shared mental model) amongst team members (Smith-Jentsch, Cannon-Bowers, Tannenbaum, & Salas, 2008). Also called *team dimensional training*, team self-correction training intends to provide a structured briefing or debriefing that is organized around an expert mental model of teamwork and focuses on both positive and negative performance examples. Smith-Jentsch et al. (2008) suggest that team briefing and debriefings can be effective if they (a) focus on general rules of behavior that are transferable across settings, (b) employ a prespecified framework to enable discussion, and (c) focus on both instances of positive and negative performance. Meta-analytic efforts suggest that guided team self-correction training is an effective team training intervention (Salas et al., 2007). Moreover, a recent meta-analysis conducted by Tannenbaum and Cerasoli (2013) showed team debriefs to have a significant positive effect on team performance. For soccer teams, as well as other teams, pre- and de-briefs can be executed before the game, at half-time, and after the game.

Stress Exposure Training. Research demonstrating the negative effects of stress has been exhibited at both the individual and team level (Driskell, Salas, & Johnston, 2006b). At the team level, stress may increase social impairment, thus potentially infringing on teamwork processes and team performance. For example, Driskell, Salas, and Johnston (1999) found that stress leads to a reduction in team perspective (i.e., a shift from a team-focus to an individual-focus perspective) and, in turn, team performance decrements. Stress training has been defined as "an intervention designed to enhance familiarity and teach skills necessary to maintain effective task performance under stress conditions" (Driskell et al., 2006b, p. 143). The general aim of stress exposure training (SET) is to combat these negative effects of stress by (a) increasing familiarity with the stress environment, (b) developing skills to maintain performance under stress, and (c) increasing confidence/self-efficacy. Stress exposure training is a model of training encompassing three phases: (1) information provision, (2) skill acquisition, and (3) application and practice. At a high-level, *information provision* provides trainees with information about stressors, the stress environment, and the effects of stress; *skill acquisition* presents trainees with techniques (e.g., guided-error training, attention-focus training, team training, etc.) that enable them to effectively perform in stressful environments;

application and practice allows trainees to apply learned skills during graduated exposure to realistic stressors. As a result, SET can be combined with other team training strategies to create a comprehensive stress training program that is directly related to training under "game" conditions. Stress exposure training can be likened to the axioms: "practice like you play" or "train like you fight."

Feedback. The provision of feedback is central to every team training intervention and should be provided both during and after training delivery. The general aim of feedback is to provide trainees with information regarding past performance so that they can adapt their behaviors for future performance. Moreover, feedback is a driver of motivation and a yardstick by which goal attainment is gauged. For teams, feedback is multilevel and multifaceted (DeShon, Kozlowski, Schmidt, Milner, & Wiechmann, 2004). Specifically, feedback can be directed at either the team members or the team; provided by teammates, the team, or an instructor; and can be outcome-oriented (e.g., how many goals a team scored) or behavior-oriented (e.g., how well did the team communicate). Despite equivocal findings, extant research has established the positive effects of well-designed and implemented feedback on training outcomes (Kluger & DeNisi, 1996). "Good" feedback is (a) accurate, (b) provided in a timely manner, (c) focused on behaviors over outcomes, (d) and constructive (Smith-Jentsch, Zeisig, Acton, & McPherson, 1998). Many of these feedback features are predicated on accurate process and performance measurement. Although describing how to evaluate team training is beyond the scope of this chapter, we note that evaluation is central to an effective team training intervention and to continuing team training efforts. For information on team performance assessment and training evaluation we refer the reader to Brannick, Salas, and Prince (1997) and Kraiger, Ford, and Salas (1993).

After-Training Reinforcement

Team training doesn't stop at the end of an intervention, it is an ongoing process. Although team training can enhance the KSAs of the individuals who partake, these KSAs may not last forever. A substantial body of literature has shown that skills degrade over time (Arthur, Bennett, Stanush, & McNelly, 1998). Consequently, it is important to take steps to mitigate this undesirable outcome. First, it is useful to stress the importance of teamwork and the application of the skills learned during training throughout the team's life-cycle. In other words, coaches and teammates should consistently encourage each other to apply team skills during practice and game-play. Encouragement may take the form of reminders of what was learned throughout the team training intervention, the provision of incentives, and continuous feedback regarding the trained skills. For example, team debriefs could be conducted after practice sessions to evaluate teamwork. Furthermore, team members should be provided ample opportunities to practice the learned skills in the performance environment (in sports teams this is typically accomplished through practice sessions). Second, refresher training can be conducted as a proactive or reactive strategy. A proactive approach would attempt to provide refresher training prior to skill decay while a reactive approach provides training when a deficiency in team competencies is identified. As a reactive strategy, performance diagnosis can be applied in order to identify where a deficiency exists, thus identifying where training should be focused. Similar to a team training intervention, refresher training should follow the science of training.

Table 2. Tips for training teams to high performance

1	**Be deliberate in selecting who you want to be on you team.**
	a. Select team members who have high levels of skill and ability. *Think*: "Hard work and determination won't always compensate for lack of ability"
	b. Consider personality traits that make skilled team members good teammates. *Think*: "A bad apple may spoil the bunch"
2	**Team members should be prepared for team training prior to the training itself.**
	a Training should be framed as an (a) advanced and (b) valuable intervention. *Think*: "The unwilling are difficult to sway"
	b Recognize trainee's past-experiences with training. *Think*: "The past predicts the future"
3	**Conduct a team-training needs analysis**
	a Identify *what* should be trained, *how* it should be trained, and *who* training should be delivered to. *Think*: "It is easier to navigate with a compass"
4	**Team training should focus on training teamwork competencies**
	a Focus on teamwork over taskwork. *Think*: "There is no 'I' in team"
	b Facilitate the development of team cognition. *Think*: "It's better to have everyone on the same page"
	c Increase adaptive team behaviors. *Think*: "If you can't adapt, you can't evolve"
	d Develop a positive team functioning perspective. *Think*: "Positive attitudes lead to positive outcomes"
5	**Select appropriate training delivery method(s)**
	a Determine if training should be delivered via information-, demonstration-, and/or practice- based methods. *Think*: "knowledge is power"; "monkey see, monkey do"; and "practice makes perfect"
6	**Choose a suitable instructional strategy**
	a The strategy to be used should be determined by the results of the needs analysis. *Think*: "Your objectives determine your approach"
7	**Provide feedback in an accurate and timely manner**
	a Feedback may be at an individual or team level, and either behavior or outcome oriented. *Think*: "It's easier to change the future when you understand the past"
8	**Be able to diagnose team performance**
	a Evaluation provides feedback and determines the efficacy of training. Accuracy is key. *Think*: "Measure twice, cut once"
9	**Encourage teamwork after team training**
	a Allow opportunities to practice team behaviors. *Think*: "If you don't use it, you lose it"
	b Re-provide training on an as needed basis. Think: "Perfection demands persistence"

CONCLUSION

Team training interventions have the potential to offer significant advantages to individuals, teams, and organizations. However, research spanning over a half-century has illustrated that in order for team training to be most effective, it must be grounded in science and be delivered systematically. Teams are currently more influential than at any other point in time and, as a consequence, training teams to high performance has been a widespread objective. This chapter outlined steps that can be taken in order to accomplish this objective. However, as with any training intervention, the strategies, tools, concepts, and focus of training varies as a function of training goals and the tasks to be trained. Nonetheless the information contained in this chapter provides a good starting point for developing a high-performing team. We conclude with a list of tips for training teams to high performance that summarize the concepts presented throughout this chapter (Table 2).

REFERENCES

Arthur Jr., W., Bennett Jr., W., Stanush, P. L., & McNelly, T. L. (1998). Factors that influence skill decay and retention: A quantitative review and analysis. *Human Performance, 11*(1), 57-101.

Austin, J. R. (2003). Transactive memory in organizational groups: The effects of content, consensus, specialization, and accuracy on group performance. *The Journal of Applied Psychology, 88*(5), 866-878. doi:10.1037/0021-9010.88.5.866

Bandura, A. (1977). *Social learning theory.* Englewood Cliffs, NJ: Prentice-Hall.

Bandura, A. (1997). *Self-efficacy: The exercise of control.* New York: Freeman.

Beal, D. J., Cohen, R. R., Burke, M. J., & McLendon, C. L. (2003). Cohesion and performance in groups: A meta-analytic clarification of construct relations. *Journal of Applied Psychology, 88*(6), 989-1004.

Bell, S. T. (2007). Deep-level composition variables as predictors of team performance: A meta-analysis. *The Journal of Applied Psychology, 92*(3), 595-615. doi:10.1037/0021-9010.92.3.595

Blickensderfer, E., Cannon-Bowers, J. A., & Salas, E. (1998). Cross-training and team performance. In J. A. Cannon-Bowers & E. Salas (Eds.), *Making decisions under stress: Implications for individual and team training* (pp. 299-311). Washington, DC: American Psychological Association.

Bowers, C. A., Braun, C. C., & Morgan, B. B. (1997). Team workload: Its meaning and measurement. In M. T. Brannick, E. Salas, & C. Prince (Eds.), *Team performance assessment and measurement: Theory, methods, and applications* (pp. 85-108). Mahwah, NJ: Erlbaum.

Bowers, C. A., Pharmer, J. A., & Salas, E. (2000). When member homogeneity is needed in work teams: A meta-analysis. *Small Group Research, 31*(3), 305-327. doi:10.1177/104649640003100303

Brannick, M., Salas, E., & Prince, C. (Eds.). (1997). *Team performance assessment and measurement: Theory, methods, and applications.* Mahwah, NJ: Lawrence Erlbaum Associates Publishers.

Burke, C. S., Salas, E., Wilson-Donnelly, K., & Priest, H. (2004). How to turn a team of experts into an expert medical team: Guidance from the aviation and military communities. *Quality and Safety in Health Care, 13*(suppl 1), i96-i104.

Burke, C. S., Stagl, K. C., Salas, E., Pierce, L., & Kendall, D. (2006). Understanding team adaptation: A conceptual analysis and model. *The Journal of Applied Psychology, 91*(6), 1189-1207. doi:10.1037/0021-9010.91.6.1189

Cannon-Bowers, J. A., Salas, E., & Converse, S. (1993). Shared mental models in expert team decision making. In N. J. Castellan Jr. (Ed.), *Individual and group decision making: Current issues* (pp. 221-246). Hillsdale, NJ: Lawrence Erlbaum Associates.

Cannon-Bowers, J. A., Tannenbaum, S. I., Salas, E., & Volpe, C. E. (1995). Defining competencies and establishing team training requirements. In R. Guzzo & E. Salas (Eds.), *Team effectiveness and decision making in organizations*, (pp. 333-380). San Francisco: Jossey-Bass.

Carron, A. V., Colman, M. M., Wheeler, J., & Stevens, D. (2002). Cohesion and performance in sport: A meta-analysis. *Journal of Sport and Exercise Psychology, 24*, 168-188.

Chiocchio, F., & Essiembre, H. (2009). Cohesion and performance: A meta-analytic review of disparities between project teams, production teams, and service teams. *Small Group Research, 40*(4), 382-420.

Cooke, N. J., Salas, E., Kiekel, P. A., & Bell, B. (2004). Advances in measuring team cognition. In E. Salas & S. M. Fiore (Eds.), *Team cognition: Understanding the factors that drive process and performance* (pp. 83-106). Washington, DC: American Psychological Association. doi:10.1037/10690-005

Currall, S. C., & Inkpen, A. C. (2000). A multilevel approach to trust in joint ventures. *Journal of International Business Studies, 33*(3), 479-495.

De Dreu, C. K., & Weingart, L. R. (2003). Task versus relationship conflict, team performance, and team member satisfaction: A meta-analysis. *Journal of Applied Psychology, 88*(4), 741-749.

De Jong, B. A., & Dirks, K. T. (2012). Beyond shared perceptions of trust and monitoring in teams: Implications of asymmetry and dissensus. *Journal of Applied Psychology, 97*(2), 391-406. doi:10.1037/a0026483

De Jong, B. A., & Elfring, T. (2010). How does trust affect the performance of ongoing teams? The mediating role of reflexivity, monitoring and effort. *Academy of Management Journal, 53*(3), 535-549. doi:10.5465/ AMJ.2010.51468649

DeChurch, L. A., & Mesmer-Magnus, J. R. (2010a). The cognitive underpinnings of effective teamwork: A meta-analysis. *Journal of Applied Psychology, 95*(1), 32-53. doi:10.1037/a0017328

DeChurch, L. A., & Mesmer-Magnus, J. R. (2010b). Measuring shared team mental models: A meta-analysis. *Group Dynamics: Theory, Research, and Practice, 14*(1), 1-14.

DeShon, R. P., Kozlowski, S. W., Schmidt, A. M., Milner, K. R., & Wiechmann, D. (2004). A multiple-goal, multilevel model of feedback effects on the regulation of individual and team performance. *Journal of Applied Psychology, 89*(6), 1035-1056.

Devine, D. J., Clayton, L. D., Philips, J. L., Dunford, B. B., & Melner, S. B. (1999). Teams in organizations: Prevalence, characteristics, and effectiveness. *Small Group Research, 30*(6), 678-711.

DiazGranados, D., Klein, C., Lyons, R., Salas, E., Bedwell, W. L., & Weaver, S. J. (2008). Investigating the prevalence, characteristics and effectiveness of teams: A U.S. sample surveyed. *Paper presented at the INGRoup: Interdisciplinary Network for Group Research*, Kansas City, MO, July 17-19.

Dirks, K. T. (1999). The effects of interpersonal trust on work group performance. *The Journal of Applied Psychology*, *84*(3), 445-455. Retrieved from http://www.ncbi.nlm.nih.gov/pubmed/10380424

Driskell, J. E., Goodwin, G. F., Salas, E., & O'Shea, P. G. (2006a). What makes a good team player? Personality and team effectiveness. *Group Dynamics: Theory, Research, and Practice*, *10*(4), 249-271. doi:10.1037/1089-2699.10.4.249

Driskell, J. E., Salas, E., & Johnston, J. (1999). Does stress lead to a loss of team perspective?. *Group Dynamics: Theory, Research, and Practice*, *3*(4), 291-302.

Driskell, J. E., Salas, E., & Johnston, J. H. (2006b). Decision making and performance under stress. In T. W. Britt, A. B. Adler, & C. A. Castro (Eds.), *Military life: The psychology of serving in peace and combat* (pp. 128-154). Westport, CT: Praeger.

Edmondson, A. (1999). Psychological safety and learning behavior in work teams. *Administrative Science Quarterly*, *44*(2), 350-383.

Edmondson, A. (2004). Psychological safety, trust, and learning in organizations: A group lens. In R. M. Kramer & K. S. Cook (Eds.), *Trust and distrust in organizations: Dilemmas and approaches* (pp. 239-272). New York: Russell Sage.

Endsley, M. (1989). *Final report: Situation awareness in an advanced strategic mission* (NOR DOC 89–32). Hawthorne, CA: Northrop Corp.

Ericsson, K. A., Krampe, R. T., & Tesch-Römer, C. (1993). The role of deliberate practice in the acquisition of expert performance. *Psychological Review*, *100*(3), 363-406.

Evans, C. R., & Dion, K. L. (1991). Group cohesion and performance: A meta-analysis. *Small Group Research, 22*(2), 175-186.

Festinger, L. (1950). Informal social communication. *Psychological Review, 57*(5), 271-282.

Fleishman, E. A., Mumford, M. D., Zaccaro, S. J., Levin, K. Y., Korotokin, A. L, & Hein, M. B. (1991). Taxonomic efforts in the description of leader behavior: A synthesis and functional interpretation. *The Leadership Quarterly*, *2*(4), 245-287. doi: 10.1016/1048-9843(91)90016-U

Forsyth, D. R. (2009). *Group dynamics* (5th ed.). Bellmont, CA: Cengage.

Gregory, M. E., Feitosa, J., Driskell, T., Salas, E., & Vessey, W. B. (2013). Designing, delivering, and evaluating team training in organizations: Principles that work. In E. Salas, S. I. Tannenbaum, D. Cohen, & G. Latham (Eds.), *Developing and enhancing high-performance teams: Evidence-based practices and advice* (pp. 441-487). San Francisco, CA: Jossey-Bass.

Gully, S. M., Devine, D. J., & Whitney, D. J. (1995). A meta-analysis of cohesion and performance: Effects of level of analysis and task interdependence. *Small Group Research, 26*(4), 497-520.

Gully, S. M., Incalcaterra, K. A., Joshi, A., & Beaubien, J. M. (2002). A meta-analysis of team-efficacy, potency, and performance: Interdependence and level of analysis as moderators of observed relationships. *Journal of Applied Psychology, 87*(5), 819-832.

Guzzo, R. A., Yost, P. R., Campbell, R. J., & Shea, G. P. (1993). Potency in groups: Articulating a construct. *British Journal of Social Psychology*, *32*(1), 87-106.

Hackman, J. R., & Wageman, R. (2005). A theory of team coaching. *Academy of Management Review*, *30*(2), 269-287.

Hollingshead, A. B. (1998). Retrieval processes in transactive memory systems. *Journal of Personality and Social Psychology, 74*(3), 659-671. doi:10.1037//0022-3514.74.3.659

Hytner, D. (2012, November 13). Dimitar Berbatov's arrival at Fulham fires sense of style and adventure. *The Guardian.* Retrieved from http://www. theguardian.com/ football/blog/2012/nov/13/fulham-dimitar-berbatov-style-adventure.

Ilgen, D. R., Hollenbeck, J. R., Johnson, M., & Jundt, D. (2005). Teams in organizations: From input-process-output models to IMOI models. *Annual Review of Psychology, 56,* 517-543.

Jehn, K., & Bendersky, C. (2003). Intragroup conflict in organizations: A contingency perspective on the conflict outcome relationship. *Research in Organizational Behavior, 25,* 187-242.

Katzenbach, J. R., & Smith, D. K. (1993). *The wisdom of teams: Creating the high-performance organization.* Boston, MA: Harvard Business School Press.

Klein, G. A., Orasanu, J., Calderwood, R., & Zsambok, C. E. (Eds.) (1993). *Decision making in action: Models and methods.* Norwood, NJ: Ablex.

Kleingeld, A., van Mierlo, H., & Arends, L. (2011). The effect of goal setting on group performance: A meta-analysis. *The Journal of Applied Psychology, 96*(6), 1289-1304. doi:10.1037/a0024315

Klimoski, R., & Mohammed, S. (1994). Shared mental model: Construct or metaphor? *Journal of Management, 20*(2), 403-437.

Kluger, A. N., & DeNisi, A. (1996). The effects of feedback interventions on performance: A historical review, a meta-analysis, and a preliminary feedback intervention theory. *Psychological Bulletin, 119*(2), 254-284. doi:10.1037/0033-2909.119.2.254.

Kozlowski, S. W. J., & Ilgen, D. R. (2006). Enhancing the effectiveness of work groups and teams. *Psychological Science in the Public Interest, 7*(3), 77-124. doi:10.1111/j.1529-1006.2006.00030.x.

Kozlowski, S. W., & Bell, B. S. (2003). Work groups and teams in organizations. In W. C. Borman, D. R. Ilgen, & R. J. Klimoski (Eds.), *Handbook of psychology: Industrial and organizational psychology* (Vol. 12, pp. 333-375). London: Wiley.

Kraiger, K., Ford, J., & Salas, E. (1993). Application of cognitive, skill-based, and affective theories of learning outcomes to new methods of training evaluation. *Journal of Applied Psychology, 78*(2), 311-328.

Kramer, W. S., Thayer, A. L., & Salas, E. (2013). Goal setting in teams. In E. A. Locke & G. P. Latham (Eds.), *New developments in goal setting and task performance* (pp. 287-310). New York: Taylor & Francis.

LePine, J. A., Piccolo, R. F., Jackson, C. L., Mathieu, J. E., & Saul, J. R. (2008). A meta-analysis of teamwork processes: Tests of a multidimensional model and relationships with team effectiveness criteria. *Personnel Psychology, 61*(2), 273-307. doi:10.1111/j.1744-6570.2008.00114.x.

Lewis, K., & Herndon, B. (2011). Transactive memory systems: Current issues and future research directions. *Organization Science, 22*(5), 1254-1265. doi:10.1287/orsc.1110.0647

Locke, E. A., & Latham, G. P. (1990). *A theory of goal setting & task performance.* Englewood Cliffs, NJ, US: Prentice-Hall, Inc.

Locke, E. A., & Latham, G. P. (2002). Building a practically useful theory of goal setting and task motivation: A 35-year odyssey. *American Psychologist, 57*(9), 705-717.

Locke, E. A., & Latham, G. P. (Eds.) (2013). *New developments in goal setting and task performance*. New York, NY: Routledge Academic.

Marks, M. A., Mathieu, J. E., & Zaccaro, S. J. (2001). A temporally based framework and taxonomy of team processes. *Academy of Management Review, 26*(3), 356-376.

Marks, M. A., Sabella, M. J., Burke, C. S., & Zaccaro, S. J. (2002). The impact of cross-training on team effectiveness. *Journal of Applied Psychology, 87*(1), 3-13.

Martens, R., & Peterson, J. A. (1971). Group cohesiveness as a determinant of success and member satisfaction in team performance. *International Review for the Sociology of Sport, 6*(1), 49-61.

Mathieu, J. E., Heffner, T. S., Goodwin, G. F., Salas, E., & Cannon-Bowers, J. A. (2000). The influence of shared mental models on team process and performance. *The Journal of Applied Psychology, 85*(2), 273-283. Retrieved from *http://www.ncbi.nlm.nih.gov/pubmed/10783543*

Mathieu, J. E., Maynard, M. T., Rapp, T., & Gilson, L. (2008). Team effectiveness 1997-2007: A review of recent advancements and a glimpse into the future. *Journal of Management, 34*(3), 410-476. doi:10.1177/0149206308316061

McIntyre, R. M., & Salas, E. (1995). Measuring and managing for team performance: Emerging principles from complex environments. In R. A. Guzzo & E. Salas (Eds.), *Team effectiveness and decision making in organizations* (pp. 9-45). San Francisco: Jossey-Bass.

Mesmer-Magnus, J. R., & DeChurch, L. A. (2009). Information sharing and team performance: A meta-analysis. *Journal of Applied Psychology, 94*(2), 535-546.

Moorman, C., Zaltman, G., & Deshpande, R. (1992). Relationships between providers and users of market research: The dynamics of trust within and between organizations. *Journal of Marketing Research, 29*(3), 314-329.

Mullen, B., & Cooper, C. (1994). The relation between group cohesiveness and performance: An integration. *Psychological Bulletin, 115*(2), 210-227.

National Science Board (2012). *Science and engineering indicators 2012*. Arlington, VA: National Science Foundation.

Oliver, L. W., Harman, J., Hoover, E., Hayes, S. M., & Pandhi, N. A. (1999). A quantitative integration of the military cohesion literature. *Military Psychology, 11*(1), 57-83.

Prince, C., Ellis, E., Brannick, M. T., & Salas, E. (2007). Measurement of team situation awareness in low experience level aviators. *International Journal of Aviation Psychology, 17*(1), 41-57.

Quiñones, M. A. (1995). Pretraining context effects: Training assignment as feedback. *Journal of Applied Psychology, 80*(2), 226-238. doi:10.1037/0021-9010.80.2.226

Ren, Y., & Argote, L. (2011). The academy of management annals transactive memory systems 1985-2010: An integrative framework of key dimensions, antecedents, and consequences. *The Academy of Management Annals, 5*(1), 189-229.

Saavedra, R., Earley, P., & Van Dyne, L. (1993). Complex interdependence in task-performing groups. *Journal of Applied Psychology, 78*(1), 61-72. doi:10.1037/0021-9010.78.1.61

Salas, E., Burke, C. S., & Cannon-Bowers, J. A. (2002). What we know about designing and delivering team training: Tips and guidelines. In K. Kraiger (Ed.), *Creating, implementing, and managing effective training and development: State-of-the-art lessons for practice* (pp. 234-259). San Francisco, CA: Jossey-Bass.

Salas, E., Burke, C. S., & Stagl, K. C. (2004). Developing teams and team leaders: Strategies and principles. In D. Day, S. J. Zaccaro, & S. M. Halpin (Eds.), *Leader development for transforming organizations: Growing leaders for tomorrow* (pp. 325-355). Mahwah, NJ: Lawrence Erlbaum.

Salas, E., & Cannon-Bowers, J. A. (2000). The anatomy of team training. In S. Tobias & J. D. Fletcher (Eds.), *Training & retraining: A handbook for business, industry, government, and the military* (pp. 312-335). New York: Macmillan.

Salas, E., DiazGranados, D., Klein, C., Burke, C. S., Stagl, K. C., Goodwin, G. F., & Halpin, S. M. (2008). Does team training improve team performance? A meta-analysis. *Human Factors: The Journal of the Human Factors and Ergonomics Society*, *50*(6), 903-933.

Salas, E., Dickinson, T. L., Converse, S. A., & Tannenbaum, S. I. (1992). Toward an understanding of team performance and training. In R. J. Swezey & E. Salas (Eds.), *Teams: Their training and performance* (pp. 3-29). Norwood, NJ: Ablex.

Salas, E., & Fiore, S. M. (Eds.) (2004). *Team cognition: Understanding the factors that drive process and performance.* Washington, DC: American Psychological Association.

Salas, E., Nichols, D. R., & Driskell, J. E. (2007). Testing three team training strategies in intact teams: A meta-analysis. *Small Group Research*, *38*(4), 471-488.

Salas, E., & Priest, H. A. (2005). Team training. In N. Stanton, H. Hendrick, S. Konz, K. Parsons, & E. Salas (Eds.), *Handbook of human factors and ergonomics methods* (pp. 44-1-44-7). London: Taylor & Francis.

Salas, E., Shuffler, M. L., Thayer, A. L., Bedwell, W. L., & Lazzara, E. H. (in press). Understanding and improving teamwork in orgnizations: A scientifically based practical guide. *Human Resource Management.*

Salas, E., Sims, D. E., & Burke, C. S. (2005). Is there a "big five" in teamwork? *Small Group Research, 36*(5), 555-599.

Salas, E., Tannenbaum, S. I., Kraiger, K., & Smith-Jentsch, K. A. (2012). The science of training and development in organizations: What matters in practice. *Psychological Science in the Public Interest*, *13*(2), 74-101.

Saunders, T., Driskell, J. E., Johnston, J., & Salas, E. (1996). The effect of stress inoculation training on anxiety and performance. *Journal of Occupational Health Psychology*, *1*(2), 170-186.

Seligman, M. E. P., & Csikszentmihalyi, M. (2000). Positive psychology: An introduction. *American Psychologist*, *55*(1), 5-14.

Shuffler, M. L., DiazGranados, D., & Salas, E. (2011). There's a science for that: Team development interventions in organizations. *Current Directions in Psychological Science, 20*(6), 365-372.

Shuffler, M. L., Pavlas, D., & Salas, E. (2012). Teams in the Military. In J. H. Laurence & M. D. Matthews (Eds.), *The Oxford handbook of military psychology* (pp. 282-310). New York, NY: Oxford University Press.

Smith-Jentsch, K. A., Cannon-Bowers, J. A., Tannenbaum, S. I., & Salas, E. (2008). Guided team self-correction: Impacts on team mental models, processes, and effectiveness. *Small Group Research*, *39*(3), 303-327. doi:10.1177/1046496408317794

Smith-Jentsch, K. A., Jentsch, F. G., Payne, S. C., & Salas, E. (1996). Can pretraining experiences explain individual differences in learning? *Journal of Applied Psychology*, *81*(1), 110-116. doi:10.1037/0021-9010.81.1.110

Smith-Jentsch, K. A, Mathieu, J. E., & Kraiger, K. (2005). Investigating linear and interactive effects of shared mental models on safety and efficiency in a field setting. *The Journal of Applied Psychology, 90*(3), 523-535. doi:10.1037/0021-9010.90.3.523

Smith-Jentsch, K. A., Zeisig, R. L., Acton, B., & McPherson, J. A. (1998). Team dimensional training: A strategy for guided team self-correction. In J. A. Cannon-Bowers & E. Salas (Eds.), *Making decisions under stress: Implications for individual and team training* (pp. 272-297). Washington, DC: American Psychological Association.

Sokolove, M. (2010). How soccer is made. *The New York Times*. Retrieved from http://www.nytimes.com/2010/06/06/magazine/06Soccer-t.html?pagewanted=all

Sorcher, M., & Goldstein, A. P. (1972). A behavior modeling approach in training. *Personnel Administration, 35*, 35-41.

Stajkovic, A. D., Lee, D., & Nyberg, A. J. (2009). Collective efficacy, group potency, and group performance: Meta-analyses of their relationships, and test of a mediation model. *Journal of Applied Psychology, 94*(3), 814-828.

Steiner, I. (1972). *Group processes and productivity*. New York, NY: Academic Press.

Tai, W. T. (2006). Effects of training framing, general self-efficacy and training motivation on trainees' training effectiveness. *Personnel Review, 35*(1), 51-65.

Tannenbaum, S. I., & Cerasoli, C. P. (2013). Do team and individual debriefs enhance performance? A meta-analysis. *Human Factors: The Journal of the Human Factors and Ergonomics Society, 55*(1), 231-245.

Tannenbaum, S. I., Salas, E., & Cannon-Bowers, J. A. (1996). Promoting team effectiveness. In M. West (Ed.), *Handbook of work group psychology* (pp. 503-529). Sussex, England: John Wiley & Sons.

Taylor, P. J., Russ-Eft, D. F., & Chan, D. W. L. (2005). A meta-analytic review of behavior modeling training. *Journal of Applied Psychology, 90*(4), 692-709.

Thompson, J. D. (1967). *Organizations in action*. New York: McGraw-Hill.

Van de Ven, A. H., Delbecq, A. L., & Koenig Jr., R. (1976). Determinants of coordination modes within organizations. *American Sociological Review, 41*(2), 322-338.

van Mierlo, H., & Kleingeld, A. (2010). Goals, strategies, and group performance: Some limits of goal setting in groups. *Small Group Research, 41*(5), 524-555. doi:10.1177/1046496410373628

Volpe, C. E., Cannon-Bowers, J. A., Salas, E., & Spector, P. E. (1996). The impact of cross-training on team functioning: An empirical investigation. *Human Factors, 38*(1), 87-100.

Wagner III, J. A. (1995). Studies of individualism-collectivism: Effects on cooperation in groups. *Academy of Management Journal, 38*(1), 152-172.

Weaver, S. J., Rosen, M. A., Salas, E., Baum, K. D., & King, H. B. (2010). Integrating the science of team training: Guidelines for continuing education. *Journal of Continuing Education in the Health Professions, 30*(4), 208-220.

Wegner, D. M. (1987). Transactive memory: A contemporary analysis of the group mind. In B. Mullen & G. R. Goethals (Eds.), *Theories of group behavior* (pp. 185-208). New York: Springer-Verlag.

Wildman, J. L., Thayer, A. L., Pavlas, D., Salas, E., Stewart, J. E., & Howse, W. R. (2012). Team knowledge research: Emerging trends and critical needs. *Human Factors: The Journal of the Human Factors and Ergonomics Society, 54*(1), 84-111.

In: Positive Human Functioning …   ISBN: 978-1-62948-974-2
Editors: A. R. Gomes, R. Resende & A. Albuquerque   © 2014 Nova Science Publishers, Inc.

Chapter 4

MENTAL TRAINING FOR ELITE ATHLETES: THEORY, RESEARCH AND IMPLICATIONS FOR PRACTICE

Robert Weinberg

Department of Kinesiology and Health, Miami University, Oxford, OH, US

ABSTRACT

When coaches and athletes lose competitions, they often attribute their loses to mental factors such as a loss in concentration, failure to cope with anxiety, or a lack of confidence. Although there is much written about specific techniques to build mental skills such as imagery, relaxation, goal-setting and self talk, less is known about how to exactly develop and implement a mental skills training (MST) program. Thus the focus of this chapter is to provide specific guidelines for the development and implementation of mental skills in sport. First, the effectiveness of mental training programs is discussed along with the knowledge base that underlies these programs and who should implement them. Then, when to implement MST as well as how long to practice different mental skills, is presented. Finally, using Poczwardowski, Sherman, and Henschen (1998) heuristic as a model, how to actually implement a MST program is presented including such things as defining one's boundaries as a sport psychology consultant, the importance of philosophy, the assessment of mental skills from both quantitative and qualitative perspectives, determining what mental skills to include, setting up a schedule for practicing mental skills and evaluating the program.

INTRODUCTION

Anyone who has participated in competitive sports knows that besides physical talent and practice there is a mental aspect that often separates the winners from losers. All one had to do was watch the 2012 Olympics from London and see that hundreds of a second in swimming and track and hundreds of a point in gymnastics and diving made the difference between getting a gold, silver or bronze medal (or no medal at all). Differences in performance, especially at the elite level, often come down to small differences and making a mental mistake (in a loss) or staying mentally strong (in a win). This can occur in competitions that might take several hours to play such as a tennis match or soccer game, where making one mental mistake or losing concentration for a moment can mean the difference between success and failure.

In the past, just like in physical talent, some performers were simply better than others in their mental skills. Fortunately, researchers and practitioners in sport psychology have been developing, evaluating and implementing mental skill programs that athletes can learn and practice to help them achieve their maximum performance both physically and mentally. This chapter has the following purposes: (1) provide empirical evidence regarding the effectiveness of psychological skills interventions (PST), (2) discuss who should implement these interventions, (3) when should PST be implemented and how much time should be spent on PST, and (4) describe in detail how one might set up and implement a mental skills training program.

Before addressing these important questions and purposes, a few general comments are warranted. When sport psychology consultants started to more consistently work with athletes on the development of mental (psychological) skills in the early 1980's there were very few empirical, controlled studies to help guide these interventions. However, in the past 30 years a number of well-controlled field-based studies have been conducted to help provide information and guidelines for conducting psychological interventions with athletes. Despite these advances there is much that we do not know about effective psychological interventions with athletes.

Many important questions still remain and some of the most important include the following: Is there an ideal time of the year to conduct psychological interventions (e.g., during season, pre-season, or post-season)? How long should the typical psychological intervention take? What specific components should be incorporated into training and how should these components be integrated? What ethical considerations should one be aware of when implementing a psychological intervention program? How young (or skillful) should athletes be to implement a mental skills program? Are certain techniques more effective in coping with certain problems (e.g., what technique(s) are most effective if the athlete is focusing too much on winning or if they start thinking ahead in a competition?). In addition, mental skills training programs can include a variety of techniques such as goal setting, relaxation/anxiety management, confidence, building, changing self-talk, routines, imagery, etc. The multitude of possibilities makes it very difficult to integrate all of these skills into one comprehensive program (or do all of these techniques need to be integrated into a mental skills intervention?).

Given the above considerations, along with and individual differences, there are really no ready-made solutions to developing the best and most effective mental skills training program. In addition to the mental skills training (MST) approach that will be discussed later in the chapter, there are also other approaches to interventions. For example, some of these are based more on a counseling approach, which focuses primarily on adjustment and personal growth. Two examples of these different approaches include a model focusing on psyhcoeducational development across a lifespan (e.g., Lerner & Lerner, 2006; Weiss, Kipp, & Bolter, 2012) and a family systems model which makes the family central to helping athletes reach their potential (e.g., Côté & Hay, 2002; Harwood, Douglas, & Minnini, 2012).

MENTAL SKILLS TRAINING (MST) AND PERFORMANCE

The first basic question that needs to be addressed before developing a mental skills intervention is to determine if these programs are, in fact, effective in enhancing performance and to some degree well-being? This is a difficult task and one that has plagued counseling and clinical psychology. Specifically, demonstrating what they do (e.g., therapy) actually produces measurable changes in the behavior and well-being of their clients is always difficult to do. For example, if a client comes into the office being clinically depressed, oftentimes the mere passage of time will result in the client feeling less depressed. So if a psychologist does therapy with a client for three months and the depression clears up, is this due to the therapy of merely the passage of time? In addition, psychologists do not have any control over what clients do outside the office and their adherence to a program might be critical in determining the effectiveness of a psychological intervention.

Conducting sport psychology interventions to improve performance and well-being often have similar problems and limitations in providing scientific data to answer questions regarding its effectiveness. What is needed are well-controlled outcome based interventions conducted in real-life competitive environments. These are inherently difficult to conduct because of time and money constraints, getting the cooperation of coaches and athletes, as well as the inability to adequately control the sporting environment. Fortunately, sport psychology researchers have been working hard to establish a database regarding the effectiveness of psychological interventions in enhancing performance. But before these intervention studies are discussed, researchers were attempting to build a knowledge base for mental skills interventions through research and experiences of elite coaches and athletes.

MENTAL SKILLS KNOWLEDGE BASE

The knowledge base for the development of MST has come from both research and applied sources. Krane and Williams (2010) and Harmison and Casto (2012) have attempted to review the literature on different psychological aspects as related to peak or elite performance. These included studies that have assessed athletes' subjective experiences during peak performances (e.g., Robazza & Bortoli, 2003; Robazza, Bortoli, & Hanin, 2004), compared more successful versus less successful athletes (e.g, Gould, Guinan, Greenleaf, Medberry, & Peterson, 1999; Gould, Weiss, & Weinberg, 1991; Greenleaf, Gould, & Diffenbach, 2001), as well as interviewing coaches, players, and scouts about what it takes from a mental perspective to be successful (e.g., Gould, Dieffenbach, & Moffett, 2002; Thomas, Hanton, & Maynard, 2007). In summarizing these different studies, Krane and Williams (2010) found that elite and successful athletes consistently reported using the following psychological skills, which likely contributed to their high-level performance: (a) imagery, (b) attentional focusing, (c) controlling anxiety and activation, (d) positive self-talk, (e) goal setting, (f) maintaining concentration, and (g) well-developed pre-competition and competition plans. Interestingly, poor performance or failure to meet one's goals was characterized by negative thoughts, worrying about losing, under or over-arousal, lack of concentration, and low levels of confidence. Finally, more successful and elite athletes adhered to their mental preparation more consistently and actually practiced their mental skills on a more consistent basis than less successful athletes. Thus, although not direct evidence regarding the effectiveness of PST on performance, these qualitative and quantitative athletes and coaches provide consistent evidence regarding the use and perceived importance of these mental skills in obtaining high levels of performance.

Before assessing the direct effect of MST interventions on performance, some recent empirical data in the area of mental toughness also provides indirect evidence regarding the importance of mental skills. The term mental toughness has been used anecdotally to describe athletes who seem to be strong from a mental perspective. However, what mental toughness really means from a scientific perspective was not really investigated until Jones, Hanton, and Connaughton's (2002) study interviewing 10 Olympic and Commonwealth Games competitors about their definition of mental toughness. Over the past 10 years there have been a number of studies investigating the definition of mental toughness as well as how to build it (e.g., Bull, Shambrook, & Brooks, 2005; Crust, 2007; Gucciardi & Gordon, 2011; Jones, Hanton, & Connaughton, 2007; Weinberg & Butt, 2011). Although there are still disagreements regarding exactly what mental toughness is and how to measure it, there seems to be a general agreement that it involves a constellation of mental skills. Although the make-up of these skills varies somewhat across studies and researchers, mental toughness seems to include mental skills such as dealing with pressure (anxiety management), attentional focus (concentration), self-belief (confidence), and motivation (goal-setting). Interviews with elite athletes (and recreational athletes) consistently demonstrate that these mental skills are critical to athletic success. Now, let's turn to the direct empirical evidence regarding the effectiveness of MST training on performance.

MST EFFECTIVENESS

The previous studies reviewed provide indirect evidence regarding MST effectiveness in enhancing performance. But the direct evidence consists of intervention studies actually testing the efficacy of PST training programs in sport. The first quantitative review of these studies was conducted by Greenspan and Feltz (1989), which included 19 published intervention studies (23 interventions) as far back as 1972. Results revealed that 87% (20/23) of the interventions reported positive results and 73% of the studies in which causality could be determined reported positive findings. More cautiously, only 18% of the studies used an adequate manipulation check of the intervention, and 35% of the studies did not use a control group. Vealey (1994) and Weinberg and Comar (1994) also conducted reviews of MST effectiveness subsequent to the Greenspan and Feltz (1989) review. Combining these three reviews, which included a variety of different sports (e.g., tennis, gymnastics, baseball, volleyball, karate, golf, skiing, boxing) 38 of 45 (85%) studies found positive performance effects although these studies did employed a wide variety of psychological techniques as part of their mental skills interventions.

In addition, Meyers, Whelan, and Murphy (1996) reported on a meta-analysis on 56 studies published between 1970 and 1989 and found an average effect size of .62 for cognitive-behavioral interventions across different treatment conditions, control conditions, dependent measures, tasks and participants. This attests to the generalizability of the positive effects of PST on performance. More recently, Martin, Vause, and Schwartzman (2005) extended the original Greenspan and Feltz (1989) analysis to include experimental studies only conducted in competitive environments through 2002. Given this more stringent inclusion criteria, results revealed positive effects in 14/15 studies (means changes ranging from 3% to 80% over baseline or control). It should be noted, however, that there is little or no information regarding the maintenance of these positive findings over time. But in conclusion, it appears that PST training is associated with or causes increases in performance and these positive effects have become stronger in more recent studies (e.g., Fournier, Calmels, Durand-Bush, & Salmela, 2005).

WHO SHOULD CONDUCT MST?

In a perfect world, a MST program should be planned, implemented, and supervised by a qualified (optimally certified) sport psychology consultant. These consultants have the advantage of having more extensive training and experience than a coach. In addition, athletes might generally be more open in discussing psychological difficulties affecting their play with a sport psychology consultant than a coach because the consultant does not make any decisions regarding the playing time of the athlete. For example, if an athlete was getting too anxious which was negatively affecting his play or was losing his confidence after a couple of failures, would he want to share these feelings with the coach? It is possible, but in most cases athletes would likely try to hide these feelings because they don't want the coach to know about these negative emotions. However, despite the fact that it is desirable for sport psychology consultants to administer a mental training program to athletes, this is not very feasible in most cases. At the professional or elite level, however, sometimes sport psychology consultants are hired by teams/individuals and even travel with them on a daily basis, which would make for the best type of implementation.

If a sport psychology consultant conducts the mental skills program it is recommended that the coaching staff attend most, or all, of the initial group training sessions. First, the coaches' presence makes it known to athletes that she thinks these sessions are important. Second, since the consultant will probably not be at most of the physical training and practice sessions, coaches can help make sure of the continuity and relatedness of mental training to physical training. Third, misunderstandings of what the consultant is doing will not likely occur because coaches will know exactly what is happening and can provide feedback if need be, regarding what needs to be done.

As noted above, many sport psychology consultants do not work with athletes/teams on a daily basis and thus are often not present to help administer mental skills training programs. Coaches, of course, have the best access to athletes on a daily basis and are thus in a position to offer MST over the course of a season. However, coaches generally do not have the background, skill, experience or knowledge to administer such a program, not to mention the time. However, Smith and Johnson (1990) developed an innovative consultation model in their work with the Houston Astros minor league program. They called this model "organizational empowerment" and it will be discussed in some detail as it provides an excellent prototype for sport psychology consultation.

In this model of service delivery the sport psychology consultant trains one or more qualified individuals within the organization to provide psychological services to coaches and athletes. The consultant then oversees the program and provides ongoing supervision to the people he is training. This really empowers the organization to provide its own psychological services unique to them, while under the supervision of a trained and or certified consultant.

In their particular situation, Smith was certified sport psychology consultant and Johnson was the manager of a minor league team who had a master's degree in psychology. It is not absolutely necessary that the person being trained have a psychology degree or training/courses in sport psychology, but they should have some background and willingness to be trained in mental skills techniques. It helped that Johnson was a "baseball person" and it was reasoned that he would have an easier time establishing credibility within the traditionally conservative culture of baseball and he also had some training in consulting and counseling which was also deemed to be important to the success of the intervention.

In terms of the actual training, Smith set up a 6-week training period before Spring Training in which Johnson was given an extensive sport psychology reading list and Smith met with him on several days focusing on the use of psychological interventions in sport. In addition, Smith accompanied Johnson to Spring Training for 10 days of hands-on training plus a series of orientation workshops for staff and players. Weekly and sometimes daily telephone supervision continued throughout the remainder of Spring Training and the regular season. Once Johnson felt comfortable with his skills, Smith worked with him to develop a MST program. Although Johnson administered the day-to-day program, Smith continued to provide support and guidance when necessary. This is an excellent model if there is a person associated with the team who has sufficient background and is willing to be taught the details of administering a MST program on a day-to-day basis.

WHEN TO IMPLEMENT A MST PROGRAM

It is best to initiate a MST program during the off-season or preseason, when there is more time to learn new skills and athletes are not so pressured about winning. Some athletes report that it can take several months to a year to fully understand new mental skills and integrate them into actual competitions. Mental training is an ongoing process that needs to be integrated with physical practice over time. Many coaches and athletes want to start a MST program in the middle of the season, usually because of some precipitating situation, such as a batter in a hitting slump. They become desperate to find a solution, but mental training in such a situation is rarely effective. Having said this, there is precedent for elite athletes being able to integrate mental skills into their training regimen one week prior to a match and show enhanced performance, as well as increased self-confidence, decreased anxiety, and more positive reinterpretation of anxiety symptoms (Thomas, Maynard, & Hanton, 2007). However, in this situation, the athletes engaged in intensive mental skills training 5 to 7 days before, 1 or 2 days before, and on the day of competition, for a total of almost 20 hours of mental practice. Such training is not likely feasible in most situations but might be possible with dedicated high level-athletes.

How Much Time Should Be Spent in MST?

The time needed to practice mental skills will typically vary according to what is being practiced and how well it is learned. For example if a new mental skill such as imagery is being introduced, special 15-30-minute training sessions 3 to 5 days a week may be necessary. As athletes become more proficient, fewer training sessions are necessary although some athletes may require individual sessions if they are having trouble learning the mental skill. The first or last 10-15 minutes of practice is often a good time to integrate mental practice into regular training sessions. As athletes become more proficient, they may be able to integrate the mental training with the typical physical practices and this need fewer special mental training sessions. Once athletes have effectively integrated a skill into physical practice, they should use it during simulated competition before using it during actual competition.

The above scenario is recommended if the sport psychology consultant is with the team on a regular basis. But many sport psychology consultants are not typically present on a daily basis, and thus scheduling adjustments may be necessary. Under such circumstances, fewer and longer mental training sessions are usually held unless a trained person (such as noted earlier in the Smith and Johnson example) can carry out the mental training program. It is typical for sport psychology consultants to start with group sessions to explain general principles and their philosophy (these might be delivered to the athletes as a team or to coaches as a group). However, research and practice has indicated that individualized sessions and individual training programs are needed to optimize the effectiveness of mental training programs (Karageorghis & Terry, 2011; Vealey, 2007). It is critical that athletes be assigned training exercises to practice during the times the sport psychology consultant is not with the team. The coach should help ensure compliance and feedback by conducting some of the training exercises, or at least providing time for players to practice. If this is not at all possible, a designated individual should remind athletes of their homework assignments and briefly discuss the athletes' reactions to the exercises once the homework has been completed. However, maximum effectiveness is likely only when designated individuals and sport psychology consultants work together as a team.

A logical question that arises after a mental training program has been put in place is "when can athletes stop mental skills training?" In the truest sense, mental skills training continues as long as the athletes participate in their sport. In this sense, mental skills are no different from physical skills. Just because a player has a great jump shot in basketball does not mean that he stops practicing his jump shot. Peyton Manning, Michael Phelps, Annika Sorenstam, Greg Maddux, Candace Parker and Wayne Gretsky- all highly skilled and talented athletes – have all been known for continually integrating the mental aspects of their sports into physical practice.

If athletes never stop MST, what is the ideal length of time for their first exposure to a formal MST program? Most sport psychology consultants would recommend an average of between 3 and 6 months because it takes time to learn these new mental skills, use them in practice and then integrate them into actual competitive situations. The specific sport, time available, existing mental skills, and commitment of the participants are factors in determining how much time to allot to the formal program. For example, I have worked with athletes who simply needed to change a small part of their mental approach and were able to do so in less than two months. In contrast, Orlick (2000) has noted that many of the Canadian Olympic athletes he has consulted with started practicing their mental training program a couple of years before the Olympic Games. Of course, their mental plans and mental preparation was much more detailed and precise than most other performers.

SETTING UP AND IMPLEMENTING A MENTAL SKILLS TRAINING PROGRAM

The sport psychology literature is replete with discussions and explanations regarding the use of different psychological interventions such as goal setting, imagery, self-talk, and relaxation. There is, however, a dearth of information regarding exactly how to implement MST programs to athletes (Weinberg & Willams, 2010 is a noted exception). As noted earlier, individual differences and unique contextual factors always need to be considered that are inherent to each athlete or team. Along these lines,, Poczwardowski et al. (1998) and Poczwardowski and Sherman (2011) proposed a general framework for sport psychology service delivery to help consultants to design, implement and evaluate a MST program focused on personal growth and/or performance enhancement in sport settings. Most of the factors they see as critical to effective sport psychology consulting are described and discussed below.

Professional Boundaries

Professional boundaries are typically defined by the type and amount of education and training sport psychology consultants received (e.g., amount of supervised work, psychology or kinesiology degree, experience with different populations, types of issues addressed). Central to professional boundaries are the ethics that help guide practice. The Association for Applied Sport Psychology (AASP) has developed an ethical code based on the one developed by the American Psychological association (APA) and consultants should adhere to these ethical guidelines in their practice. One's ethical guidelines (e.g., confidentiality, assessment procedures, athletes' rights) should be clearly conveyed not only to the athletes, but to the organization (e.g., professional team, University athletic department, club managers/owners) that hires you. In summary, when recognizing one's professional boundaries sport psychology consultants should include their initial training, supervised practice, ongoing peer supervision/consultation.

Philosophy

When most people hear the word philosophy it typically brings up boring and complicated thoughts or images. However, one of the most important things for any consultant (or coach or CEO) is to be very clear of their philosophy and approach to their particular domain. But before discussing one's philosophy, it is important for sport psychology consultants to clearly spell out what sport psychology consultation is really about.

The focus is on "regular" athletes who simply are having an issue, which focuses on the mental side of performing (e.g., concentration, anxiety, mental preparation). It is important to make sure athletes (especially younger ones) understand that sport psychology is not about "head cases" or "psychos" because there are many misconceptions about what sport psychologists do. In fact, personally, I never use the word psychology or psychologist, because for many people it has a negative connotation that you are weak mentally. I prefer to call myself a mental coach. Staying after practice to work on one's ball control skills in soccer should be applauded; similarly, spending extra me developing concentration skills should also be applauded.

Getting back to one's philosophy, service philosophy refers to the consultant's beliefs about the nature of reality and the nature of human behavior change. This could include a behavioral approach, social learning approach, rational-emotive approach, person-centered approach, or cognitive-behavioral approach (just to name a few). For sport psychology consultants, it is important to spell out their approach in dealing with psychological issues in sport and exercise. In addition to the specific approaches noted above, within a sport psychology setting, there are two basic approaches in working with athletes. One is clinical in nature and focuses on more serious mental issues (e.g., substance abuse, eating disorders), which are not that prevalent in sport. Most sport psychology consultants do not take this approach and will refer out to a clinical psychologist or appropriate mental health specialist if a serious clinical issue arises.

The other approach is termed educational and deals with building and enhancing mental skills such as goal setting, imagery, concentration and confidence. I like to explain the educational approach using a triangle. At one end of the triangle are physical/technical skills and coaches usually teach these to athletes. Athletes uniformly agree that this is important to success. A second point of the triangle is physical conditioning and either coaches or trainers are in charge of getting athletes into shape. Again they all agree that this is important for success. The third point of the triangle is mental skills such as concentration, coping, and goal setting. Once again athletes note that these are essential for success. I inform them that this is what I do. In essence, I see myself as a mental coach and I am in charge of teaching them these skills. I note that some coaches try to teach these skills but oftentimes they simply don't have time and/or the expertise to do so.

Making Contact

Gaining entry into a sports team is not an easy task. For example, Ken Ravizza (2001), who is now a very successful sport psychology consultant had to initially talk to the wrestling coach for months before the coach would even allow him in the wrestling room. From a definitional point of view, gaining entry refers to athletes' coaches' and organizations' willingness to readily accept the consultant into their environment. Getting one's "foot in the door" has always been a critical part of any business trying to sell their services or product to another business. Sport psychology is certainly a service business and thus establishing respect, credibility, and trust is essential. This can be accomplished through demonstrating knowledge or experience in the sport (including any limitations), clarifying your role and services to be provided, opening lines of communication along with the consultant's role, maintaining confidentiality, as well as outlining timelines and implementation specifics.

Besides direct contact with the team or organization, there are a number of other ways to "get in the door" and make your services known. For example, in today's technological society, it is essential that sport psychology consultants have an up-to-date website which highlights their experience, educational background, services offered along with other useful information. People often turn first to the internet for many services and sport psychology is no exception. If a sport psychology consultant is not skilled in creating a website then he or she should hire a specialist to set one up. Getting your website to come up early in the search for sport psychologists in your area would most likely really help your business.

Another way to make your services known is through giving presentations and writing. There are usually opportunities to give presentations to a variety of sport (e.g., Little League, youth sport organizations, sport and exercise/fitness clubs, sports medicine facilities, physical therapy organizations) and non-sport (Kiwanis Club, Lions Club, Civic Organizations, Chamber of Commerce) groups. These presentations could be something that both sport and non-sport organizations might be interesting in hearing such as leadership, group cohesion, mental toughness, communication skills or developing talent. Also, to make contacts, you might also join some of these organizations. You never know who might be in the audience who likes what you had to say and offers you an opportunity to work with a team or a group. Regarding writing, of course if you write a book on a specific topic like "coaching the mental part of sport" or "parenting your superstar" gives you automatic credibility with that audience. But also writing applied articles for specific sport magazines that are read by coaches and parents (e.g., USA gymnastics, swimming technique, tennis, football quarterly) also will provide visibility.

Especially when getting started as a sport psychology consultant, you often have to give away your services because people are not often willing to pay for an "unknown". So volunteering for a sport organization or doing an internship is often helpful in eventually landing a job. In fact, in many areas of business, internships are a key way for individuals to demonstrate to employers that they are capable and competent. Employers also feel that they know what they are getting when someone has served as an intern for many months. In my experience, many graduate students who took internship positions in sport psychology have used these as a springboard to either opening up their own practice or for being hired for a full-time position (sometimes with another organization).

Assessment

Assessment refers to identifying the athlete, coach, or organization's needs, wants, strengths and weaknesses with respect to the psychological aspects that are critical to individual or collective growth within the sport environment. In first evaluating athletes' psychological strengths and weaknesses, bear in mind that not only psychological factors influence performance. A baseball player, for example, may attribute his slump to being overly anxious when in reality his problem is biomechanical, relating to a "hitch in his swing". Similarly, a gymnast who more frequently falls off the balance beam may not have developed an anxiety problem; rather she might just have experienced a growth spurt in which she has yet to adjust. Thus, input from coaches, biomechanists, physiologists, and teachers, is often useful. Two clues that an athlete might benefit from mental training are that the athlete performs better in practice than in competition or performs more poorly in important competitions than in unimportant ones.

An oral interview and written psychological inventories can provide useful subjective and objective information. Taylor (1995) summarized the strengths and limitations of both subjective and objective assessments in evaluating athletes' mental skills (see Table 1).

Table 1. Assessing athletes' needs

Type	Strenghts	Limitations
Subjective assesment		
Interviewing (client)	Establishes trust and rapport Reveals self-perceptions, beliefs, and attitudes Provides in-depth knowledge about sport participation and life issues	Includes self-presentational bias Is affected by lack of self-awareness Is affected by poor insight
Interviewing (others)	Provides new perspective of athlete Establishes consensus	Involves subjectivity bias Is affected by alternative agenda
Observation	Provides unambiguous behavioral data Enables comparison of behavioral with expressed perceptions Reveals patterns of behavior Reveals relationship between practice and competitive performance Provides cross-situational consistency	Includes observer bias Depends on representativeness of observed behaviors Is affected by observational time limitations
Objective assessment		
Sport specific	Provides impartial evaluation	Is affected by resistance by athlete
General	Confirms subjective assessment	Is hampered by self-presentational bias Uses non-sport-specific inventories
Trait versus state	Assesses sport-specific issues Uncovers new issues Uses time efficiently Provides ease of administration	Uses nondiagnostic inventories Lacks a relationship with performance Measures only traits Has restricted test usage

Adapted, by permission, from J. Taylor, 1995, "A conceptual model for integrating athletes' needs and sport demands in the development of competitive mental preparation strategies," *The Sport Psychologist* 9(3): 342.

In addition, Beckman and Kellmann (2003) discussed the different factors that sport psychologists should consider before administering questionnaires and other formal assessments to athletes. These include the reliability and validity of the questionnaire, the usefulness of the questionnaire as seen by the athletes, and the honesty that athletes show in completing the questionnaire. Furthermore, Singer and Anshel (2006) provided some guidelines and ethical concerns when using psychological tests in mental skills training program. The exact format and integration of objective and subjective assessments depend on the expertise of the sport psychologist as well as the rapport and trust between the athlete and the sport psychologist. Using both subjective and objective assessments helps consultants find consistencies (and inconsistencies) between oral and written statements. However, in general, I recommend the semi-structured interview, which includes general questions with opportunities to use the athlete's responses to form follow-up questions (Orlick, 2000). The interview is a good time to determine the areas in which the athlete needs help and to start building the trust critical to any therapeutic relationship. The following are sample interview items.

- Tell me about your involvement in your sport, summarizing what you consider important events, both positive and negative (This is a good starting point because it lets athletes talk about themselves and become comfortable)?
- Describe in detail the thoughts and feelings surrounding your best and worst performances. What do you believe is your greatest psychological strength? Your biggest weakness?
- Try to describe any psychological problems you are having now. What is your relationship with your coach? Do you feel comfortable talking to your coach?

It is my experience (and that of others) that this interview typically lasts approximately one hour, although there are always individual differences. This initial interview is not only important to find out where the athlete needs help but also is a place to start building the trust that is critical for any therapeutic relationship. As the old says goes, "athlete don't care what you know until they know that you care". Furthermore, it is helpful that the sport psychology consultant has a good working knowledge about the sport, even if he or she does not have much practical experience. I have, at times, had to read up, do some observation, or look at videos to help me better understand a sport with which I was not familiar (e.g., cricket, cutting horse, snowboarding). This helps build credibility from the athletes; point of view because it gives them a sense that the consultant can understand their point of view.

In addition, as noted by Simons (2013), a sport psychology consultant should ask who, what, when, how, and where, questions but not "why" questions on the initial interview. The client may not know the answer to "why" questions (and experience embarrassment and confusion) or the answer to a "why" question might cause emotional conflict and cause the client to withdraw. The important thing is to build a strong relationship and rapport with the client at the outset.

Furthermore, many sport psychology consultants also use some psychological inventories to assess various skills. A recent article (Woodcock, Duda, Cumming, Sharp, & Hollanmd, 2012) provides some excellent recommendations for effective psychometric assessment to help practitioners more accurately assess athletes' mental skills. These are some of the most popular assessments with sport psychology consultants:

- Test of Attentional and Interpersonal Style (Nideffer, 1976)
- Sport Anxiety Scale (Smith, Smoll, & Schutz, 1990)
- Test of Performance Strategies (Thomas, Murphy, & Hardy, 1999)
- Trait–State Confidence Inventory (Vealey, 1986)

Sport psychology consultants should consider a number of factors before administering questionnaires or other formal assessments to athletes (Beckman & Kellmann, 2003). For example, to be used effectively, inventories should be reliable and valid for the individual athlete or team. For example, if a sport psychology consultant were working with a 12 year-old female gymnast, a scale that was developed and normed on adult males would be inappropriate. The scale should also be seen as useful by the athletes and completed honesty, as some athletes will give socially desirable responses (i.e., tell the investigator what he wants to hear). Finally, consultants need to provide athletes with a clear identification of the purpose of the assessment and make sure the athlete (and coach if applicable) is committed to the assessment.

Some sport- and situation-specific inventories have also been developed, such as the Baseball Test of Attentional and Interpersonal Style (Albrecht & Feltz, 1987), the Officials Stress Test (Goldsmith & Williams, 1992), and the Gymnastics Efficacy Measure (McAuley, 1985). Along these lines, Dosil (2006) provided specific information for implementing mental skills training programs for different sports. Although there are certain similarities in mental skills training programs for specific sports, programs can differ somewhat depending on the exact nature of the sport. For example, golf is a closed sport that is very predictable and not time stressed, whereas soccer is an open sport with lots of uncontrolled factors and is time stressed. Thus, you can have golfers work on their thinking process between shots because there is lots of time, whereas soccer players need to react quickly to changing conditions on the field and cannot do as much thinking while on the field of play. In addition, as noted earlier, to evaluating the athlete's mental skills, you should consider the unique physical, technical, and logistical demands of the sport itself in order to maximize the effectiveness of the psychological intervention (Taylor, 1995). For example, sports that involve explosiveness and anaerobic output (e.g., the 100 meter dash) differ greatly from those that require endurance and aerobic output (e.g., marathon running). Sports that rely on fine motor skills (e.g., archery) differ from ones involving gross motor skills (e.g., powerlifting).

Along these lines it is important to observe athletes while they are competing and practicing their sport throughout the consultation process. These observations not only provide the consultant with important information regarding how athletes are reacting in different situations, but it also helps build the relationship between consultant and athlete as it demonstrates the commitment the consultant has to the athlete. Watson and Shannon (2013) provide excellent guidelines for conducting systematic observations including when, where, and what to observe for both individual and team sport athletes.

After completing the interview and psychological assessment, written feedback should be provided to each athlete that highlights his or her psychological strengths and areas of improvement as they relate to sport performance and personal growth. This assessment should be given to athletes in a second one-on-one meeting and athletes should be provided an opportunity to react to it. This provides an opportunity to get consensual validation from athletes in terms of the evaluation. Sometimes oral and written evaluations are contrary and this is a good time to address any discrepancies and resolve it with the athlete. The assessment should conclude with recommendations for the type of skills and intervention program that the consultant thinks would be suit the athlete's needs.

An alternative approach to the typical interview or questionnaire assessment, is known as *performance profiling* (Butler & Hardy, 1992). A detailed description of this technique is beyond the scope of the present chapter but essentially it involves athletes identifying the mental skills associated with the best athlete in their specific sport. They then rate themselves on these mental skills compared to this best performer which provides a sense of self-determination not always seen in other types of assessments. The responses of the player would then be transferred to a "psychological profile" which provides a visual representation of the player's strengths and personal areas of improvement.

CONCEPTUALIZING ATHLETES' CONCERNS AND POTENTIAL INTERVENTIONS

This area has not received much attention in the sport psychology literature. But at times, issues with respect to performance problems may be different from problems identified during an initial interview, psychometric testing and observation. Specifically, "the root causes are rarely discovered during the initial exploration process. Generally, the causes of performance decrements are complex and multiple in nature" (Ogilvie & Henschen, 1995, p. 48). As a result, determining the real issues may dramatically improve services provided.

For example, an athlete may say that he has a concentration problem, as he seems to focus on the wrong things in critical situations. He starts to either think forward (future-oriented thinking) or think in the past (past-oriented thinking). Thus he is thinking about possibly failing or on a mistake that he just made. But the real problem is that he lacks confidence in himself because the coach has been constantly criticizing and yelling at him when he makes a mistake. This has totally undermined his confidence and that is the real issue.

As noted earlier, meeting the specific needs of athletes and teams cannot be accomplished effectively by a standard mental skills training package. Although the general outline of a program may remain similar, a sport psychology consultant should be prepared to compensate, adjust, and individualize mental skills training to meet the specific needs of the client. Although a packaged program will use many of the strategies at the disposal of consultants (e.g., imagery, anxiety management techniques, changing self-talk, developing routines, setting goals), inattention to individual and organizational differences (often identified through assessment) can severely limit the effectiveness of any intervention. An experienced sport psychology consultant will adjust his intervention to meet individual needs and remain flexible throughout the intervention period.

DETERMINING WHICH MENTAL SKILLS TO INCLUDE

Once the assessment is complete, the consultant must decide how many of the mental skills to emphasize. This decision should be based on when the program is first being implemented (e.g., preseason off-season, competitive season) and how much time the athlete and coach are willing to devote to mental skills training. This decision should be based on the coaches' and athletes' answers to these questions:

- How many weeks of practice or preseason are available?
- How much practice time will be devoted weekly to PST?
- How interested are the athletes in receiving PST?
- Will there still be time to practice mental skills after the competitive season begins?

When sufficient time is not available for a comprehensive training program, it is best to prioritize objectives and emphasize a few skills initially rather than superficially working on all the needed skills. A model proposed by Vealey (2007), developed from research over the past 25 to 30 years, emphasizes the development of mental skills to achieve performance success as well as personal well-being. In this model, Vealey differentiates between skills and methods. *Skills* are qualities to be obtained while *methods* are procedures or techniques employed to develop these skills. Methods contain many of techniques which sport psychology consultants typically use like relaxation, goal setting, imagery, and self-talk. Unfortunately, if the skill to be learned is optimal arousal, sometimes consultants focus on a particular method such as progressive relaxation. However, there are many methods which may help an athlete achieve optimal arousal such as stress inoculation training, interpretation of the stressful situation as facilitative, the relaxation response, and reframing using self-talk. This model emphasizes that multiple types of mental skills are important for success and well-being in coaches and athletes, including foundation, performance, personal development, and team skills.

Foundation skills represent those qualities that are basic and necessary psychological skills. For example, without an individual's desire to succeed (achievement drive), there is little hope that any MST program would be successful because it takes commitment to practice the skills and carry out the program. The method of goal setting is one good way to enhance motivation. *Performance skills* are traditional psychological skills that most sport psychology consultants attempt to achieve. The premise is that exceptional performance is most likely to occur when these skills are learned and integrated into an athlete's actual competitive performance. *Facilitative (personal development)* skills have unfortunately been left out of many MST programs. Although these don't always directly affect sport performance, they can facilitate behavior in sport and other areas of life. For instance, communication skills might help a captain talk with his teammates or an athlete talk to her coach. These same communication skills might be helpful in relationships where communication breakdowns are often the cause of problems. Finally, *team skills* focus on group cohesion and building an effective team climate. Building what is called collective efficacy (confidence in your team and teammates) is an important part of making a group of individuals a tem. A list of these psychological skills is noted below.

- *Foundation skills* are intrapersonal resources that are the basic mental skills necessary to achieve success. These skills include the following:
  - Achievement drive
  - Self-awareness
  - Productive thinking
  - Self-confidence
  - Self-esteem
- *Performance skills* are mental abilities critical to the execution of skills during sport performance. These skills include the following:
  - Energy management
  - Attentional focus
  - Perceptual-motor skill
  - Optimal mental arousal

- ***Personal development skills*** are mental skills that represent significant maturational markers of personal development allowing for high-level psychological functioning through clarity of self-concept, feelings of well-being, and a sense of relatedness to others. These skills include the following:
  - Identity achievement
  - Interpersonal competence
- ***Team skills*** are collective qualities of the team that are instrumental to an effective team climate and overall team success. These skills include the following:
  - Leadership
  - Cohesion
  - Team confidence

DEVELOPING AN IMPLEMENTATION SCHEDULE

After assessing athlete skills and determining the strategies to implement it is now time to develop a training schedule. Before or after practice 1 or 2 days a week might serve as a formal meeting time for educating participants on various other psychological skills. In general, it is better to hold frequent, short meetings rather than less frequent, long meetings. Informal meetings can occur during social events, on bus or plane rides to competitions, at the hotel, at meals, or at any other time and place. These informal meetings complement the structured meetings and individualize content to each athlete. Some athletes are still not comfortable going into an office and speaking about mental issues. Therefore, many consultants find that impromptu meetings like noted above often is the best (and sometimes only) time to hear athletes out. So consultants need to be around a lot (if possible) so athletes get used to them being around and feel more comfortable talking with them about important, and sometimes sensitive, issues.

A critical point in setting up a training schedule is determining when to start and how long the training should last. As was noted earlier, it is best to develop psychological skills just before the season begins or during the off-season, but the key is to systematically schedule MST as part of the daily practice regimen. Holliday and colleagues (2008) have proposed a systematic periodization approach to the development of mental skills, similar to the periodization model used to train physical skills for many sports. Periodization refers to planned variation in key training variables, particularly volume and intensity, over predetermined training cycles. The aim is to maximize long-term development and "peak performance" for targeted competitions while minimizing training problems such as burnout, overtraining, and injury. Periodization has been proposed as a method to train mental skills through the preparatory, competitive, and peaking phases. This is an example of using imagery for a soccer player:

- ***Preparatory phase***: The soccer player performs high-volume, low-intensity imagery exercises every day, focusing on improving imagery vividness and controllability or making small adjustments in controlling the ball in his mind.
- ***Competitive phase***: The soccer player performs imagery less frequently (i.e., decreased volume). He now images himself on the soccer pitch getting ready for a

penalty kick instead of imaging himself playing away from the soccer pitch (e.g., practicing on a grass field). In addition, soccer-related imagery predominates, focusing on developing effective passing strategies from the midfield to the offensive end (increased intensity), for example.

- *Peaking phase*: The soccer player imagines himself performing against specific players and teams in speicifc situations (i.e., high intensity).

EVALUATION OF PROGRAM EFFECTIVENESS

It is not an easy task to evaluate the effectiveness of an MST program. However, evaluation is essential for improving a training program and the skills of the individual in charge of the program. Aside from the accountability demands that ethically oblige consultants to evaluate the effectiveness of what they do (see Smith, 1989), practical considerations are also important as noted below.

- An evaluation provides feedback for gauging the program's effectiveness and for then modifying the program as necessary.
- An evaluation allows participants to suggest changes in how the program is conducted.
- An evaluation is the only way to objectively judge whether the program has achieved its goals.

A more formal total evaluation should occur at the end of the MST program. Ideally, the evaluation should include interviews and written rating scales to supply both qualitative and quantitative feedback. The evaluation should focus on the players' assessment of the value of the program from both a psychological and performance perspective. Also useful to coaches and athletes are objective performance data. For example, if one of the program goals was to help a tennis player relax while serving second serves under pressure, then percent double faults in critical situations (e.g., when on serve and the player is serving when the game score is at least 4-5 or 5-4) would be a good statistic for evaluation. Possibly the percentage of 2nd point serves won under the same conditions might also be a good statistic because if a player does not put much on his second serve then the receiver might hit a return winner or place the server at a disadvantage because of a big return off a weak second serve. One of the things that should be asked of athletes is how often they actually practiced mental skills because many programs fail to meet expectations simply because of a lack of athlete practice and participation. In addition, the following questions are useful for evaluating the effectiveness of a MST program:

- What techniques appeared to work best?
- Was enough time allotted to practice the psychological skills?
- Was the consultant available?
- Was the consultant knowledgeable, informative, and easy to talk with?
- Should anything be added to or deleted from the program?
- What were the major strengths and weaknesses of the program?

An article by Anderson, Miles, Mahoney, and Robinson, (2002) suggests that a practitioner administered case study approach to evaluating should be employed. This would ideally use a number of effectiveness indicators to accommodate the constraints of a practice setting and fulfill the functional criteria for evaluating practice. More specifically, effectiveness indicators should be broken down into four distinct categories. These include the quality of support (e.g., consultant effectiveness), psychological skill and well-being (e.g., anxiety control optimism), response to support (e.g., changes in knowledge and attitude), and performance (e.g., objective, subjective). This presents a more well-rounded view of evaluation than simply performance, which is the focus and bottom line of many interventions.

CONCLUSION

The theme to this edited text revolves around positive human functioning. The present chapter certainly contributes to this end by providing guidelines for successful and effective mental training interventions. When providing mental training for athletes, the goal should not only be focused on improving performance (although this is most certainly important for elite athletes). Probably more importantly, in the long run, is having the athlete experience positive personal growth and development. Thus, teaching skills such as goal-setting, relaxation, imagery, self-talk, and routines can help the athlete as an individual function more effectively in other areas of life. In addition, the guidelines put forth in this chapter are meant to facilitate a positive consultant-athlete relationship. In essence, this consulting experience should help the athlete as a person as well s an athlete. Frankly, our goal as sport psychology consultants should be to help the effective functioning of our clients. Creating a trusting relationship with open communication and mutual respect would certainly help athletes grow as individuals, preparing them for the challenges of life that lay ahead.

REFERENCES

Albrecht, R. R., & Feltz, D. L. (1987). Generality and specificity of attention related to competitive anxiety and sport performance. *Journal of Sport Psychology*, 9, 241–248.

Anderson, A., Miles, A., Mahoney, C., & Robinson, P. (2002). Evaluating the effectiveness of applied sport psychology practice: Making the case for a case study approach. *The Sport Psychologist, 16,* 432-453.

Beckman, J., & Kellmann, M. (2003). Procedures and principles of sport psychological assessment. *Journal of Sport & Exercise Psychology, 17,* 338-350.

Bull, S., Shambrook, C., &James, J. (2005). Towards an understanding of mental toughness in elite English cricketers. *Journal of Applied Sport Psychology*, *17*, 209-227.

Butler, R., & Hardy, L. (1992). The performance profile: Theory and application. *The Sport Psychologist, 6,* 253-264.

Côté, J., & Hay, J. (2002). Children's involvement in sport: A developmental perspective. In J. Silva & D. Stevens (Eds.), *Psychological foundations of sport* (pp. 484-502). Boston MA: Allyn & Bacon.

Crust, L. (2007). Mental toughness in sport: A review. *International Journal of Sport and Exercise Psychology, 5,* 270-290.

Dosil, J. (2006). *The sport psychologist's handbook: A guide for sport-specific performance enhancement.* West Sussex, UK: Wiley.

Fournier, J., Calmels, C., Durand-Bush, N., & Salmela, J. (2005). Effects of a season-long PST program on gymnastic performance and psychological skill development. *International Journal of Sport and Exercise Psychology, 3,* 59-78.

Goldsmith, P. A., & Williams, J. M. (1992). Perceived stressors for football and volleyball officials from three rating levels. *Journal of Sport Behavior,* 15, 106–118.

Gould, D., Diffenbach, K., & Moffett, A. (2002). Psychological characteristics and their development in Olympic champions. *Journal of Applied Sport Psychology, 14,* 172-204.

Gould, D., Guinan, Greenleaf, C., Medberry, R., & Peterson, K. (1999). Factors affecting Olympic performance: Perceptions of athletes and coaches from more and less successful teams. *The Sport Psychologist, 13,* 371-394.

Gould, D., Weiss, M., & Weinberg, R. (1981). Psychological characteristics of successful and non-successful Big 10 wrestlers. *Journal of Sport Psychology, 3,* 69-81.

Greenleaf, C., Gould, D., & Diffenbach, K. (2001). Factors influencing Olympic performance: Interviews with Atlanta and Nagano U.S. Olympians. *Journal of Applied Sport Psychology, 13,* 154-184.

Greenspan, M., & Feltz, D. (1989). Psychological interventions with athletes in competitive situations: A review. *The Sport Psychologist, 3,* 219-236.

Gucciardi, D., & Gordon, S. (2011). *Mental toughness in sport: Developments in research and theory.* London: Routledge.

Harmison, R., & Casto, K. (2012). Optimal performance: Elite level performance in "the zone." In S. Murphy (Ed.), *The Oxford handbook of Sport and Performance Psychology* (pp. 707-724). New York: Oxford University Press.

Harwood, C., Douglas, J., & Minniti, A. (2012). Talent development: The role of the family. In S. Murphy (Ed.), *The oxford handbook of sport and performance psychology* (pp. 476-492). New York: Oxford University Press.

Holliday, B., Burton, D., Sun, G., Hammermeister, J., Naylor, S., & Freigang, D. (2008). Building the better mental training mousetrap: Is periodization a more systematic approach to promoting performance excellence? *Journal of Applied Sport Psychology, 29,* 199-219.

Jones, G., Hanton, S., & Connaughton, D. (2002). What is this thing called mental toughness? An investigation of elite sport performers. *Journal of Applied Sport Psychology, 14,* 205-218.

Jones, G., Hanton, S., & Connaughton, D. (2007). A framework of mental toughness in the world's best performers. *The Sport Psychologist, 9,* 201-211.

Karageorghis, C., & Terry, P. (2011*). Inside sport psychology.* Champaign, IL: Human Kinetics.

Krane, V., & Williams, J. (2010). Psychological characteristics of peak performance. In J. Williams (Ed.), *Applied sport psychology: Personal growth to peak performance* (6th ed., pp. 169–188). Mountain View: Mayfield.

Lerner, R., & Lerner, J. (2006). Toward a new vision and vocabulary about adolescence: Theoretical, empirical and applied bases for a positive youth development perspective. In

I. Baker & C. Tamis Lamoda (Eds.), *Child psychology: A handbook of contemporary issues* (pp. 449-465). New York: Psychology Press.

Martin, G., Vause, T., & Schwartzman, L. (2005). Experimental studies of psychological interventions with athletes in competition Why so few? *Behavior Modification, 29,* 615-641.

McAuley, E. (1985). Modeling and self-efficacy: A test of Bandura's model. *Journal of Sport Psychology, 7,* 283–295.

Meyers, A., Whelan, J., & Murphy, S. (1996). Cognitive behavioral strategies in athletic performance. *Progress in Behavior Modification, 30,* 137-16.

Nideffer, R. (1976). Test of attentional and interpersonal style. *Journal of Personality and Social Psychology, 34,* 394-404.

Ogilvie, B., & Henschen, K. (1995).The art of application of psychological enhancing principles. In K. Henschen & W. Straub (Eds.), *Sport psychology: An analysis of athlete behavior* (2nd ed., pp. 45-54). Longmeadow, MA: Mouvement Publications.

Orlick, T. (2000) *In pursuit of excellence: How to win in sport and life through mental training* (3rd ed.). Champaign, IL: Human Kinetics.

Poczwardowski, A., & Sherman, C. P. (2011). Revisions to the Sport Psychology Service Delivery (SPSD) Heuristic: Explorations with experienced consultants. *The Sport Psychologist, 25*(4), 511-531.

Poczwardowski, A., Sherman, C., & Henschen, K. (1998). A sport psychology service delivery heuristic: Building on theory and practice. *The Sport Psychologist, 12,* 191-207.

Ravizza, K. (2001). Reflections and insights from the field of performance enhancement consulting. In G. Tenenbaum (Ed.), *Reflections and experiences in sport and exercise psychology* (pp. 197-213). Morgantown, WV: Fitness Information Technology.

Robazza, C., & Bortoli, L. (2003). Intensity, idiosyncratic content and functional impact of performance-related emotions in athletes. *Journal of Sport Science, 21,* 171-189.

Robazza, C., Bortoli, L., & Hanin, Y. (2004). Pre-competition emotions, bodily symptoms, and task-specific qualities as predictors of performance in high-level karate athletes. *Journal of Applied Sport Psychology, 15,* 151-165.

Simons, J. (2013). The applied sport psychology intake. In S. Hanrahan & M. Andersen (Eds.), *Routledge handbook of applied sport psychology* (pp. 81-89), New York: Routledge.

Singer, R., & Anshel, M. (2006). An overview of interventions in sport. In J. Dosil (Ed.), *The sport psychologist's handbook: A guide for sport-specific-performance enhancement* (pp. 63-88). New York: Wiley.

Smith, R. (1989). Applied sport psychology in the age of accountability. *Journal of Applied Sport Psychology, 1,* 166-180.

Smith, R., & Johnson, J. (1990). An organizational empowerment approach to consultation in professional baseball. *The Sport Psychologist, 4,* 347-357.

Smith, R., Smoll, F., & Schutz, B. (1990). Measurement and correlates of sport-specific cognitive and somatic train anxiety: The Sport Anxiety Scale. *Anxiety Research, 2,* 263-280.

Taylor, J. (1995). A conceptual model for integrating athletes' needs and sport demands in the development of competitive mental preparation strategies. *The Sport Psychologist, 9,* 339-357.

Thomas, O., Hanton, S., & Maynard, I. (2007). Anxiety responses and psychological skill use during time leading up to competition. *Journal of Applied Sport Psychology*, *19*, 379-397.

Thomas, O., Maynard, I., & Hanton, S. (2007). Intervening with athletes during the time leading up to competition: Theory to practice. *Journal of Applied Sport Psychology, 19*, 398-418.

Thomas, O., Murphy, S., & Hardy, L. (1999). Test of performance strategies: Development and preliminary validation of a compre-hensive measure of athletes' psychological skills. *Journal of Sport Sciences*, 17(9), 697–711.

Vealey, R. (1986). Conceptualization of sport-confidence and competitive orientation: Preliminary investigation and instrument development. *Journal of Sport Psychology, 8*, 221-246.

Vealey, R. (1994). Current status and prominent issues in sport psychology interventions. *Medicine and Science in Sport and Exercise, 26*, 495-502.

Vealey, R. (2007). Mental skills training in sport. In G. Tenenbaum & R. Eklund (Eds.), *Handbook of sport psychology* (3 ed., pp. 287-309). New York: Wiley.

Watson, J., & Shannon, V. (2013). Individual and group observations: Purposes and processes. In S. Hanrahan & M. Andersen (Eds.), *Routledge handbook of applied sport psychology* (pp. 90-100). New York: Routledge.

Weinberg, R., & Butt, J. (2011). Building mental toughness. In D. Gucciardi & S. Gordon (Eds.), *Mental toughness in sport: Developments in research and theory* (pp. 212-230). London: Routledge.

Weinberg, R., & Comar, W. (1994). The effectiveness of psychological interventions in competitive sport. *Sports Medicine Journal, 18*, 406-418.

Weinberg, R., & Williams, J. (2010). Integrating ad implementing a psychological skills training program. In J. Williams (Ed.), *Sport psychology: Personal growth to peak performance* (6 ed., pp. 525-457). New York: McGraw Hill.

Weiss, M., Kipp. L., & Bolter, N. (2012). Training in life: Optimizing positive youth development through sport and physical activity. In S. Murphy (Ed.), *The Oxford Handbook of Sport and Performance Psychology* (pp. 448-475). New York: Oxford University Press.

Woodcock, C., Duda, J., Cumming, J., Sharo, L., & Holland, M. (2012). Assessing mental skill and technique use in applied intervention: Recognizing and minimizing threats to psychometric properties of the TOPS. *The Sport Psychologist, 26*, 1-15.

LEADERS

In: Positive Human Functioning …   ISBN: 978-1-62948-974-2
Editors: A. R. Gomes, R. Resende & A. Albuquerque   © 2014 Nova Science Publishers, Inc.

Chapter 5

COACHING YOUNG ATHLETES TO POSITIVE DEVELOPMENT: IMPLICATIONS FOR COACH TRAINING

Stewart Vella[1] and Wade Gilbert[2]

[1]Interdisciplinary Educational Research Institute, Faculty of Social Sciences,
University of Wollongong, Australia
[2]Department of Kinesiology, California State University, Fresno, US

ABSTRACT

Youth sport settings can, and should, be viewed as principle settings for nurturing a wide range of positive developmental outcomes. Coaches are increasingly being called upon to assume this responsibility. The purpose of this chapter is to provide positive youth development guidelines for youth sport coaches and coach educators. The guidelines are based on a comprehensive review of conceptual and empirical literature related to positive youth development in sport and across youth development settings. The Social Cognitive Theory of Achievement Motivation (Dweck, 1999), and implicit beliefs about ability in particular, provides the conceptual framework for our positive youth development guidelines. Insights gleaned from this framework are used to make recommendations for youth sport coaching practice and coach education design. More specifically, six instructional strategies designed to facilitate positive youth development through sport are discussed: (1) a focus on effort and persistence, (2) promoting challenge, (3) promoting the value of failure, (4) defining success as giving your best effort, (5) promoting learning, and, (6) providing high performance expectations. In order to best equip coaches to facilitate positive developmental outcomes a blended approach to coach training has been outlined. According to this approach, foundational training designed to impart generic and sport-specific professional and interpersonal knowledge should be supplemented by opportunities for formal and guided reflection to increase self-awareness.

INTRODUCTION

Organized youth sport has long been considered a primary venue for youth development. Comprehensive and diverse organized youth sport programming has been woven into the daily life and cultural fabric of most countries around the world for many decades now (De Knopp, Engström, Skirstad, & Weiss, 1996). It is widely believed that participation in organized youth sport can lead to physical, social, psychological/emotional, and intellectual development. Indeed there is research evidence demonstrating that participation in youth sport can result in a wide array of positive developmental outcomes (see reviews of this research by Fraser-Thomas, Côté, & Deakin, 2005; Gould & Carson, 2008; and Weiss, 2008). Some groups have gone so far as to proclaim that life skill development should be the primary goal of youth sport, taking precedence over the development of sport skills (Perkins & Noam, 2007). The constellation of personal attributes, or life skills, believed to be developed or derived through participation in organized sport has variously been described as the '5Cs' (Lerner, Fisher, & Weinberg, 2000) or the '4Cs' (Côté, Bruner, Erickson, Strachan, & Fraser-Thomas, 2010). Virtually every review of positive youth development and sport in the past decade traces the origin of this movement to the writings of Lerner and colleagues who organized developmental outcomes into the '5Cs': competence, confidence, connection, character, and caring/compassion. Lerner and colleagues, however, did not focus exclusively on sport settings. In an attempt to adapt the '5Cs' model specifically to youth sport settings Côté and colleagues conducted a comprehensive review of the youth sport-specific literature and concluded that 'caring/compassion' and 'character' should be combined into one broad outcome referred to as 'character'; hence the '5Cs' was transformed to the '4Cs' specific to sport settings.

At least three attempts have been made to empirically test the '5Cs / 4Cs' models with youth sport participants. In 2009 Jones and Lavallee conducted focus groups with athletes (n=19) – some of whom were youth sport athletes – coaches (n=10) and sport psychologists (n=4) in England. Their qualitative analysis revealed two broad categories of positive youth development outcomes: interpersonal life skills and personal life skills. Interpersonal life skills encompassed social skills, respect, leadership, and family interaction skills. Personal skills included self-organization, discipline, self-reliance, goal-setting, managing performance outcomes, and motivation. In Canada, 250 youth sport summer camp participants between 12 and 16 years of age were surveyed by Jones, Dunn, Holt, Sullivan, and Bloom (2011). They did not find support for the '5Cs / 4Cs' model and instead concluded that positive youth development outcomes in sport settings might more practically be regrouped into two broad outcome categories: pro-social values and confidence/competence. Pro-social values included items such as caring, character, and family connection. Around the same time in Australia 22 youth sport coaches were interviewed about the desired outcomes for youth sport participants (Vella, Oades, & Crowe, 2011). Contrary to the findings of Jones et al. who found evidence for collapsing the '5Cs / 4Cs', Vella and colleagues found evidence for expanding the developmental outcome categories. Based on the responses from the coaches in the Vella et al. study, eight positive youth development themes were identified as desirable outcomes: (1) competence, (2) confidence, (3) connection, (4) character, (5) life skills, (6) climate, (7), positive affect, and (8) psychological capacities. It is impossible to make firm conclusions at this point about a single classification system for positive youth development outcomes that may be achieved through youth sport participation. The few available studies used different methodologies (confirmatory factor analysis, focus groups, individual qualitative interviews), different samples (summer camp youth participants, youth sport athletes, coaches, sport psychologists), and were conducted in different youth sport settings (Australia, Canada, and England). What can be concluded at this time, however, is that despite these methodological and contextual differences, all studies did in fact show support either for the attainment or expected attainment of positive youth development outcomes through youth sport.

Regardless of how positive youth developmental outcomes through sport are classified, the belief that youth sport can and should be a source of positive youth development has been referred to as a 'sport evangelistic' view of youth sport settings. Scholars such as Coakley have argued that this 'sport evangelistic' view lacks credible supporting evidence and is narrowly focused on individual development (Coakley, 2011). Coakley advocates for a much broader approach to positive youth development through sport; one that extends beyond personal development to community and civic development. Admittedly this is a tall order for youth sport programs, which typically operate on small budgets and are administered by an untrained (or lightly trained) volunteer or part-time workforce. Irrespective of one's view on the role and impact of youth development through sport, the consensus is that positive youth development through participation in organized youth sport is contingent upon a myriad of factors (Coakley, 2011; Holt, 2011). For example, in their recent study of 297 youth sport participants Gould and Carson (2011) found significant differences on athlete reported development outcomes based on variables such as athlete gender and sport type (individual vs. team sport). The one constant across all youth sport experiences, though, is the presence of a coach. Therefore, the most likely determinant of positive youth development outcomes realized through youth sport participation is the philosophy and behavior of the youth sport coach.

A growing body of scientific evidence shows that youth sport coaches do in fact believe that a coach's role should extend beyond teaching sport specific skills to teaching for a wide range of positive youth developmental outcomes (Camiré, Trudel, & Forneris, 2012; Gould, Collins, Lauer, & Chung, 2007; Holt, 2008). This approach may be considered athlete-centered coaching as opposed to a coach-centered approach. In athlete-centered coaching the developmental needs and well-being of the athletes drive coaching decisions and behaviors. The goal is to develop young people who are empowered – through their sport experience – to lead a fully engaged and productive life (Kidman, 2005). It is questionable however if youth sport coaches are adequately trained to assume this responsibility. Although formal coach education programs have existed in many developed countries since the 1970s, there is very limited evidence showing that participation in these coach education programs translates into coaching behaviors that result in positive youth developmental outcomes (Trudel, Gilbert, & Werthner, 2010). Published evaluations of coach education programs are extremely rare, and conclusions must be drawn instead from isolated intervention studies (e.g., Coatsworth & Conroy, 2006; Falcão, Bloom, & Gilbert, 2012; MacDonald, Côté, & Deakin, 2010; Smith, Smoll, & Curtis, 1979). Evidence from these types of small-scale intervention studies regularly show that it is possible to design coach education programs that effectively teach youth sport coaches how to create environments that contribute to positive changes in youth developmental outcomes.

The purpose of this chapter is to provide positive youth development guidelines for youth sport coaches and coach educators. The guidelines are based on a comprehensive review of conceptual and empirical literature related to positive youth development in sport and across youth development settings.

CONCEPTUAL FOUNDATION FOR POSITIVE YOUTH DEVELOPMENT THROUGH SPORT

In order to provide a strong conceptual foundation for positive youth development through sport, a theory should: (1) be able to address the various domains that underpin positive youth development through sport, such as competence, confidence, connection and character, (2) have demonstrated efficacy and applicability in each domain, especially with children, and (3) be easily understood and applied within the sporting context, and in particular, within coaching practice. One theory which fulfils these criteria is Dweck's Social Cognitive Theory of Achievement Motivation (Dweck & Leggett, 1988). According to this theory, fundamental implicit beliefs about the nature of human abilities have significant short- and long-term implications for individuals' motivational frameworks, including their cognitions, affect and behavior (Dweck, 1999, 2006; Dweck & Leggett, 1988). Implicit beliefs are unconscious conceptions or theories about the nature of human abilities. They provide a framework for the interpretation of events that occur within an achievement context and dictate the subsequent behavioral and motivational responses (Dweck & Leggett, 1988). There are two basic implicit beliefs: incremental beliefs and entity beliefs. Those who hold incremental beliefs assume that ability is a malleable and increasable quality that can be trained and developed. In contrast, those who hold entity beliefs assume that ability is fixed and unable to be developed (Dweck, 1999).

Research over multiple domains associated with positive youth development, including sports, education, personality, and morality has consistently shown that incremental beliefs (as opposed to entity beliefs) are associated with the acquisition of developmental assets. Such assets include: higher rates of motivation, persistence, and effort, a greater preference for challenge, and, an ability to generate strategies for improvement (Blackwell, Trzesniewski, & Dweck, 2007; Chiu, Dweck, Tong, & Fu, 1997; Chiu, Hong, & Dweck, 1997; Dweck & Leggett, 1988; Gunderson et al., in press). Incremental beliefs are also particularly powerful predictors of motivational and behavioral responses following a failure or setback (Dweck & Leggett, 1988). This is important because positive youth development is contingent upon the acquisition of agency, which is the ability to regulate behavior over extended periods of time in order to meet long-term goals in complex contexts that lend themselves to both failures and setbacks (Larson, 2011). As a consequence, incremental beliefs in human abilities both facilitate the direct acquisition of developmental assets (such as mastery and self-regulation) and provide the necessary conditions under which developmental assets are acquired (such as motivation and persistence).

On the surface, a belief that human abilities are malleable is at the heart of effective coaching in any context. In fact, the very definition of effective coaching stipulates that coaches apply their knowledge in order to *improve* athletes' competence, confidence, connection, and character (Côté & Gilbert, 2009). Chase (2010) has persuasively argued that all coaches should adopt a belief in the incremental nature of human abilities, and although the argument is set within the context of coach development, the basic premise is fundamental to effective coaching practice: coaches' beliefs in the nature of human abilities dictate their behaviors, and ultimately, their effectiveness. This premise is most poignantly highlighted by Côté and colleague's Coaching Model (Côté, Salmela, Trudel, Baria, & Russell, 1995). According to the Coaching Model, a coach's mental model of athlete potential is the determinant of athlete development. A coach will draw upon their own personal characteristics, athlete characteristics and contextual factors to make an estimate of athlete potential, and will regulate their actions accordingly over varying contexts. These actions will facilitate the ultimate goal of athlete development. Thus, if a coach believes that ability is a stable, fixed, and concrete entity, they will regulate their actions accordingly, and athlete development will be hindered. In contrast, if coaches believe that ability can be acquired through hard work they will also regulate their actions accordingly and athlete development will be maximised.

Two fictional examples are used to highlight the impact of different views about human abilities on coaching behaviors. The first is Coach Lauren. Coach Lauren has a strong belief in innate ability, or "natural talent", and believes that young athletes "either have it or they don't". She has a strong desire to win because winning is the true indicator of success. Subsequently, when Coach Lauren wants to build a winning team her pre-season recruitment strategy is to recruit only young athletes who are proven performers – she must recruit "the best" in order to have a winning team. In the absence of the most highly skilled athletes, her team is unlikely to win. If Coach Lauren's team suffers a heavy loss in their first game, it is because the other team is more talented, more skilful, and there is little hope that her team can overcome the disparity in talent – the situation is hopeless and there is little that Coach Lauren can do about it. When her athletes don't execute a skill correctly it is an indication that they are not up to the task of performing to a high level – they don't possess the required skills and are unlikely to do so in the future because they "just don't have it". If Coach Lauren wants to improve her team, she must recruit more talented athletes. The likely outcomes for Coach Lauren's athletes are a fear of failure, a reluctance to engage in challenging tasks, decreases in self-efficacy following a failure, declines in persistence and motivation, and a focus on winning (Dweck, 1999).

Example number two is Coach Kelly. Coach Kelly believes that ability and mastery are a product of effort, persistence and learning. She has a strong desire to teach and believes that success is defined by effort and learning. For her pre-season recruitment strategy Coach Kelly is non-selective because she believes that she can teach the skills that are required. Coach Kelly is inclusive and is willing to take young athletes that "need some work". If her team suffers a heavy loss in their first game Coach Kelly will draw important lessons from the loss, emphasize continued learning, and promote deliberate practice. When her athletes fail to execute a skill in training, Coach Kelly will provide a strategy for improvement and reinforce the value of practice, thereby providing the conditions that are necessary for skill acquisition. As such, if Coach Kelly wants to improve her team she has a range of strategies that can be applied and that are founded upon learning, effort, persistence, and practice. The likely outcomes for Coach Kelly's athletes are an ability to appraise performance and set new goals, a belief in the value of persistence and effort, a focus on learning rather than winning, and self-efficacy that is derived from controllable factors such as hard work (Dweck, 1999).

Clearly, the vast differences in coaching behaviors that are brought about by opposing beliefs about the nature of ability will have significant repercussions for positive youth development. As stipulated by Larson (2011), sustained positive youth development requires the ability to regulate actions over time in service of a long-term goal, including assets such as cognitive skills, the ability to regulate emotions, and persistent motivation. Alternatively, Benson (2007) has articulated the internal assets that are indicative of positive youth development, including a commitment to learning, positive values, and social competencies. Each of the assets articulated by both Larson and Benson are much more likely to be facilitated by Coach Kelly. Her focus on persistence, learning, and developing strategies for improvement lend themselves to positive youth development and can play a causal role in facilitating positive functioning. However, incremental beliefs in human ability do not always translate into behaviors that are either consistent with these beliefs or promote these beliefs to athletes. Gunderson and colleagues (Gunderson, et al., in press) have shown that parents who held incremental beliefs were unlikely to articulate these to their children. In fact, parents who held incremental beliefs were likely to communicate with their children in ways that were consistent with entity beliefs, and as a result their children were more likely to adopt entity beliefs about their ability. Further, Gundersen et al. have shown that the way parents communicate to children as young as 14 months of age is a strong predictor of their motivational frameworks up to five years later. For these reasons, it is imperative that coach education programs provide coaches with guidance on how to develop and maintain instructional strategies that are consistent with incremental beliefs about human abilities in order to facilitate positive youth development through sport.

In the following section we review positive youth development coaching practices that are consistent with an incremental view of ability, and suggest six general coaching strategies designed to promote positive youth development through sport.

KEY POINTS FOR COACHING PRACTICE

There is a growing, albeit limited, body of research on how youth sport coaches attempt to nurture positive youth developmental outcomes for sport participants. Undoubtedly the most comprehensive line of research on this topic is the work of Ronald Smith, Frank Smoll, and their colleagues that has spanned nearly four decades (Smith & Smoll, 2011).Their work has been guided by a mediational model of coach-athlete interactions, whereby coaching behaviors influence athlete developmental outcomes and evaluative reactions, which are filtered through athlete perceptions of coaching behaviors. They have identified five specific coaching principles that are associated with positive changes in youth attitudes toward the sport experience and their coach, self-esteem, achievement-goal orientation, and performance anxiety. These five principles, collectively referred to as the Mastery Approach to Coaching (MAC), are:

1   Developmentally oriented philosophy of winning (effort and fun versus winning at all costs);
2   A positive approach to coaching characterized by high frequency of positive reinforcement and technical instruction;
3   Establishment of group norms that emphasize athletes' mutual obligations;
4   Shared decisional responsibility with the athletes; and,
5   Increased coach self-awareness and reflection.

In their review of the literature on coaching life skills, Gould, Carson, and Blanton (2013) distinguish between direct and indirect coaching strategies for teaching positive youth development outcomes through youth sport. When coaches explicitly discuss specific life skills they expect athletes to develop while also reinforcing these skills, they are engaging in direct coaching strategies. Indirect coaching strategies are described as situations in which a coach creates conditions designed to nurture positive youth development outcomes without formally directing the athletes. Referring to their 2007 study of award-winning American youth football coaches, Gould et al. identified examples both of direct and indirect coaching strategies. Direct coaching strategies included strategies aimed at building quality relationships with athletes (e.g., treating them like young adults and communicating with care and tact) and reinforcing life skills (e.g., emphasizing the importance of academic progress and talking to players about being disciplined). Indirect coaching strategies focused on exhibiting the desired outcomes (e.g., serving as a role model or using others as mentors to teach about life skill transfer).

More recently Camiré and colleagues (2011) summarized strategies for helping coaches facilitate youth development through sport, based on a review of the literature and findings from their own research in this area. They identified five general coaching strategies: (1) carefully develop your coaching philosophy, (2) develop meaningful relationships with your athletes, (3) intentionally plan developmental strategies in your coaching practice – analogous to 'direct coaching strategies' described by Gould et al. (2013), (4) don't just talk about life skills, make athletes practice them, and (5) teach athletes how life skills transfer to non-sport settings. In their 2012 interview study of youth sport coaches (n=9) and student-athletes (n=16), Camiré and colleagues found direct evidence for the strategies coaches use to teach life skills to their athletes. In addition to having a coaching philosophy that values the importance of teaching life skills, the coaches stressed the importance of making time to get to know your athletes and their unique learning needs and profile – referred to as the athlete's 'preexisting makeup'. Some specific strategies used by the coaches were athlete peer evaluations, providing frequent opportunities for athletes to display their skills, modeling the core life skills values themselves, taking advantage of teachable moments, and having athletes complete volunteer work. 'Volunteerism' as a strategy for developing life skills through sport has also been identified in other studies (e.g., Boon & Gilbert, 2010). Using the United Nation's Millennium Development Goals as a conceptual framework, Boon and Gilbert found that soccer coaches could easily identify numerous practical coaching strategies for teaching citizenship through youth soccer. The 14 coaches identified strategies such as pre-season equipment exchanges (passing on used equipment to younger or less fortunate athletes and their families), setting aside one soccer practice weekly to help each other with school homework, scheduling scrimmages against opposite-gender teams, and implementing a post-practice / post-game team trash pick-up program (clean the field and surrounding area).

Based on our review both of the literature that can inform positive youth development through sport and examples of youth sport coaching research on this topic, we offer six broad instructional strategies for teaching positive youth development through sport. These strategies are summarized in Table 1. Given the highly context-dependent nature of effective coaching (Côté & Gilbert, 2009), the successful application of these broad instructional strategies is likely to be highly variable. We encourage readers to supplement our suggestions with the detailed behavioral checklists for positive youth development coaching behaviors created by Harwood (2008).

Table 1. A summary of instructional strategies to promote positive youth development through sport

Strategy		Description	Coaching Examples
1	Focus on effort and persistence	Promote and praise effort and persistence. Provide opportunities for the deliberate practice of life skills and sport-specific skills.	• Use process praise (and avoid person praise) – see Gunderson et al., in press • Make time for the deliberate practice of life skills during practice, such as goal setting
2	Promote challenge	Promote young people's engagement with difficult tasks that offer a chance to master new skills and provide feedback on performance.	• Set practices at a difficult level • Facilitate a mastery climate • Set challenging goals for young people
3	Promote the value of failure	Interpret failures and setbacks as valuable opportunities to learn important skills such as behavioral regulation, planning and monitoring.	• Attribute failures to controllable factors that can be improved, and set practices accordingly • Use failure to monitor goal attainment
4	Define success as controllable	Define success by controllable factors such as effort and persistence.	• Set self-referenced goals and judge success by their attainment • Don't look at the scoreboard when determining satisfaction with performance
5	Promote learning	Promote learning goal orientations and a mastery climate (see Smith and Smoll, 2011).	• Focus on learning rather than winning • Share decisional responsibility with athletes • Use a high frequency of positive reinforcement, particularly process praise, and technical instruction
6	Provide high performance expectations	Communicate expectations of athletes that are above current performance levels, and deliver them from within a supportive environment.	• Set difficult goals for young athletes, preferably process goals • Communicate high levels of belief in young athletes' ability to improve

Focus on Effort and Persistence

At their very core, incremental beliefs in human abilities are a belief that mastery and skill acquisition are under one's own control, and are therefore dependent upon practice. Deliberate practice is defined as a highly structured activity that requires cognitive or physical effort over long periods in order to promote skill development (Ericsson, Krampe, & Tesch-Römer, 1993) – if one wants to develop ability then one must invest effort and persistence into its acquisition. The implication of this is that the promotion of effort, persistence, and deliberate practice is a key strategy in facilitating incremental beliefs. In fact, research has shown that children who receive praise for their effort believe that the source of their success is deliberate practice. In contrast, children who receive praise for their ability believe that the source of their success is a fixed and internal entity (Zentall & Morris, 2010).

The promotion of effort and persistence may be particularly important following a setback. Given that positive youth development requires the regulation of motivation and behaviors over an extensive period the need to maintain effort and persistence following demotivating events is critical (Larson, 2011). Children who are high in entity beliefs tend to disengage from tasks following a setback because setbacks are indicative of low ability. This typically "helpless" response may also led to low levels of self-efficacy (Lirgg, Chase, George, & Ferguson, 1996), with both high levels of entity beliefs and low levels of self-efficacy likely to lead to the belief that the potential to master new skills is minimal (Ommundsen, 2003). Such beliefs are detrimental to positive youth development because they have significant negative impacts on developmental assets such as identity. According to Benson (2007), a positive identity is constituted by the belief that a young person can control their future and a positive view of the future. However, those high in entity beliefs and low in self-efficacy are not likely to acquire either of these developmental assets. The promotion of effort and persistence, especially to those high in entity beliefs and low in self-efficacy can send clear messages to youth that they are in control of their own learning, and are able to work towards positive long-term goals (Skinner, 1995).

While it is important that the promotion of effort and persistence as the means to mastery is explicit, it need not be sport-specific. Vella and colleagues (Vella et al., 2011) have shown that youth sport coaches aim to facilitate a broad array of competencies that are consistent with positive youth development, including technical, tactical and performance skills, and life skills such as communication and decision-making skills. A coach-facilitated mastery climate in youth sports is associated with the acquisition of critical developmental and life skills including the development of identity and initiative (Gould & Carson, 2011; Gould, Flett, & Lauer, 2012). Furthermore, non-sport specific promotion of effort and persistence may aid in the generalisation of these key life skills across other domains such as schooling because beliefs about ability are consistent across multiple domains (Fry & Duda, 1997).

Promote Challenge

Children who hold incremental theories of ability are attracted to difficult and challenging tasks because they offer a chance to learn and master new skills. In contrast, those who hold entity beliefs shy away from difficult and challenging tasks because the potential failure would invalidate their ability (Dweck, 1999; Dweck & Leggett, 1988). This may be particularly so for individuals who also have low levels of self-efficacy (Ommundsen, 2003), and detracts from the developmental asset that Benson (2007) has described as a commitment to learning. Challenge is one of the most important motives for participation in youth sports (Gould, Feltz, & Weiss, 1985) and is potentially a key reason why youth sports offer a greater number of learning experiences than other domains such as schooling or social clubs (Hansen, Larson, & Dworkin, 2003). However, approximately one third of children would choose to participate in an easy game over a challenging one (Fry, 2000) and would therefore miss out on the important skills that can be derived from such opportunities.

Challenging tasks provide important feedback on skills, and as such, offer instances through which young people can learn the skills of behavioral regulation and strategy generation – both of which are integral to positive youth development (Larson, 2011). In fact, children who engage in challenging tasks with the potential to increase mastery have higher levels of developmental assets, including higher rates of competence and physical self-concept. These skills may be critical to positive youth development because they enable the development of resilience, which is at the core of positive development (Peterson, 2004). Furthermore, such skills are associated with problem-solving abilities which are key to the effectiveness of programs of positive youth development (Catalano, Berglund, Ryan, Lonczak, & Hawkins, 2004). In contrast, those who avoid challenging tasks are unlikely to gain critical skills such as behavioral regulation and are more likely to experience amotivation (Conroy, Kaye, & Coatsworth, 2006). They are also more likely to experience deficits in identity and self-esteem as described by Benson (2007). This may be because they are unlikely to experience performance accomplishments if they continually withdraw from challenging tasks because performance accomplishments are an important source of self-efficacy (Bandura, 1997). Lastly, learning activities that provide optimal challenge-skills balance are reported to be a hallmark of optimal experiences. This challenge-skill balance is referred to as the 'golden rule of flow experiences' (Jackson & Csiksentmihalyi, 1999).

Promote the Value of Failure

Those who subscribe to incremental beliefs in human abilities share a firm understanding of the value of failure. Dweck (1999) has poignantly demonstrated this by showing that the performance of those who subscribe to either entity or incremental beliefs is parallel, but only until failure occurs. Following failure, subscribers to an entity theory exhibit maladaptive response patterns, including decreased self-efficacy, decreased motivation, and ultimately, withdrawal from tasks (Dweck, 1999). This is because from an entity perspective, failure is viewed as an enduring indication of inadequate levels of ability. As such, a fear of failure provides those who hold entity views with significant deficits in developmental assets. For example, research has demonstrated that the perceived aversive consequences of failure include a diminished perception of self, a diminished sense of achievement, and significant emotional costs (Sagar, Lavallee, & Spray, 2007). In contrast, those who hold incremental views approach failure as a temporary setback that provides important opportunities for performance feedback. As a consequence they exhibit adaptive responses such as increased effort and motivation, goal setting, and behavioral regulation, all of which are important developmental assets (Benson, 2007; Dweck, 1999).

Children and adolescents who hold an incremental theory of ability and understand the value of failure are more likely to acquire the developmental assets associated with positive youth development. Ommundsen (2003) has shown that physical education students who hold an incremental theory of ability are more likely to plan, monitor and regulate their cognitions over different learning tasks than their entity-theory peers. Furthermore, these skills are enhanced following setbacks, and lead to the perception that one is in control of their own learning. Additionally, those who believe that failure does not constitute a setback or an enduring indication of insufficient ability are more likely to maintain healthy levels of self-esteem following sub-par performances (Dweck, 1999). In contrast, those who subscribe to entity beliefs see failure as a negative evaluation that is to be avoided at all costs. As such, failure inevitably induces the "helpless" response amongst those who hold entity views, and can lead to a range of negative beliefs and behaviors, including depression (Seligman, 1975). Therefore, a firm understanding in the value of failure is a critical component in facilitating resilience and positive developmental assets, and avoiding the negative consequences that result from the inevitable failures that occur within complex and messy real-world contexts.

Define Success as Controllable

Young people enjoy activities at which they are able to succeed (Lepper, Master, & Quin Yow, 2008). However, the motivational powers of feelings of competence are delicate, and this is especially so when success is not under one's own control. When young people feel that their success is out of their control they experience the helpless response (Seligman, 1975). Therefore, feelings of control and competence are heavily dependent upon attributions for success that emphasize factors that are able to be controlled, including effort, persistence, and hard work. Those who make external attributions for success, including other-referenced ideals such as winning may be led to believe that effort and hard work are futile endeavours (Ommundsen, 2003). Legendary coach John Wooden made success attainable by defining success as peace of mind which is a direct result of self-satisfaction in knowing that you made the effort to become the best of which you are capable (Wooden & Jamison, 2004). Thus, Wooden firmly placed the conditions for success under the control of each of his athletes, and thereby maintained their motivation, enjoyment, and development. This approach is consistent with those who subscribe to incremental beliefs of human abilities because these individuals typically set self-referenced goals in order to judge success. In contrast, entity theorists attribute success to natural talent – if one wants to be successful they must be endowed with high levels of ability. The result of this belief is a set of maladaptive responses to perceived failures that includes decreases in motivation, disengagement, and low levels of self-efficacy (Sarrazin et al., 1996).

The belief that one can control their own successes is a key developmental asset for a number of reasons. The key asset of self-worth, often referred to as confidence (Jelicic, Bobek, Phelps, Lerner, & Lerner, 2007), is diminished if one believes success is not under their control. This may be because other important developmental assets such as initiative and optimism are also both diminished if one believes that the future is not controllable. Without initiative and optimism young people are unlikely to seek out difficult tasks, and are therefore unlikely to experience the feelings of success which are key to healthy levels of self-efficacy. Indeed, the underlying belief that the future is under one's control is the foundation of self-efficacy (Bandura, 1997), and aspects of mental health (Seligman, 1975). Furthermore, the belief that the future is under one's control also provides the foundation upon which a range of other important developmental assets can be garnered, including goal setting, behavioral regulation, commitment to learning, resilience, and optimism. By defining success as "giving your best effort" behaviors such as hard work and persistence are reinforced, both of which are key underpinnings of deliberate practice and skill mastery.

Promote Learning

The benefits of adopting learning goal orientations in youth sport contexts are well established. A learning goal orientation is constituted by a desire to improve one's ability or master new skills, in contrast to a desire to seek validation or favourable judgements of one's ability through performance (referred to as a performance goal orientation). Learning goal orientations are associated with increased levels of perceived competence, motivation, enjoyment, and effort, as well as decreased levels of anxiety and immoral behavior (Duda, 2005; Newton & Duda, 1999). According to Dweck's Social Cognitive Model of Achievement Motivation there is a close relationship between incremental beliefs and learning goal orientations (Dweck & Leggett, 1988). Young people who hold incremental beliefs of human ability are more likely to adopt learning goal orientations, and as a result, are also more likely to acquire a range of developmental assets. For example, the promotion of learning goals can increase students' preference for engaging in challenging tasks, levels of satisfaction, positive attitudes, and can increase motor skill development (Morgan & Carpenter, 2002; Robinson, 2011). Furthermore, the adoption of learning goals are also associated with other indicators of positive youth development, including increases in perceived peer acceptance, perceived ability, sport enjoyment, the development of achievement strategies, and satisfaction with one's performance, as well as decreases in friendship conflict (Roberts, Hall, Jackson, Kimiecik, & Tonymon, 1995; Smith, Balaguer, & Duda, 2006).

Learning goals have been consistently associated with higher rates of pro-social behaviors and lower rates of immoral behaviors. Pro-social behavior is central to many conceptualisations of positive youth development. The development of character and caring are central components of the '5Cs' of positive youth development promoted by Jelicic et al. (2007), and the '4Cs' promoted by Côté and colleagues in the sport and coaching domains (Côté et al., 2010; Côté & Gilbert, 2009). Additionally, positive values such as caring, integrity, honesty, responsibility, and restraint are key internal assets articulated by Benson (2007) within the theory of developmental assets. Learning goal orientations have been associated with higher rates of moral standards, moral functioning, sporting behaviors, disciplined behaviors, respect for the game and opponents, and character development, as well as lower rates of unsporting behaviors, sex discrimination, and cheating (Cervello, Jimenez, del Villar, Ramos, & Santos-Rosa, 2004; D'Arripe-Longueville, Rantaleon, & Smith, 2006; Gano-Overway, Guivernau, Magyar, Waldron, & Ewing, 2005; Giraud, 2006; Greenwood, 2009; Kavussanu & Ntoumanis, 2003; Kavussanu & Roberts, 2001; Van Yperen, Hamstra, & van der Klauw, 2011). By promoting self-referenced goals such as mastery young athletes are less inclined to engage in immoral behaviors because the mechanism by which they can achieve success is under their control. When young people seek goals that require reference to others they are more likely to engage in immoral behaviors in order to be perceived as successful. If winning is promoted over learning, young people may come to value winning at any cost, and are therefore also more likely to engage in immoral or cheating behaviors. Alternatively, the promotion of learning, particularly when generalised outside of the sports domain, can equip young athletes to become a contributing member of society – one key goal of positive youth development (Peterson, 2004).

Provide High Expectations

Anecdotal evidence suggests that children can be transformed through the provision of appropriately high expectations (Dweck, 2006). This evidence shows that children can be inspired, motivated, and filled with self-belief when respected and influential adults provide them with high expectations. Such provisions facilitate incremental beliefs in human abilities because they often require the need for mastery of addition skills. Furthermore, the provision of high expectations can provide a platform for positive youth development because the attainment of high expectations inherently requires the skills of positive youth development. In particular, the attainment of high expectations requires agency, which Larson (2011) has described as the "abilities to organize and regulate actions over time to work toward a long term goal, as an individual or with others, in complex real world contexts" (p. 18). The provision of high expectations may also work to induce visions of positive 'possible future selves', which is associated with key developmental assets such as resilience and optimism, and important life-skills such as the ability to self-reflect (Walsh, 2008). Lastly, high performance expectations have important theoretical links to the development of self-efficacy (Avolio & Bass, 2002). Slater and colleagues (Slater, Spray, & Smith, 2012) suggest that, in line with Bandura's Social Cognitive Theory (Bandura, 1997) the provision of appropriately high expectations facilitates the experience of positive performance accomplishments and vicarious experiences which serve to increase self-efficacy. High performance expectations may also work as a form of verbal persuasion regarding ability level and may also serve to increase self-efficacy (Bandura, 1997).

It must be noted that simply providing young people with high expectations is unlikely to lead to the skills necessary for positive youth development in and of itself. High expectations should be delivered in conjunction with specific strategies for the attainment of goals, and from within a caring climate that promotes independence and self-management of behaviors. The provision of high performance expectations in the absence of one or both of these contextual variables can be harmful for child development by inducing pressure, fear, anxiety and feelings of helplessness (Hall, Kerr, & Matthews, 1998). For these reasons, high performance expectations have typically not been associated with positive youth development within the youth sports context (Vella, Oades, & Crowe, 2012). In contrast, if high performance expectations are delivered in conjunction with strategies for their attainment and from within a caring climate young people can acquire foundational skills that will serve to promote and sustain their development. Skills that are fundamental to both the attainment of high performance expectations and positive youth development include goal setting, developing learning strategies, performance monitoring, behavioral regulation, and sustaining effort and deliberate practice over the long-term. In addition, research shows that the caring climate itself can promote positive youth development. Gano-Overway and colleagues have shown that the caring climate influences rates of pro-social and antisocial behavior by developing youths' ability to monitor, manage, and control positive affect, which in turn enhances their belief in their ability to empathize (Gano-Overway et al., 2009).

Despite evidence from some studies that youth sport coaches can identify, and in some cases regularly integrate, positive youth development strategies into their practice, there also is evidence to suggest that many challenges and barriers remain before this can become common practice. For example, in a recent study examining the use of autonomy-supportive coaching behaviors in a youth soccer program designed to explicitly promote life skills, the authors found that even with some supplementary training, experienced coaches tended to revert to traditional authoritarian and ego-involving behaviors (Cowan, Taylor, McEwan, & Baker, 2012). In the next section of this chapter we provide suggestions for designing coach education experiences that we believe have great potential for addressing some of these challenges and helping coaches adopt an incremental ability mindset.

PRACTICAL IMPLICATIONS FOR COACH EDUCATION

It should be clear at this point that the role of the youth sport coach, and arguably a sport coach at any level, must include an emphasis on holistic athlete development. The role of the sports coach is now expected to extend well beyond development of athlete technical and tactical sport-specific skills. This is clearly articulated in the recently created International Sport Coaching Framework (International Council for Coaching Excellence [ICCE] and the Association of Summer Olympic International Federations [ASOIF], 2012). For example, it is recognized in the Framework that "a coach who instills a sense of discipline or who unifies a group for a common purpose is every bit as successful as the league title-winning coach" (p. 10). How, then, should coach education programs be designed to help youth sport coaches understand and adopt this enhanced role?

Large-scale coach education programs have long included modules and resources specific to teaching positive youth development outcomes. For example, the two largest coach education programs in the United States – the American Sport Education Program (Martens, 2012) and the NFHS Fundamentals of Coaching (Barnson, 2011) – include course sections related to coaching for character, goal setting, confidence, and creating effective motivational climates. However, evaluation studies documenting the effectiveness of these types of programs on improving coaches' ability to teach these life skills to athletes in the field are absent. Careful review of coach education intervention research, however, does provide some insight into approaches that may be useful for coach education designers to consider.

Perhaps the earliest, and most comprehensive, example of a coach education intervention designed specifically to teach youth sport coaches how to coach for the 5Cs is Harwood's (2008) study with four soccer coaches in England. In this intervention, 90-minute workshops were created for each of the 5Cs, and coaches were assessed pre- and post-workshops on their 5Cs coaching efficacy. Coaches were also asked to write reflections on their ability to implement 5Cs coaching strategies into their soccer practices, and rate their athletes on a 5Cs behavioral rating scale. Although there was wide variation among the four coaches in terms of changes in 5Cs coaching efficacy (i.e., their belief in their ability to teach the 5Cs), every coach reported that their athletes' 5Cs behaviors increased following each workshop. This study illustrates the complexity and challenge of changing coaches' philosophy and adoption of 5Cs coaching behaviors, but also shows that with even a single 90-minute workshop acute positive changes in athlete 5Cs behaviors can be obtained. Harwood recommended that the 90-minute coach education workshops be supplemented with ongoing coach education opportunities that provide youth sport coaches with regular opportunities for dialogue and reflection.

Another example comes from MacDonald and colleagues (2010) who surveyed youth sport programs in Canada that either trained ($n=4$) or did not train ($n=6$) their coaches on how to teach life skills. The survey included questions about the type of life skill training provided to the coaches. Athletes who played for the trained coaches ($n=41$) were then compared to athletes who played for the untrained coaches (n=68) using their responses on the Youth Experience Survey for Sport (YES-S). Significant differences between the groups were found, but only for the personal and social skill development dimensions of the YES-S. Results show that even with informal coach training, such as discussion of life skills in coach meetings and mentoring from experienced coaches, youth sport coaches may be able to effectively create settings that result in positive youth development outcomes such as personal and social skills. Coach meetings and mentoring afford coaches opportunities to discuss and reflect upon coaching strategies and their roles as coaches. These coach education strategies are consistent with current views on coach education design and constructivist learning approaches.

It appears that views on coach education design have shifted in the past decade to place more emphasis on what is referred to as a 'constructivist' learning approach (Cushion & Nelson, 2013; Trudel, Culver, & Werthner, 2013). From this perspective, each coach's unique learning biography is recognized as they enter and proceed through a coach education system (Trudel & Gilbert, 2006; Trudel et al., 2010). A coach's learning biography includes their prior experience as an athlete and / or as a coach and knowledge and skills they acquired across other work and life experiences. When coaches are viewed as adult learners with unique learning biographies, they are provided with guided opportunities to structure and control their own learning, and the coach education curriculum is driven by each coach's particular learning needs (Lauer & Dieffenbach, 2013). From this perspective, ongoing coach reflection becomes critical to coach development and specifically to learning how to coach for positive youth development outcomes.

Reflection on one's coaching philosophy is suggested as a good place to start the reflective process when training coaches on how to coach for positive youth development outcomes (Holt, 2011). Practical suggestions for helping coaches become more reflective and increase self-awareness about their coaching philosophies are available in the literature (e.g., Gilbert & Trudel, 2006) and most recently have been organized around two broad types of reflection – reflective practice and critical reflection (Gilbert & Trudel, 2013). Coach education programs can and should include infrastructure to support both reflective practice (thinking about how to resolve everyday coaching issues) and critical reflection (deep self-analysis to re-organize personal mental models / philosophies of coaching). Coach education activities designed to stimulate and support critical reflection will perhaps be most beneficial to helping youth sport coaches create environments conducive to fostering positive youth developmental outcomes. Holt (2011, p. 260) provides a list of critical reflection questions that could easily be integrated into coach education workshops ("Can you clearly explain your coaching philosophy? What factors make it difficult for you to prioritize youth development? What specific activities do you give to your players to promote their development? Can you use sport to teach lessons that will be valuable in other areas of athletes' lives?"). Erhamm, Erhmann, and Jordan (2011) refer to the critical reflection process as 'InsideOut Coaching'; you have to engage in critical self-analysis first before you can expect to transform the lives of young athletes. Some examples of critical reflection questions from Erhmann that could also be used in coach education workshops include: (1) Why do I coach?, (2) Why do I coach the way I do?, (3) What does it feel like to be coached by me?, and (4) How do I define success?.

Most recently ethnodrama has been suggested as an effective pedagogical tool for stimulating coach reflection on positive youth development scenarios (Morgan, Jones, Gilbourne, & Llewellyn, 2013). Morgan and colleagues have experimented with having actors perform live demonstrations of coaching scenarios in front of coaching students, who then debrief a series of reflective questions such as: What are the issues in the scene? Have you altered your perceptions? What are your 'solutions'? and What informs your thinking? The authors reported that the coaching students "universally agreed that the ethnodrama scenes were successful in depicting the multifaceted complex nature of coaching" (p. 492). The authors concluded that the production of DVD-based scenes could be a viable tool for scaling-up the use of this teaching method.

An important outcome, and purpose, of coach reflection is to help coaches increase not only self-awareness, but awareness of the preferences and learning styles of their athletes. Recall that learning about athlete needs and personal profiles is the central tenet of an athlete-centered coaching approach (Kidman, 2005). Studies with youth sport athletes and coaches show that congruency between athlete preferred and coach actual behaviors directly influences athlete perceptions of the motivational climate (Stein, Bloom, & Sabiston, 2012). It is important that coach education programs provide coaches with reflection, or self-monitoring (Smith & Smoll, 2011), experiences and practical tools they can continue to use once they return to the field. Unfortunately, results from coach education research designed to teach coaches how to engage in regular reflection or self-monitoring shows extremely poor, or non-existent, compliance once coaches return to the field (Trudel et al., 2010).

Even when reflective practice is built into large-scale coach education programs and supported with centralized resources, coaches often struggle with adopting a constructivist learning approach (Paquette, Hussain, Trudel, & Camiré, in press). Triathlon Canada recently modified some of their coach education programs by re-structuring the experience to give the coaches more ownership of the learning experience. Once coaches reach a certain level of certification, coaches are required to develop and reflect on personalized learning portfolios. Results from a case study with four coaches show that despite all of the supporting infrastructure Triathlon Canada has put in place for the coaches, many of the coaches were still very uncomfortable with this level of introspection and instead were expecting their coach education experience to provide them with 'answers' and feedback on their coaching. These results, when viewed collectively with results from other coach education intervention studies that have attempted to formalize coach reflection (e.g., Knowles, Tyler, & Gilbourne, 2006), show that coach education is still a long way off from identifying and creating practical and effective learning experiences that develop truly reflective coaches. It can be argued, then, that until coach education can resolve this situation youth sport settings will fail to realize their potential as positive youth development environments. Effectively teaching a range of complex positive youth development outcomes will most surely require coaches who are comfortable with, and adept at, managing and reflecting on the constantly shifting needs, personalities and learning preferences of their youth sport athletes. It should be noted though that coach reflection, considered the intrapersonal knowledge component of coaching effectiveness, rests upon a foundation of well-developed professional and interpersonal knowledge (Côté & Gilbert, 2009). That is, we cannot expect youth sport coaches to engage in high quality reflection if they do not first have basic knowledge of their sport, sport science, athlete development, and coaching methodology (e.g., instructing, planning, organizing). In sum, it is recommended that coach education programs continue to offer educational experiences that first teach coaches generic and sport-specific professional and interpersonal knowledge and then gradually shift coach education offerings to more coach-centered experiences that include formal and guided coach reflection. This mix of learning experiences is referred to as a 'blended approach' to coach education which is firmly grounded in the coach education literature and is the advocated approach in the 2012 International Sport Coaching Framework (ICCE and ASOIF, 2012).

CONCLUSION

The consensus is that youth sport settings can, and should, be viewed as principal settings for nurturing a wide range of positive youth development outcomes. Youth sport coaches, who serve as the primary teacher in these settings, are increasingly being called upon to assume responsibility for teaching positive youth development outcomes to their young athletes. The role of the youth sport coach has evolved from a focus on sport specific skill development to holistic youth development. One way that youth sport coaches may be able to maximize positive youth development through sport is to adopt the six instructional strategies outlined in this chapter. These instructional strategies are grounded in Dweck's conception of incremental beliefs about ability (Dweck, 1999), and also incorporate the Mastery Approach to Coaching (Smith & Smoll, 2011) and work relevant to goal orientations (Duda, 2005). According to this conceptual framework incremental beliefs about the nature of human abilities underpins a motivational and behavioral framework that impacts young people's acquisition of positive developmental assets. The instructional strategies that have been derived from this conceptual foundation are: (1) focus on effort and persistence, (2) promote challenge, (3) promote the value of failure, (4) define success as giving your best effort, (5) focus on learning, and (6) provide high performance expectations.

At present there still remains a considerable gap between best-practice recommendations based on theory, emerging research and everyday practice and training of youth sport coaches. It is encouraging to note that recent studies show a subtle shift in how coaches, and youth sport administrators, describe their coaching philosophies and the role of the youth sport coach. It is also encouraging to observe a concurrent movement across coach education systems to a blended approach to coach training that includes training both in foundational sport and human development as well as guided opportunities for reflection to increase self-awareness.

REFERENCES

Avolio, B. J., & Bass, B. M. (2002). *Developing potential across a full range of leadership: Cases on transactional and transformational leadership.* Mahwah, NJ: Lawrence Erlbaum Associates.

Bandura, A. (1997). *Self-efficacy: The exercise of control.* New York: W.H. Freeman and Company.

Barnson, S. C. (2011). *Supplement for fundamentals of coaching.* Indianapolis, IN: National Federation of State High School Associations.

Benson, P. L. (2007). Developmental assets: An overview of theory, research and practice. In R. K. Silbereisen & R. M. Lerner (Eds.), *Approaches to positive youth development.* (pp. 3-58). Los Angeles: Sage Publications.

Blackwell, L. S., Trzesniewski, K. H., & Dweck, C. S. (2007). Implicit theories of intelligence predict achievement across adolescent transition: A longitudinal study and an intervention. *Child Development*, 78, 246-263. doi: 10.1111/j.1467-8624.2007.00995.x

Boon, A., & Gilbert, W. (2010). Using the United Nation's Millennium Development Goals to teach citizenship in youth soccer. *Journal of Coaching Education*, 3(3), 37-55.

Camiré, M., Forneris, T., Trudel, P., & Bernard, D. (2011). Strategies for helping coaches facilitate positive youth development through sport. *Journal of Sport Psychology in Action*, 2, 92-99. doi: 10.1080/21520704.2011.584246

Camiré, M., Trudel, P., & Forneris, T. (2012). Coaching transferring life skills: Philosophies and strategies used by model high school coaches. *The Sport Psychologist*, 26, 243-260.

Catalano, R. F., Berglund, M. L., Ryan, J. A. M., Lonczak, H., & Hawkins, J. D. (2004). Positive youth development in the United States: Research findings on evaluations of positive youth development programs. *Annals of the American Academy of Political and Social Science*, 591, 98-124.

Cervello, E. M., Jimenez, R., del Villar, F., Ramos, L., & Santos-Rosa, F. J. (2004). Goal orientations, motivational climate, equality and discipline of Spanish physical education studnets. *Perceptual & Motor Skills,* 99(1), 271-183.

Chase, M. A. (2010). Should coaches believe in innate ability? The importance of leadership mindset. *Quest*, 62(3), 296-307.

Chiu, C., Dweck, C. S., Tong, J. Y., & Fu, J. H. (1997). Implicit theories and conceptions of morality. *Journal of Personality and Social Psychology*, 73(5), 923-940. doi: 0022-3514/97/53.00

Chiu, C., Hong, Y., & Dweck, C. S. (1997). Lay dispositionism and implicit theories of personality. *Journal of Personality and Social Psychology & Health*, 73, 19-30.

Coakley, J. (2011). Youth sports: What counts as "positive development?" *Journal of Sport and Social Issues*, 35, 306-324. doi: 10.1177/0193723511417311.

Coatsworth, J. D., & Conroy, D. E. (2006). Enhancing the self-esteem of youth swimmers through coach training: Gender and age effects. *Psychology of Sport and Exercise*, 7, 173-192.

Conroy, D. E., Kaye, M. P., & Coatsworth, J. D. (2006). Coaching climates and the destructive effects of mastery-avoidance achievement goals on situational motivation. *Journal of Sport & Exercise Psychology*, 28(1), 69-92.

Côté, J., Bruner, M., Erickson, K., Strachan, L., & Fraser-Thomas, J. (2010). Athlete development and coaching. In J. Lyle and C. Cushion (Eds.), *Sports coaching: Professionalisation and practice* (pp.63-83). Edinburgh: Churchill Livingstone Elsevier.

Côté, J., & Gilbert, W. (2009). An integrative definition of coaching effectiveness and expertise. *International Journal of Sports Science and Coaching*, 4, 307-323.

Côté, J., Salmela, J., Trudel, P., Baria, A., & Russell, S. (1995). The coaching model: A grounded assessment of expert gymnasic coaches' knowledge. *Journal of Sport & Exercise Psychology*, 17(1), 1-17.

Cowan, D. T., Taylor, I. M., McEwan, H. E., & Baker, J. S. (2012). Bridging the gap between self-determination theory and coaching soccer to disadvantaged youth. *Journal of Applied Sport Psychology,* 24(4), 361-374. doi: 10.1080/10413200.2011.650820

Cushion, C., & Nelson, L. (2013). Coach education and learning: Developing the field. In P. Potrac, W. Gilbert, & J. Denison (Eds.), *Routledge handbook of sports coaching* (pp. 359-374). London: Routledge.

D'Arripe-Longueville, F., Rantaleon, N., & Smith, A. L. (2006). Personal and situational predictors of sportspersonship in young athletes. *International Journal of Sport Psychology*, 37(1), 38-57.

De Knopp, P., Engström, L-M., Skirstad, B., & Weiss, M. (Eds.). (1996). *Worldwide trends in youth sport.* Champaign, IL: Human Kinetics.

Duda, J. L. (2005). Motivation in sport: The relevance of competence and achievement goals. In A. J. Elliot & C. S. Dweck (Eds.), *Handbook of competence and motivation* (pp. 318-335). New York: Guildford Publications.

Dweck, C. S. (1999). *Self-theories: Their role in motivation, personality, and development.* Philadelphia: Psychology Press.

Dweck, C. S. (2006). *Mindset: The new psychology of success.* New York: Random House.

Dweck, C. S., & Leggett, E. L. (1988). A social-cognitive approach to motivation and personality. *Psychological Review*, 95, 256-273.

Ehrmann, J., Ehrmann, P., & Jordan, G. (2011). *InsideOut coaching: How sports can transform lives.* New York: Simon & Schuster.

Ericsson, K. A., Krampe, R. T., & Tesch-Römer, C. (1993). The role of deliberate practice in the acquisition of expert performance. *Psychological Review*, 100, 363-406.

Falcão, W. R., Bloom, G. A., & Gilbert, W. D. (2012). Coaches' perceptions of a coach training program designed to promote positive youth developmental outcomes. *Journal of Applied Sport Psychology*, 24, 429-444. doi:10.1080/10413200.2012.692452

Fraser-Thomas, J. L., Côté, J., & Deakin, J. (2005). Youth sport programs: An avenue to foster positive youth development. *Physical Education and Sport Pedagogy*, 10(1), 19-40.

Fry, M. D. (2000). A developmental examination of children's understanding of task difficulty in the physical domain. *Journal of Applied Sport Psychology*, 12(2), 180-202.

Fry, M. D., & Duda, J. L. (1997). A developmental examination of children's understanding of effort and ability in the physical and academic domains. *Research Quarterly for Exercise & Sport*, 68(4), 331-344.

Gano-Overway, L. A., Guivernau, M., Magyar, T., Waldron, J. J., & Ewing, M. E. (2005). Achievement goal perspectives, perceptions of the motivational climate, and sportspersonship: Individual and team effects. *Psychology of Sport and Exercise*, 6(2), 215-232.

Gano-Overway, L. A., Newton, M., Magyar, T. M., Fry, M. D., Kim, M., & Guivernau, M. R. (2009). Influence of caring youth sport contexts on efficacy-related beliefs and social behaviors. *Developmental Psychology*, 45(2), 329-340.

Gilbert, W., & Trudel, P. (2006). The coach as a reflective practitioner. In R. L. Jones (Ed.), *The sports coach as educator: Re-conceptualising sports coaching* (pp. 113-127). London: Routledge.

Gilbert, W., & Trudel, P. (2013). The role of deliberate practice in becoming an expert coach: Part 2 – Reflection. *Olympic Coach Magazine*, 24(1), 35-44.

Giraud, C. (2006). *Achievement goal orientations and moral functioning in elite athletes. Dissertation Abstracts International: Section B: The Sciences and Engineering*, 67(4-B), 2278.

Gould, D., & Carson, S. (2008). Life skills development through sport: Current status and future directions. *International Review of Sport and Exercise Psychology*, 1, 58-78.

Gould, D., & Carson, S. (2011). Young athletes perceptions of the relationship between coaching behaviors and developmental experiences. *International Journal of Coaching Science*, 5(2), 3-29.

Gould, D., Carson, S., & Blanton, J. (2013). Coaching life skills. In P. Potrac, W. Gilbert, & J. Denison (Eds.), *Routledge handbook of sports coaching* (pp.259-270). London: Routledge.

Gould, D., Collins, K., Lauer, L., & Chung, Y. (2007). Coaching life skills through football: A study of award winning high school coaches. *Journal of Applied Sport Psychology*, 19, 16-37.

Gould, D., Feltz, D., & Weiss, M. (1985). Motives for participating in competitive youth swimming. *International Journal of Sport Psychology*, 16(2), 126-140.

Gould, D., Flett, R., & Lauer, L. (2012). The relationship between psychosocial development and the sports climate experienced by underserved youth. *Psychology of Sport & Exercise*, 13, 80-87. doi: 10.1016/j.psychsport.2011.07.005

Greenwood, P. (2009). Character and caring in the context of American football: An examination of the relationship between positive youth development and achievement goal theory. *Dissertation Abstracts International Section A: Humanities and Social Sciences*, 69(9-A), 3738.

Gunderson, E. A., Gripshover, S. J., Romero, C., Dweck, C. S., Goldin-Meadow, S., & Levine, S. C. (in press). Parent praise to 1- to 3-year-olds predicts chidlren's motivational frameworks 5 years later. *Child Development*, 1-16. doi: 10.1111/cdev.12064

Hall, H. K., Kerr, A. W., & Matthews, J. (1998). Precompetitive anxiety in sport: The contribution of achievement goals and perfectionism. *Journal of Sport & Exercise Psychology*, 20(2), 194-217.

Hansen, D. M., Larson, R. W., & Dworkin, J. B. (2003). What adolescents learn in organized youth activities: A survey of self-reported developmental experiences. *Journal of Research on Adolescence*, 13, 25-55.

Harwood, C. (2008). Developmental consulting in a professional football academy: The 5Cs Coaching Efficacy Program. *The Sport Psychologist*, 22(1), 109-133.

Holt, N. (2008). (Ed.). *Positive youth development through sport*. Abingdon, UK: Routledge.

Holt, N. L. (2011). Sport and positive youth development. In I. Stafford (Ed.), *Coaching children in sport* (pp. 256-266). London: Routledge.

International Council for Coaching Excellence [ICCE] and the Association of Summer Olympic International Federations [ASOIF]. (2012). *International sport coaching framework*. Champaign, IL: Human Kinetics.

Jackson, S., & Csiksentmihalyi, M. (1999). *Flow in sports: The keys to optimal experiences and performances*. Champaign, IL: Human Kinetics.

Jelicic, H., Bobek, D. L., Phelps, E., Lerner, R. M., & Lerner, J. V. (2007). Using positive youth development to predict contribution and risk behaviors in early adolescence: Findings from the first two waves of the 4-H Study of Positive Youth Development. *International Journal of Behavioral Development*, 31, 263-273. doi: 10.1177/0165025407076439

Jones, M. I., Dunn, J. G. H., Holt, N. L., Sullivan, P. J., & Bloom, G. A. (2011). Exploring the '5Cs' of positive youth development in sport. *Journal of Sport Behavior*, 34(3), 250-267.

Jones, M. I., & Lavallee, D. (2009). Exploring the life skill needs of British adolescent athletes. *Psychology of Sport and Exercise*, 10(1), 159-167.

Kavussanu, M., & Ntoumanis, N. (2003). Participation in sport and moral functioning: Does ego orientation mediate their relationship? *Journal of Sport & Exercise Psychology*, 25(4), 501-518.

Kavussanu, M., & Roberts, G. C. (2001). Moral functioning in sport: An achievement goal perspective. *Journal of Sport & Exercise Psychology*, 23(1), 37-54.

Kidman, L. (2005). *Athlete-centred coaching: Developing inspired and inspiring people.* Christchurch, NZ: Innovative.

Knowles, Z., Tyler, G., Gilbourne, D., & Eubank, M. (2006). Reflecting on reflection: Exploring the practice of sports coaching graduates. *Reflective Practice*, 7(2), 163-179.

Larson, R. W. (2011). Positive development in a disorderly world. *Journal of Research on Adolescence*, 21, 317-334.

Lauer, L., & Dieffenbach, K. (2013). Psychosocial training interventions to prepare youth sport coaches. In P. Potrac, W. Gilbert, & J. Denison, *Routledge handbook of sports coaching* (pp. 451-462). London: Routledge.

Lepper, M., Master, A., & Quin Yow, W. (2008). Intrinsic motivation in education. In S. Karabenick & T. C. Urdan (Eds.), *Advances in motivation and achievement* (pp. 521-555). Bingley, UK: Emerald Group Publishing.

Lerner, R. M., Fisher, C. B., & Weinberg, R. A. (2000). Toward a science for and of the people: Promoting civil society through application of developmental science. *Child Development*, 71, 11-20.

Lirgg, C. D., Chase, M. A., George, T. R., & Ferguson, R. H. (1996). Impact of conception of ability and sex-type of task on male and female self-efficacy. *Journal of Sport & Exercise Psychology*, 18, 426-434.

MacDonald, D. J., Côté, J., & Deakin, J. (2010). The impact of informal coach training on the personal development of youth sport athletes. *International Journal of Sports Science & Coaching*, 5(3), 363-372.

Martens, R. (2012*). Successful coaching (4th ed.).* Champaign, IL: Human Kinetics.

Morgan, K., & Carpenter, P. (2002). Effects of manipulating the motivational climate in physical education lessons. *European Physical Education Review*, 8(3), 207-229.

Morgan, K., Jones, R. L., Gilbourne, D., & Llewellyn, D. (2013). Innovative approaches in coach education pedagogy. In P. Potrac, W. Gilbert, & J. Denison (Eds.), *Routledge handbook of sports coaching* (pp. 486-496). London: Routledge.

Newton, M. L., & Duda, J. L. (1999). The interaction of motivational climate, dispositional goal orientation and perceived ability in predicting indices of motivation. *International Journal of Sport Psychology*, 30, 63-82.

Ommundsen, Y. (2003). Implicit theories of ability and self-regulation strategies in physical education classes. *Educational Psychology: An International Journal of Experimental Educational Psychology*, 23(2), 141-157.

Paquette, K. J., Hussain, A., Trudel, P., & Camiré, M. (in press). A sport federation's attempt to restructure a coach education program using constructivist principles. *International Sport Coaching Journal*

Perkins, D. F., & Noam, G. G. (2007). Characteristics of sports-based youth development programs. In D. F. Perkins and S. Le Menestrel (Eds.), *New directions for youth development: Theory, research, practice* (pp. 75-84). Hoboken, NJ: Wiley & Sons.

Peterson, C. (2004). Preface (to the positive youth development issue). *The Annals of the Amercian Academy of Political and Social Science*, 591, 6-12.

Roberts, G. C., Hall, H. K., Jackson, S. A., Kimiecik, J. C., & Tonymon, P. (1995). Implicit theories of achievement and the sport experience: Effect of goal orientations on achievement strategies and perspectives. *Perceptual & Motor Skills*, 81(1), 219-224.

Robinson, L. E. (2011). Effect of a mastery climate motor program on object control skills and perceived physical competence in preschoolers. *Research Quarterly for Exercise and Sport*, 82(2), 355-359.

Sagar, S. S., Lavallee, D., & Spray, C. M. (2007). Why young elite athletes fear failure: Consequences of failure. *Journal of Sports Sciences*, 25(11), 1171-1184.

Sarrazin, P., Biddle, S., Famose, J. P., Cury, F., Fox, K., & Durand, M. (1996). Goal orientations and conceptions of the nature of sport ability in children: A social cognitive approach. *British Journal of Social Psychology*, 35, 399-414.

Seligman, M. (1975). *Helplessness*. San Francisco: Freeman.

Skinner, E. A. (1995). *Perceived control, motivation and coping*. Thousand Oaks: Sage.

Slater, M. J., Spray, C. M., & Smith, B. M. (2012). "You're only as good as your weakest link": Implicit theories of golf ability. *Psychology of Sport and Exercise*, 13, 280-290. doi: 10.1016/j.psychsport.2011.11.010

Smith, A. L., Balaguer, I., & Duda, J. L. (2006). Goal orientation profile differences on perceived motivational climate, perceived peer relationships, and motivation-related responses of youth athletes. *Journal of Sports Sciences*, 24(12), 1315-1327.

Smith, R. E., & Smoll, F. L. (2011). Cognitive-behavioral coach training: A translational approach to theory, research, and intervention. In J. K. Luiselli and D. D. Reed (Eds.), *Behavioral sport psychology: Evidence-based approaches to performance enhancement* (pp. 227-248). New York: Springer.

Smith, R. E., Smoll, F. L., & Curtis, B. (1979). Coach effectiveness training: A cognitive-behavioral approach to enhancing relationship skills in youth sport coaches. *Journal of Sport Psychology*, 1, 59-75.

Stein, J., Bloom, G. A., & Sabiston, C. M. (2012). Influence of perceived and preferred coach feedback on youth athletes' perceptions of team motivational climate. *Psychology of Sport and Exercise*, 13, 484-490.

Trudel, P., Culver, D., & Werthner, P. (2013). Looking at coach development from the coach-learner's perspective: Considerations for coach development administrators. In P. Potrac, W. Gilbert, & J. Denison (Eds.), *Routledge handbook of sports coaching* (pp. 359-374). London: Routledge.

Trudel, P., & Gilbert, W. D. (2006). Coaching and coach education. In D. Kirk, M. O'Sullivan, & D. McDonald (Eds.), *Handbook of Physical Education* (pp. 516-539). London: Sage.

Trudel, P., Gilbert, W., & Werthner, P. (2010). Coach education effectiveness. In J. Lyle, & C. Cushion (Eds.), *Sport coaching: Professionalisation and practice* (pp. 135-152). London: Elsevier.

Van Yperen, N. W., Hamstra, M. R., & van der Klauw, M. (2011). To win, or not to lose, at any cost: The impact of achievement goals on cheating. *British Journal of Management*, 22(Suppl 1), S5-S15.

Vella, S. A., Oades, L. G., & Crowe, T. P. (2011). The role of the coach in facilitating positive youth development: Moving from theory to practice. *Journal of Applied Sport Psychology*, 23, 33-48.

Vella, S. A., Oades, L. G., & Crowe, T. P. (2012). Validation of the Differentiated Transformational Leadership Inventory as a measure of coach leadership in youth soccer. *The Sport Psychologist*, 26(2), 203-224.

Walsh, D. (2008). Helping youth in underserved communities envision possible futures: An extension of the teaching personal and social responsibility model. *Research Quarterly for Exercise & Sport*, 79(2), 209-221.

Weiss, M. R. (2008). "Field of dreams": Sport as a context for youth development. *Research Quarterly for Exercise and Sport*, 79, 434-449.

Wooden, J. R., & Jamison, S. (2004*). My personal best: Life lessons from an aAll-American journey*. New York: McGraw-Hill.

Zentall, S. R., & Morris, B. J. (2010). "Good job, you're so smart": The effects of inconsistency of praise type on young children's motivation. *Journal of Experimental Child Psychology*, 107, 155-163.

In: Positive Human Functioning ...   ISBN: 978-1-62948-974-2
Editors: A. R. Gomes, R. Resende & A. Albuquerque   © 2014 Nova Science Publishers, Inc.

Chapter 6

COACHING HIGH PERFORMANCE ATHLETES: IMPLICATIONS FOR COACH TRAINING

Gordon A. Bloom, William R. Falcão and Jeffrey G. Caron

Department of Kinesiology and Physical Education, McGill University, Montreal, Quebec, Canada

ABSTRACT

In addition to teaching sport-specific skills, coaches must teach and instill life skills such as leadership, teamwork, and character building to their athletes. These are important skills to promote the development of positive human functioning. A growing body of research on coaches of high performance athletes has revealed their role entails more than producing a great win-loss record and champion athletes (e.g., Bloom, Durand-Bush, Schinke, & Salmela, 1998; Vallée & Bloom, 2005). Although winning is an expected outcome for these coaches, some have managed a successful win-loss record while balancing the personal and professional development of their athletes (e.g., Côté, Salmela, Trudel, Baria, & Russell, 1995; Duchesne, Bloom, & Sabiston, 2011; Vallée & Bloom, 2005).

The purpose of this chapter is to explain some of the methods and strategies that coaches of high performance athletes have used to help their athletes attain high levels of success both on and off the playing surfaces. A diagram of coaching effectiveness owing its roots to the work of Côté and Gilbert (2009) will help frame the discussion in this chapter. More specifically, the diagram outlines how coaches' knowledge (i.e., professional, interpersonal, and intrapersonal) and athletes' outcomes (competence, confidence, connectedness, character/caring) are influenced by the context (high performance sport) in which they coach. Using this diagram as a foundation, the contexts of coaching Intercollegiate, Olympic/Paralympic, Professional, and Masters athletes will be provided by describing research and conceptual frameworks specific to each elite level of competition. Finally, recommendations and implications for coach training/education will be presented.

INTRODUCTION

Coaches take on many different roles, which include teacher, mentor, role model, friend, and community leader. All of these roles have an enormous effect on the development of athletes. The role of the coach allows them to teach and instill life skills such as leadership, teamwork, and character building to their athletes, which are important to their overall growth and development outside of sport (Bloom, Durand-Bush, Schinke, & Salmela, 1998; Bloom & Salmela, 2000; Vallée & Bloom, 2005).

Former University of North Carolina basketball coach Dean Smith echoed these sentiments when reflecting on his enjoyment of coaching, citing that "…what I enjoyed most were the pursuit of the championships and the journeys each team traveled together – coaches and players – in quest of the dream" (Smith, 2002, p. xix). Many of the greatest team sport athletes in the last century have credited their athletic success to great coaching. More specifically, baseball player Derek Jeter, basketball player Michael Jordan, hockey player Wayne Gretzky, and soccer player David Beckham have frequently praised many of their great coaches for teaching them technical, tactical, and psychological skills that helped them achieve success both on and off their playing fields.

Aside from the anecdotal testimonials of world-class athletes, a look at some of the early research on talent development highlights the important role of the coach in one's rise to prominence. For example, the seminal work of Benjamin Bloom (1985) on the development of talented performers provided insights into the career paths of expert swimmers and tennis players. Bloom indicated that talented youth in any performance domain exhibited similar developmental patterns. Central to this evolution of expertise was the role of the coach or mentor at each stage in the individual's career. Research by Ericsson and colleagues (Ericsson & Charness, 1994; Ericsson, Krampe, & Tesch-Römer, 1993; Ericsson & Lehmann, 1996) also examined the development of expertise in various domains, in which they posited the key component to reaching a level of expertise was deliberate practice. More specifically, they stated "the amount of time an individual is engaged in deliberate practice activities is monotonically related to that individual's acquired performance" (Ericsson et al., 1993, p. 368). Of critical importance in the development of exceptional performance was the input and teaching by coaches, because these levels were rarely achieved without quality instruction.

Aside from being expert strategists and pedagogues, there is a growing body of research on expert coaches that has revealed that their role entails more than just producing a great win-loss record and champion athletes (e.g., Bloom et al., 1998; Bloom & Salmela, 2000; Côté, Bruner, Erickson, Strachan, & Fraser-Thomas, 2010; Duchesne et al., 2011; Gould & Carson, 2008; Vallée & Bloom, 2005). Although winning is an expected outcome of the job requirements for coaches of high performance athletes, some have managed to balance successful win-loss records with a balance on the holistic development of their players (e.g., Duchesne et al., 2011; Vallée & Bloom, 2005). Legendary American college basketball coach John Wooden was an advocate of this coaching philosophy in which he said, "when I think of all the attorneys that played for me and the doctors that played for me… the dentists that played for me… the teachers that played for me… the businessmen that played for me… it's good. Their joys are my joys. Their sorrows and disappointments were my sorrows and disappointments. I'm happy that not a day goes by without a call from one of my players" (Nater & Gallimore, p. xvii).

The purpose of this chapter is to explain some of the methods and strategies that coaches of high performance athletes have used to help them attain high levels of success both on and off the playing surfaces. The chapter will begin by looking at some landmark coaching profiles and biographies to try and determine the characteristics of expert coaches. Following this, a diagram of effective coaching that owes its roots to the work of Côté and Gilbert (2009) will be reported. The next section will integrate aspects of this model by separating the results of coaching into the domains of Intercollegiate athletes, Olympic/Paralympic athletes, Professional athletes, and Masters athletes. The final section will provide implications for coach training/education.

CHARACTERISTICS OF EXPERT COACHES

Some significant retrospective profiles and biographies of successful coaches were published in the last 30 years that shed valuable strategies, philosophies, and recommendations on coaching high-level athletes (e.g., Jackson & Delehanty, 1995; Kimiecik & Gould, 1987; Mechikoff & Kozar, 1983; Nater & Gallimore, 2006; Riley, 1993; Torre & Verducci, 2009; Walton, 1992; Wooden, 1988; Wrisberg, 1990). For example, Kimiecik and Gould interviewed James "Doc" Counsilman, the dean of American swim coaches, who coached 6 NCAA team championships and 23 Big Ten championships. He was head coach of the men's U.S. Olympic swimming team on several occasions, his swimmers held world records in every swimming event, and his scientific advancements in swimming helped revolutionize the sport. Councilman stressed the importance of implementing a positive, athlete-centered coaching style that included helping his athletes set realistic goals and build confidence (Kimiecik & Gould, 1987). Using a similar framework, Wrisberg (1990) interviewed Pat Summitt, who at the young age of 38 had already coached three NCAA championship teams and a gold medal winning American Olympic basketball team. The interview focused on coaching style, such as how to prepare athletes for a game, how to conduct practices, and how to interact with players. This work offered coaches, athletes, players, sport administrators, and mental performance consultants' insights on the knowledge of an elite coach in such crucial areas as player development, leadership style, goal-setting tasks, and the relationship between sport psychology consultants and coaches and players. In sum, both the research of Kimiecik and Gould and Wrisberg provided important information on how coaches think and apply their knowledge in certain situations. Valuable information was also presented in two books, in which a number of highly successful coaches from both team and individual sports were profiled (Mechikoff & Kozar, 1983; Walton, 1992). Some of the individuals studied included football coaches Bear Bryant, Vince Lombardi, and Lou Holtz, basketball coaches John Wooden and Abe Lemmons, and track and field coaches Brutus Hamilton and Payton Jordan. Important coaching information and strategies emerged regarding athlete selection, athlete discipline, and their pre- and post-competition procedures. Like other coaches who preceded them, they also noted there were no definitive set of concepts or principles for them to follow and that most of their knowledge was acquired through coaching experience and from other successful coaches and mentors.

FRAMEWORK FOR UNDERSTANDING COACHES OF HIGH PERFORMANCE ATHLETES

Given the increased empirical research in coaching science in the last 30 years, it is somewhat surprising that scholars have had a difficult time reporting on good or effective coaching. A recent publication from Côté and Gilbert (2009) may help solve this elusive puzzle. Drawing on the different conceptual models of coaching and the empirical coaching science literature, Côté and Gilbert offered an integrative definition of coaching effectiveness and expertise that has yet to be challenged or reproduced. The authors defined coaching effectiveness and expertise as "the consistent application of integrated professional, interpersonal, and intrapersonal knowledge to improve athletes' competence, connection, and character in specific coaching contexts" (p. 316). This definition is based on years of research and practice, and borrows from teaching, positive psychology, and coaching literature. The following sections will describe each of the three key aspects of Côté and Gilbert's definition in more detail.

Coaches' Knowledge

Collinson (1996) reviewed literature on expert teachers and found they encompassed *professional, interpersonal,* and *intrapersonal* knowledge. Given that coaches are in many ways similar to teachers (Nater & Gallimore, 2006; Wilson, Bloom, & Harvey, 2010), Côté and Gilbert (2009) suggested that coaching effectiveness and expertise also involves professional, interpersonal, and intrapersonal facets of knowledge.

Professional knowledge -focuses on sport-specific aspects (e.g., technical and tactical skills) that are acquired in coach certification programs, clinics, and workshops. Côté and Gilbert (2009) suggested that effective coaches must also acquire interactional (i.e., interpersonal and intrapersonal) aspects of knowledge. Interpersonal encompasses both group and individual interactions and involves a number of daily interactions with many people, including athletes, officials, parents, and sport administrators. Strong interpersonal skills allow coaches to communicate appropriately and effectively with diverse individuals who vary in age, background, education, and competitive levels. Côté and Gilbert also said that strong intrapersonal skills are an important part of coaching knowledge. This refers to a coach's ability to review, revisit, and reflect on their coaching practice. Taken together, coaches who incorporate these three aspects of knowledge in their teaching/coaching habits develop "maturity, wisdom, and capacity to reason and make judgments" (p. 311).

Athletes' Outcomes

Horn (2008) postulated that coaches were most effective when athlete's achieved successful sporting performances and positive psychological responses. More specifically, performance was measured by win-loss percentages, player development, and success at the national and international level, whereas psychological responses referred to high sport enjoyment, self-esteem, and satisfaction. Although these athlete outcomes were desirable for defining coaching effectiveness and expertise, Côté and Gilbert (2009) felt it lacked the specificity required to influence coaches' daily practice. Therefore, the authors selected Côté and colleagues' (2010) 4 C's framework (Competence, Confidence, Connection, and Character/Caring) to describe athletes' outcomes in all sporting environments.

Athletes' feelings of sport-related competence were an important outcome of effective coaching. In turn, increased competency influences one's feelings of connectedness (Ryan & Deci, 2000), which refers to positive bonds and social relationships with people inside and outside of sport. Confidence was defined as an internal sense of positive self-worth, where effective coaches should empower their athletes to be confident, self-reliant members of their sport and society. Finally, character/caring engendered respect for their sport and others, integrity, empathy, and responsibility. In sum, Côté and Gilbert (2009) indicated that effective coaches should aspire to involve athlete outcomes congruent with the 4 C's. Moreover, the authors noted that a coach's implementation of the 4 C's over an extended period of time would be "the hallmark of expert coaching" (p. 313).

Coaching Context

Just as coaches' knowledge and athlete outcomes are integral aspects of defining coaching effectiveness and expertise, so too is the coaches' sporting context. Specifically, sporting context refers to the unique setting in which coaches seek to develop athletes. Trudel and Gilbert (2004) proposed three contexts of sport: (a) recreational sport, (b) developmental sport, and (c) elite sport. Lyle (2002) offered similar classifications, however he suggested two distinct paths: participation and performance. Participation coaches focused on short-term goals, enjoyment, and health-related outcomes for their athletes. Performance coaches expected higher degrees of specificity from their athletes, and sought to influence athlete's performance variables. Côté, Young, North, and Duffy (2007) combined the earlier frameworks (Lyle, 2002; Trudel & Gilbert, 2004) and formed developmentally appropriate coaching contexts, which were included as part of Côté and Gilbert's (2009) definition of coaching effectiveness and expertise. More precisely, Côté and colleagues specified four coaching contexts, which were subdivided into participation and performance. Participation coaches for (a) children (i.e., sampling years) and (b) adolescents and adults (i.e., recreational years), and performance coaches for (c) young adolescents (i.e., specializing years) and (d) older adolescents and adults (i.e., investment years). Together, this framework posits a continuum for participation and performance spanning childhood to adulthood. Côté and Gilbert noted that coaching effectiveness "should be defined according to how coaches meet their athletes' needs and help them fulfill their goals, as defined be the specific coaching context" (p. 315).

Côté and Gilbert's (2009) definition of coaching effectiveness and expertise influenced the conceptualization of Figure 1. This figure highlights the three categories that impact good coaching. The current chapter will focus on the *contexts* of coaching Intercollegiate, Olympic/Paralympic, Professional, and Masters Athletes. Authors Vella and Gilbert focused on aspects of recreational youth sport coaching in the previous chapter.

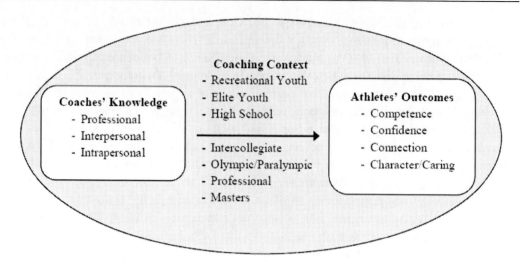

Figure 1. Diagram of coaching effectiveness.

INTERCOLLEGIATE ATHLETES

Many studies in coaching science have used intercollegiate athletes as participants (Gilbert & Rangeon, 2012; Gilbert & Trudel, 2004). This has become a common practice in coaching research which is undoubtedly partially attributable to the accessibility scholars have to student-athletes and intercollegiate coaches. This section will use Vallée and Bloom's (2005) conceptual model of intercollegiate coaching to address coaching at the University and College levels.

Conceptual Model of Intercollegiate Coaching

Vallée and Bloom's (2005) model offers a unique blend of theory to practice for intercollegiate coaching. The three main components of their model are called *coaches' attributes*, *individual growth*, and *organizational skills*. These elements are held together by a fourth element called *vision*. According to the authors, the successful balance of these components leads to the holistic (i.e., personal and athletic) development of athletes. Each component of the model and its outcome will be discussed.

Coaches' Attributes
Vallée and Bloom (2005) found that expert coaches had a wide range of traits, personalities, characteristics, and leadership styles. Years before their findings, the Multidimensional Model of Leadership (MML: Chelladurai, 1990) examined more directly the complex relationship between coach behaviors, preferred coaching styles, and team success. The MML suggests that successful coaching depends on the congruence between coaches' behaviors and athletes' preferred behaviors. Horn, Bloom, Berglund, and Packard (2011) studied American intercollegiate student-athletes and found they had a broad range of preferred coaching styles that correlated closely with their motivation. Thus, it is the match

between coach and athlete characteristics and preferences that affects athletes' personal satisfaction and ultimately team success.

In a study on preferred coaching styles of intercollegiate football players, Riemer and Chelladurai (1995) found different preferences of coaches' behaviors according to the athletes' role/position on their team. For example, defensive players preferred democratic leadership styles more than offensive players, which they attributed to defensive players having to react to changes in the environment as opposed to running set plays (as occurs with offensive players). Riemer and Chelladurai also found the football players were most satisfied when their perceptions of their coaches' leadership styles were congruent with their preferences.

Pat Summitt was a successful female intercollegiate coach who was tough, offered a lot of social support, and understood her athletes' preferences.. Coach Summitt, the former head women's basketball coach of the University of Tennessee, is the all-time winningest coach in American collegiate basketball history with 1098 wins and 208 losses. She won eight American collegiate national championships, was named coach of the century by the Naismith Memorial Basketball Hall of Fame, was ranked number 11 on the list of the 50 greatest coaches of all time by the American Sporting News, and was recently inducted to the International Basketball Federation Hall of Fame (www.patsummitt.org). She was famous for having an authoritarian coaching style, which can be exemplified by quotes such as "I don't give out compliments easily" and "I'm a coach, so I take the issue of control personally". Despite having a tough coaching style, coach Summitt had an excellent relationship with her players, was very committed to the program, and always sought their well-being. According to Packer and Lazenby (1998), Summit said "...my philosophy and the system that we have here at Tennessee is that we see three dimensions that we must be prepared to deal with: the person, the player, the student" (p. 149). Other popular quotes such as "Class is more important than a game" and "If I was renowned as a tough coach, I also wanted to be a caring one" also illustrate Coach Summit's care for her athletes. Her coaching style and successful career are examples of the importance of the alignment between coaches' behaviors and athletes' preferred behaviors, having a positive coach-athlete relationship, and prioritizing individual growth over athletic success.

Individual Growth

Individual growth referred to the coaches' principles of fostering athlete development. Vallée and Bloom's (2005) study revealed intercollegiate coaches spent a substantial amount of time building self-confidence, enhancing maturity, and creating a sense of ownership in their student-athletes. Recent developments of coaching literature have also emphasized individual growth in addition to athletic performance (e.g., Côté et al., 2010; Gould & Carson, 2008; Papacharisis, Goudas, Danish, & Theodorakis, 2005). Further to this, Côté and Gilbert (2009) found that effective coaching entailed fostering athletes' competence, confidence, connection, and character, while Horn (2008) stressed other psychological responses such as building athletes' self-esteem, intrinsic motivation, enjoyment, and satisfaction. These characteristics of effective coaching can be seen in the practice of many intercollegiate coaches, including American basketball icon, John Wooden.

Coach Wooden won ten American intercollegiate national championships in a twelve year span. He was named collegiate basketball coach of the year six times and ended his career with a record of 664 wins and 162 losses. He was famous for his holistic coaching philosophy (Gilbert, 2010) and by maxims such as: "What you are as a person is far more important than what you are as a basketball player" and "The best way to improve the team is to improve ourselves" (www.coachwooden.com). The philosophy of developing the individual as well as developing the athlete was a common theme in coach Wooden's practices and coaching philosophy (cf. Wooden, 1988) and one of the main characteristics attributed to his success as an intercollegiate coach and humanitarian.

Organizational Skills

Organizational skills entailed aspects of planning and management. Planning referred to creating a seasonal plan, preparing practices, and getting athletes ready for competition. Management was the execution of the seasonal plan (Vallée & Bloom, 2005). The responsibility of intercollegiate coaches in North America goes beyond training athletes. For example, Davies, Bloom, and Salmela (2005) found that administrative duties were a large part of Canadian intercollegiate coaches' duties and profoundly influenced their level of job satisfaction. More recently, Dieffenbach, Murray, and Zakrajsek (2011) investigated the internship experiences of American intercollegiate coach interns and found their management activities outweighed their sport-specific coaching responsibilities. These research findings reinforce the notion that organizational skills are an integral part of the sport coaching profession.

Vision

The vision involves the coaches' goals and direction of their program. It begins as soon as a coach takes over the reins of a new program. The vision is fundamental to coaching success as it guides the other three components of the model. The vision is influenced by how the coach sells the vision, organizes the season, and creates a philosophy of athlete growth and development.

Sullivan and Kent's (2003) study on leadership style and coaching efficacy among intercollegiate coaches has many similarities with Vallée and Bloom's (2005) model. Sullivan and Kent found that coaches' perceived efficacy (i.e., their attributes) influenced their focus on athlete development (i.e., individual growth) and their coaching styles (i.e. organizational skills). More specifically, they suggested that novice coaches who were less confident in their coaching skills relied more on autocratic instructions and organizational skills. More experienced and confident coaches used more positive feedback and focused more on athlete development. In turn, their confidence and use of positive feedback was related to greater motivation and teaching efficacy. In sum, as coaches gained experience and became more confident in their coaching attributes, they used more positive feedback and appropriate training instructions, which in turn influenced their focus on athlete development.

Gary Barnett is an example of an American intercollegiate coach who successfully implemented a vision to turn around an unsuccessful program. In the early 1990's he took over as head coach of the football team at Northwestern University who had lost 49 consecutive games. While others laughed at him, Barnett told his players and school to expect victory. In only four years, Barnett turned the team into conference champion and national contenders (www.garybarnettfoundation.org). Barnett's (1996) philosophy focused on effective teaching practices and ensuring that everyone knew and accepted the team vision. Barnett's vision motivated and encouraged his players to succeed through adversity (Moskal, 1997). His vision was reinforced by his mission statement: "to take the student-athlete where he cannot take himself and foster an environment that teaches young men to relentlessly pursue and win the championship, appreciate and embrace cultural diversity, and achieve an exemplary foundation of leadership and academic success" (Barnett, 1996, p. 19). By creating a vision for his team and encouraging his players to believe in it, Barnett transformed Northwestern's football into a prominent and successful program.

Holistic Development

According to Vallée and Bloom (2005), the appropriate execution of the four components of the model will lead to the desired holistic development of the athlete. Holistic coaching is an emerging topic in the coaching literature, which has gained increased attention (Cassidy, 2010). While there is no consensus operational definition for holistic coaching, researchers have begun to reveal the main elements of this concept (Cassidy, 2013; Duchesne et al., 2011; Potrac, Brewer, Jones, Armour, & Hoff, 2000). Recently, Cassidy (2013) described holistic practices as those in which coaches integrated the social, cognitive, and physical aspects of their players. Duchesne and colleagues discussed the importance of holistic development in intercollegiate settings. In their study, intercollegiate coaches from the highest competition level of American university sport shared their experiences coaching international student-athletes. The results suggested that coaching international student-athletes involved an additional responsibility of mentoring players to improve as students, athletes, and members of their communities. The responsibility of the coach went beyond the playing field by helping athletes adjust to a new country and culture. This was exemplified by the following quote from one coach in their study: "…they need to feel that this is a home for them away from their home" (p. 9).

Key Points for Coaching Practice

The practical implications of this model can be seen in Chantal Vallée's coaching career. After completing her Master's degree, Vallée accepted a position as the head coach of the women's basketball program at University of Windsor, which consistently ranked among the lowest in Canada. In her sixth year at the helm of this program, Vallée won the first of three consecutive Canadian intercollegiate national championships. She has also been nominated Canadian coach of the year and has won nine regional and local 'coach of the year' awards. These outstanding results reflect Vallée's practice guided by the model developed in her study.

As described in her model, Vallée's vision was set early when she took over the program and proclaimed they would be national champions in five years. This broad proclamation for team success on the court was also going to involve success off the court by becoming involved with their community which was struggling in a recession. Coach Vallée motivated her athletes to work hard on and off the court. The impact they had in their community was evident when they received a civic reception in their return to Windsor after winning a national championship.

Coach Vallée's plan was executed following her principles of athlete growth and development on and off the basketball court. Her organizational skills, including her ability to recruit, plan and run practices, and prepare her players for competitions helped the team achieve success. Her coaching practices were assisted by her attributes of staying positive and building athletes' confidence. The balance between these elements of her model allowed Coach Vallée to build positive interactions between her players, foster their holistic development, and build a successful basketball program.

In sum, the model of expert intercollegiate coaching provides a specific framework for professionals coaching at the intercollegiate level. Having a vision and developing the necessary skills to fulfill one's vision is critical to becoming a successful intercollegiate coach. Also, the recent literature and practical examples have shown that successful intercollegiate coaching involves fostering the holistic development of athletes, individually, academically, and athletically, like Pat Summitt, John Wooden, and Chantal Vallée have shown is possible.

OLYMPIC/PARALYMPIC ATHLETES

This section addresses aspects of coaching athletes who represent their countries by competing at the Olympic and Paralympic levels. As highlighted previously in this chapter, a positive coach-athlete relationship is essential for athletic success. The 3 + 1 Cs model focuses on this relationship and was developed using data from Olympic athletes (Jowett & Cockerill, 2003). As such, it will be used as the framework for this section.

3 + 1 Cs Model

Jowett and colleagues created the 3 + 1 Cs model in order to measure relationships between coaches and athletes at the emotional, cognitive, and behavioral levels (Jowett, 2003; Jowett & Lavallee, 2007; Jowett & Meek, 2000). The model has undergone a number of transformations since its original conceptualization by Jowett and Meek (2000). The most recent version of the 3 + 1 Cs model has four constructs that are labeled *closeness*, *commitment*, *complementarity*, and *co-orientation* (Jowett & Lavallee, 2007).

Closeness is the emotional component of the model and was defined as the connection or attachment between coaches and athletes. This construct involved terms such as liking, trust, intimacy, respect, and belief in one another (Jowett & Lavallee, 2007). More specifically, the model suggested that belief was very important to achieving closeness, and the coaches' beliefs regarding the athlete were crucial to the relationship (Jowett & Cockerill, 2003). Commitment was described as the cognitive component of the coach-athlete relationship. It represented the perceptions and expectations of their attachment, as well as coaches' and athletes' intentions to maintain the relationship (Jowett & Lavallee, 2007). Complementarity referred to the behavioral component of the coach-athlete relationship. This construct involved mutual hard work and cooperative behaviors between coaches and athletes (Jowett & Lavallee, 2007). According to Jowett and Cockerill, it is essential that coaches and athletes have a clear understanding of each other's roles, tasks, and that they support each another in order to establish a positive and fruitful relationship.

Co-orientation was described as the shared knowledge and understanding between coaches and athletes, and represented the mutual perceptions of the three previous constructs (closeness, commitment, and complementarity) (Jowett & Cockerill, 2003; Jowett &

Lavallee, 2007). Co-orientation allowed for an evaluation of the degree of agreement between coaches and athletes (Jowett & Cockerill, 2003). According to Jowett and Lavallee, there were three dimensions of co-orientation: *assumed similarity*, which reflected the degree to which coach and athlete assumed they shared the same feelings, thoughts, and behaviors; *actual similarity*, which reflected how much they actually shared feelings, thoughts, and behaviors; and *empathic understanding*, which reflected how much understanding coach and athlete showed towards each other.

According to Jowett and Lavallee (2007), the coach and athlete relationship was "interdependent if both experience high levels of trust and respect (closeness); wished to remain attached and committed to each other in the future (commitment); and behaved in a responsive, friendly and easygoing manner (complementarity)" (p. 15). Results from research that has used the 3 + 1 Cs model indicated that the coach-athlete relationship was an important factor related to performance, particularly for Olympic athletes (Greenleaf, Gould, & Dieffenbach, 2001; Jowett & Cockerill, 2003; Philippe & Seiler, 2006).

Olympic Athletes

Greenleaf and colleagues (2001) interviewed 15 Olympic athletes regarding factors that positively and negatively impacted their performance. The authors found that coaching, psychological and physical preparation, team unity, and support positively impacted performance, whereas coach issues, overtraining, media distraction, and lack of support detracted from performance. Specific to coaching, athletes mentioned that contact, trust, friendship, feedback, availability, and having a good plan positively affected their performance. One participant said the most effective coaches were also their good friends (Greenleaf et al., 2001). Other Olympians mentioned that power conflicts, lack of access, and selection controversy were coaching issues that negatively impacted their performance.

Jowett and Lavallee's (2007) 3 + 1 Cs model describes the nature of the coach-athlete relationship and has been used as a framework to study Olympic athletes. For example, Jowett and Cockerill (2003) interviewed 12 Olympic medalists to understand the nature of the coach-athlete relationship based on closeness, complementarity, and co-orientation. The results indicated that coaches and athletes invested great emotional care and concern, and developed mutual feelings – often times personal – with one another. This was what the authors referred to as closeness, which is related to the holistic approach to coaching (cf. Vallée & Bloom, 2005) where coaches must show "interest in the welfare and development of the athlete" (Jowett & Cockerill, 2003, p. 320). Similarly, Philippe and Seiler (2006), who interviewed five Olympic male swimmers, found that respect, esteem, admiration, appreciation, and regard were requirements to establishing a good coach-athlete relationship.

Jowett and Cockerill (2003) also found that Olympic athletes felt successful coaches provided technical instruction in a manner that inspired and nurtured them. These findings were related to complementarity and reinforced the notion that athletes positively perceived coaches who were knowledgeable and caring. Similarly, Philippe and Seiler (2006) found that Olympic swimmers considered mutual acceptance the most important factor in establishing a positive coach-athlete relationship. As described by the 3 + 1 Cs model, Olympic swimmers also emphasized the importance of coaches and athletes respecting and accepting their roles in preparation for a competition.

Jowett and Cockerill (2003) determined that communication between coach and athlete was essential to develop mutual understanding and shared knowledge. Athletes felt their coaches' understanding and knowledge allowed them to react appropriately to their needs, aspirations, and problems. This was related to co-orientation and referred to the synergy between coach and athlete expectations. Likewise, Philippe and Seiler (2006) noticed that Olympic swimmers stressed the importance of communication and goal setting in establishing balance in their relationship. Olympic swimmers also identified communication as a key factor for achieving performance (Philippe & Seiler, 2006).

The 3 + 1 Cs model provides a valuable framework for identifying elements of the coach-athlete relationship that affect Olympic athletes' performance. The coaching literature suggests the most effective and liked coaches are those who demonstrate the knowledge to respond appropriately to athletes' needs and problems, and who build a positive relationship through trust, friendship, availability, and care. Also, Olympic athletes prefer holistic coaches who not only attend to their athletic needs, but also to their personal and emotional development. Finally, communication ensures a negotiation and clarity of the roles, responsibilities, goals, and expectations of both coaches and athletes, and was frequently mentioned as an essential aspect of a balanced relationship. In conclusion, Olympic coaches' knowledge, focus on holistic development and ability to communicate with their athletes helps build a symbiotic coach-athlete relationship that positively impacts performance.

Paralympic Athletes

Sport was originally constructed as an able-bodied activity. As a result, there are limited opportunities for individuals with a disability to participate (DePauw & Gavron, 2005). An estimated 600 million people, or 10% of the world's population, have some degree of physical disability or impairment (DePauw & Gavron, 2005). In Canada, approximately 4.4 million people have a physical disability (Statistics Canada, 2007). Sport Canada (2006) reported that less than 1% of individuals with a physical disability (age 16+) are involved in organized sport or physical activity programs compared to approximately 31% of Canadians without a disability in the same age group (Statistics Canada, 2002). These statistics highlight the need to increase the number of resources available to individuals with a disability. While there is much research on Olympic athletes the same cannot be said for Paralympic athletes (Burkett, 2013), and even fewer investigations on coaches of athletes with a disability.

In recent years, research on coaches of athletes with a disability has begun to appear (Burkett, 2013; Gilbert & Rangeon, 2012), although there is no central model or framework specific to coaching Paralympic athletes. As such, Paralympic coaching studies have used theoretical frameworks originally designed for able-bodied populations, including the MML, the Coaching Model (CM), and Self-Determination Theory (SDT) (e.g., Banack, Sabiston, & Bloom, 2011; Cregan, Bloom, & Reid, 2007; Tawse, Bloom, Sabiston, & Reid, 2012). More details of these frameworks can be found at their original sources (i.e., MML: Chelladurai, 1990; CM: Côté et al., 1995; SDT: Deci & Ryan, 2000). The remainder of this section will focus on research findings specific to coaching Paralympic athletes.

Studies on Paralympic coaches have found they adapted their knowledge and behaviors from able-bodied sport experiences using a combination of innovation, intuition, and creativity (Burkett, 2013). For example, Burkett and Mellifont (2008a, 2008b) adapted coaching techniques for Paralympic cyclists and swimmers using biomechanical and physiological measures. Their adaptations were unique to the disabilities of each athlete. For the Paralympic cyclists, adaptations to the bike included height of the seat, seat tube angle, and cleating of the feet, which resulted in their athlete's achieving best performances (Burkett & Mellifont, 2008a). For the Paralympic swimmers, information about stroke rate, stroke length, and segmental velocity allowed coaches and athletes to adjust race strategies that improved their turn times and racing strategies (Burkett & Mellifont, 2008b). According to Burkett and Mellifont (2008a, 2008b), a crucial part of their success was attributed to the receptiveness of both the coaches and athletes.

Studies focusing on the psychological aspects of coaching athletes with a disability have also revealed the importance of coaches' adapting their behaviors and strategies to meet the needs of their athletes (Banack et al., 2011; Cregan et al., 2007; Tawse et al., 2012). For example, Tawse and colleagues revealed the knowledge and strategies used by wheelchair rugby coaches to develop their athletes personally and athletically. The coaches encouraged their elite athletes to set goals in sport as well as in their personal lives, which included promoting their independence and integration into their community. In another study, Banack et al. investigated the motivation of Canadian Paralympic athletes. Their results suggested Paralympic athletes' perceptions of control predicted their feelings of independence and their connection to the coach and other athletes. Also, athletes' perceptions of ability and control predicted their inherent enjoyment of the sport. These findings highlight the importance of Paralympic coaches fostering holistic development and feelings of independence on building a positive coach-athlete relationship and a respectful team environment. If these occur, successful individual and team performances are likely to follow.

In summary, the research cited in this section indicates the coach-athlete relationship is an important element common to both Olympic and Paralympic athletes. Players seem to feel a greater connection and commitment to their coaches and athletic goals when they feel their coaches care about them as people, on and off the playing surface. A unique aspect of Paralympic coaching is the coaches' ability to adjust to their athletes' individual needs. The findings presented in this section suggest that the 3 + 1 Cs (Jowett & Lavallee, 2007) model could be used to understand the coach-athlete relationship in both Olympic and Paralympic settings.

Key Points for Coaching Practice

The development of the coach-athlete relationship and a holistic coaching approach are common themes in Olympic/Paralympic research. Two individuals have appeared to adopt many of the same coaching approaches to build a positive relationship with their athletes and achieve high performance success. The coaching practices of Anson Dorrance and Andy Banks will be explained.

Anson Dorrance coached the USA women's soccer team between 1986 and 1994. Under his leadership, the USA team won the first FIFA women's world championship in 1991 and was honored with the USA Soccer Hall of Fame Medal of Honor. Coach Dorrance had a record of 66 wins, 22 loses, and 5 ties with the National team. Throughout his career he has won eight National and nine regional coach of the year awards. Wang and Straub (2012) examined the coaching approach used by Coach Dorrance and identified some of his successful coaching practices. According to the authors, Coach Dorrance: (a) used a democratic coaching style and included players in team decisions, (b) promoted discipline and created a positive team environment by setting team values that ensured athletes exhibited positive behaviors, (c) created a competitive environment using objective measures that avoided team conflicts, (d) fostered psychological skills such as self-disciple, competitive fire, and self-belief, and (e) facilitated the development of elite athletes by fostering players' physical, technical, mental, and independent decision-making skills, among other things. In addition, Coach Dorrance's positive approach to coaching fostered confidence, eliminated anxiety, and allowed his athletes to perform at the highest level. Coach Dorrance shows how a positive coaching style that includes a holistic approach to coaching can lead to success at the world class level.

Another example is Andy Banks, coach of the UK diving team at the 2008 Beijing Olympics and many other international competitions. Coach Banks is famous for raising the profile of diving in the UK and coaching renowned athletes such as Tom Daley, Tonica Couch, and Brooke Graddon. Dixon, Lee, and Ghaye (2012) interviewed Coach Banks about his coaching practices and found a process-oriented coaching philosophy that focused on helping athletes do their best. To accomplish his goal, Coach Bank's developed a positive coach-athlete relationship that was also fostered in his practices, which helped athletes focus and deal with high pressure situations (Dixon et al., 2012). Coach Banks also has a holistic approach to coaching that emphasizes the development of the person before the athlete (Dixon et al., 2012).

Examination of the coaching practices of Dorrance and Banks reinforces the importance of the coach-athlete relationship at the Olympic/Paralympic level. The 3 + 1 Cs model offers a strong guideline for building positive relationships between coaches and Olympic/Paralympic athletes based on closeness, commitment, complementarity, and co-orientation. Finally, the practical examples presented support the use of a positive and holistic approach to coaching as a strategy to build positive relationships that will motivate and encourage athletes to perform at the highest levels.

PROFESSIONAL ATHLETES

When most of his peers were still attending high school classes, 16 year-old Wayne Rooney scored his first goal in one of the top professional soccer leagues in the world (English Premier League). Fortunately for Mr. Rooney, his many personal (i.e., educational) and social (i.e., gatherings with friends and family) sacrifices paid off, as he has enjoyed a successful and prosperous professional career. However, the transition to the professional level can be overwhelming for both players and coaches, as the focus of sport often shifts from intrinsic motivation and playing for fun to extrinsic motivation and playing for pay. Specifically, ticket sales, long competitive seasons, television-broadcasting rights, and interactions with media help to generate revenue for professional sports teams and may also affect how professional sport coaches interact with their athletes (Draper, 1996). Moreover, players with the highest salaries can influence ownership with their personal or professional agendas, which may undermine the coach's authority and affect the coach-athlete relationship (Draper, 1996).

Not surprisingly, research has found that professional athletes experience daily stressors from a variety of sources that include job security, and interpersonal relationships with family, friends, coaching staff, and the media (Gearity & Murray, 2011; Kristiansen, Roberts, & Sisjord, 2012; Nicholls, Holt, Polman, & Bloomfield, 2006; Noblet & Gifford, 2002). Poor performance in professional sport often leads to intense scrutiny from spectators, media, and coaches, that could result in reduced playing time or dismissal, and can lead to unemployment. Taken together, the professional sporting environment contains a number of intricate relationships and needs that make playing at this level much different than other elite contexts.

Although very little empirical research exists on coaching professional athletes, Fasting and Pfister (2000) noted that playing professional sports "can be rewarding, but it can also be stressful and demanding" (p. 91). This section will focus on professional sport, including whether it's possible to implement holistic coaching strategies with professional athletes in a manner that was reported with Intercollegiate and Olympic/Paralympic athletes.

The Coaching Model

The Coaching Model (CM; Côté et al., 1995) will be used to understand some of the unique attributes of the professional sporting context. This model has served as a theoretical framework for much recent coaching research, allowing for a connection to be made between the knowledge accumulated on how and why coaches work as they do. The CM conceptualizes that coaches approach their job by developing a model of their athlete's or team's potential, which influences their course of action. This estimate of team potential is often influenced by the peripheral factors, called Coach's Personal Characteristics, Athlete's Personal Characteristics, and, most significantly to this chapter, Contextual Factors. The coach then integrates these three components into his/her mental model, to determine how to act in the three primary components of coaching: Organization, Training, and Competition. Due to its relevance to the content contained in this chapter, a detailed description of contextual factors will be provided before exploring research on professional athletes and their coaches.

Contextual Factors

Few empirical articles have explicitly investigated the unique contextual factors associated with various levels of coaching, and how they ultimately influence athletes' personal growth, development, and performance. One study from Davies and colleagues (2005) interviewed six male Canadian University basketball coaches on factors that influenced their job satisfaction. Coaches felt that some contextual factors affected their job, including objectives and preferences of their athletic director, prominence of their basketball program, as well as multiple administrative roles and duties. With respect to professional sport, Draper (1996) interviewed professional team sport coaches who said that professional athletes clearly "had their own agendas" (p. 195) and were not necessarily willing to work towards to a common goal, which led to many coaching stresses and adaptations. The coaches also knew they had very little job security and that they were easier to replace than the players (Draper, 1996).

In sum, these examples from both University and professional sport illustrate how coaching contexts vary depending on level of competition (Côté & Gilbert, 2009). Further, they demonstrate how contextual factors can influence a coach's primary responsibility, which is athlete growth and development (Côté et al., 1995). Now that a definition of contextual factors has been provided, literature on athletes and coaches in professional sport will be described in more detail.

Research on Professional Athletes

"I think people have this perception that professional athletes or celebrities are not susceptible to the same problems as everyone else. There's a lot of travel, there's a lot of demands, there's a lot of pressure – both internal and external." – Landon Donovan (American Professional Soccer player).

To date, research on professional athletes has largely focused on their perceived stressors, such as those caused by fear of poor performance (Nicholls et al., 2006). Professional athletes have also reported stress due to interpersonal relationships and performance expectations (Gearity & Murray, 2011; Noblet & Gifford, 2002), as well as scrutiny from their coaches (Kristiansen et al., 2012). Nicholls and colleagues analyzed the diary entries of eight professional European rugby players over a 28-day period. Among their results, the athletes reported experiencing stress due to coach criticism at both practices and games. Kristiansen and colleagues interviewed three European professional soccer goaltenders to understand how they coped with negative media attention. Interestingly, although the athletes indicated negative media attention was detrimental to their confidence, the athletes were more concerned with negative feedback from their coach. Another study from Noblet and Gifford (2002) with 32 professional Australian footballers found athletes experienced both competition and non-competition-related stress, including failing to meet expectations from coaches. Taken together, these studies suggest that professional athletes experience a great deal of stress, much of which is related to performance expectations from their coaches.

Research on Coaching Professional Athletes

"I had to meet one-on-one with my guys. I felt I had to know about them. And I had a rule with myself: The player doesn't have to understand me; I have to understand him. That's my job. I don't play. But it's my job to understand everything I can about him. As much as I can about his family, his upbringing, everything I could understand about him. I felt then I could solve some of his needs." – Sparky Anderson (Hall of Fame Major League Baseball Manager).

Research on coaches of professional athletes has investigated a number of factors related to team success and performance (e.g., Keshtan, Ramzaninezhad, Kordshooli, & Panahi, 2010; Mielke, 2007; Potrac, Jones, & Armour, 2002; Potrac, Jones, & Cushion, 2007; Thelwell, Weston, Greenlees, & Hutchings, 2008; White, Persad, & Gee, 2007). For example, Mielke noted that although few head coaches of professional teams enjoyed long tenures with the same team, those who had stronger interpersonal relationships with their players lasted longer with the same team compared to those that did not. Potrac and colleagues (2002) used a combination of observation and interviews to understand one English professional soccer coach's methods of communication. In a similar study, Potrac et al. (2007) observed four professional male English soccer coach's behaviors and found the more successful coaches (i.e., those with long tenures) praised their athletes more than non-successful coaches. This led the authors to conclude, "more can be achieved by coaches using positive rather than negative interactions" (p. 41). Taken together, these findings suggest that coaches of professional athletes have achieved success using positive forms of feedback and communication.

Furthermore, Bennie and O'Connor (2010) interviewed six coaches and 25 athletes who competed in Australian professional cricket and rugby. The results indicated that coaches strived to develop their athletes on and off the field by using a holistic or athlete-centered approach. Moreover, coaches emphasized achieving personal goals while de-emphasizing winning. In turn, professional athletes felt comfortable interacting with their coaches regarding both sport and non-sport matters. Results from Bennie and O'Connor's study on professional athletes were in accordance with existing research on coaching effectiveness and expertise presented in earlier parts of this chapter (Côté & Gilbert, 2009; Côté et al., 2007). Moreover, it appears that it is possible for coaches of professional athletes to reinforce the 4C's to maximize athletes' development and performance both on and off the field, despite the higher stakes that are a part of professional sport.

Key Points for Coaching Practice

While the majority of professional coaching tenures are short, and filled with intense scrutiny from the media, spectators, management, and ownership, it is possible to follow many of the similar coaching philosophies attributed to the coaches of Intercollegiate and Olympic/Paralympic athletes. More specifically, coaches of professional athletes who have strong interpersonal relationships with their athletes have longer tenures with their teams (Mielke, 2007), and have athletes that achieve greater personal and professional satisfaction with their sport (Bennie & O'Connor, 2010; Potrac et al., 2002, 2007). Coaches may be surprised to learn that holistic coaching styles are possible at the professional level, and according to our research, even recommended.

MASTERS ATHLETES

According to Warburton, Ashe, Miller, Shi, and Marra (2009), approximately 75% of adults and seniors are physically inactive. In addition, physical inactivity is linked to a number of negative health-related outcomes that can include increased hospitalizations and healthcare visits (Warburton et al., 2009). Aside from engaging in recreational activities, some adults and seniors have begun competing in a variety of sports against athletes of similar age and skill levels. At the highest levels of competition these individuals are referred to as Masters athletes. Masters athletics is a class of sport where athletes, aged 35 and above, engage in competitions that are separated into age-specific categories at intervals of five or ten years (e.g., 35–40, 50–60). Common Masters sports include swimming, track and field, and athletics. To date, the most important competition for Masters athletes is the World Championships, which has been held biannually since 1975 (World Masters Athletics, 2013). The first edition took place in Toronto, Canada and was attended by 1427 competitors. The 20th World Championships in Porto Alegre, Brazil are expected to include approximately 5000 competitors. Evidently, the Masters athletics movement has grown in size and popularity since its inception. In addition to the many health benefits of Masters sport, it has allowed researchers the unique opportunity to study healthy, active aging populations.

Physiological Factors

To date, the majority of research on Masters athletes has focused on physiological variables (e.g., Baker & Schorer, 2010; Fell & Williams, 2010; Krampe & Ericsson, 1996; Tarpenning, Hamilton-Wessler, Wiswell, & Hawkins, 2004). For example, the relationship between maximal oxygen consumption and muscle recovery and performance (Fell & Williams, 2010; Tarpenning et al., 2004), and the relationship between sport performance and age related decline (Baker & Schorer, 2010; Krampe & Ericsson, 1996). One concern for Masters athletes is that normal human aging is associated with a decline in neuromuscular function and performance (Vandervoort, 2002), referred to as sarcopenia. Research on Masters swimmers has shown that resistance training interventions partially reverses the effects of sarcopenia (Porter, Vandervoort, & Lexell, 1995; Vandervoort, 2002). Although this line of inquiry is still in its early stages, research on Masters athletes' physiological outcomes demonstrate a number of important health benefits associated with sport participation.

Psychological Factors

In addition to Masters athletes' physical health, research has also begun to examine psychological aspects of their sport participation. Related to motivation, studies using achievement goal theory (i.e., task or ego orientations) (cf. Nicholls, 1989) found that Masters athletes were mostly task-oriented, which was associated with greater enjoyment and commitment to their sport (Hodge, Allen & Smellie, 2008; Medic, 2010). Other studies used SDT (Deci & Ryan, 1985) to indicate that Masters athletes were motivated by health and weight control, as well as their affiliation with other athletes (Ogles & Masters, 2000). Similarly, Stevenson (2002) found Masters athletes were intrinsically motivated for reasons related to competition, training, and forming positive social relationships with their peers (Stevenson, 2002). Taken together there is evidence suggesting these athletes have unique motives for their sport participation that include leading an improved healthy, active, and social lifestyle.

Intrinsic motivation is considered the ideal type of motivation, and has been associated with higher life satisfaction, enjoyment, and personal fulfillment (Deci & Ryan, 1985). Medic, Young, Starkes, and Weir (2012) investigated the coach's role in fostering intrinsic motivation among Masters athletes. Using quantitative measures, they found that athletes who had a coach had greater intrinsic motivation compared to athletes who did not have a coach.

Similarly, although using qualitative measures, Stevenson (2002) found that Masters athletes with a coach received more encouragement to continue training, which fostered a positive environment that included sound technical instruction. In sum, these findings highlight the role of the coach in motivating Masters athletes to adhere to their training programs by creating a positive training environment.

Key Points for Coaching Practice

A number of negative health-related outcomes have been linked to physical inactivity (Warburton et al., 2009). Additionally, Warburton and colleagues found that physical activity greatly reduces co-morbidities associated with many chronic diseases. As such, Masters athletes can serve as role models for their peers. Research on Masters athletes has discovered their participation is linked to intrinsic and task-oriented variables. Moreover, coaches of Masters athletes have fostered their intrinsic motivation for sport participation, although access to full-time coaches is limited at this time.

In sum, coaches of Masters athletes must understand their athletes' motives for participating in sport generally include skill mastery, enjoyment, and living healthy lifestyles. Implementing a task-oriented coaching approach is recommended. Furthermore, coaches should be aware of the many physiological impacts of aging. Masters athletes have benefitted from increased resistance exercises by reducing muscle mass decline. Thus, the coaching recommendations posed in this section are likely to increase the chances of their athletes achieving positive human functioning and development.

PRACTICAL IMPLICATIONS FOR COACH EDUCATION

Education and training are essential for creating effective training sessions that shape the development and effect future success in any profession (Lyle, 2002). In Canada, coach education and development is governed by the Coaching Association of Canada (CAC: www.coach.ca). Created in 1970, the CAC promotes quality coaching to enhance the experiences of Canadian athletes. This organization provides the foundation of skills, knowledge, and attitudes to ensure effective coaching across all levels of the Canadian sport system (Bloom, 2007). In 1974, this association launched the National Coaching Certification Program (NCCP) to equip coaches with tools to become competent and successful community leaders. Since then, the program has undergone several revisions to keep it up-to-date with scientific findings, including a shift to a competency-based approach in 2008 (CAC, 2013). The newest NCCP approach is a knowledge- and course-based program made up of three streams, which are called community sport, instruction, and competition. The competition stream is designed for individuals who have previous coaching experience and who intend to work with athletes at the provincial/state, national, and international levels.

Although the competition stream is designed to teach coaches how to focus on the long-term development of athletes (CAC, 2013), there are no specific examples for teaching these principles to Intercollegiate, Olympic/Paralympic, Professional, or Masters athletes. The information in this chapter has indicated that there are unique aspects to coaching in each of these contexts, and as such, coach education training would benefit by addressing the unique context of each elite level of coaching. Moreover, the need is exemplified with the recent advancements of both the Paralympic and Masters movements. How many countries have specific coaching courses for coaches working with athletes at these levels of competition? Moreover, how many coaching education courses around the world are geared for aspiring coaches of professional athletes? Needless to say, while coach education and training remains a valuable learning tool, the information presented in this chapter demonstrates that the unique characteristics of each elite level of competition needs to be implemented into the highest streams of coach education in every country if coaches are expected to create the ideal training environments that will enhance athlete's growth and development.

CONCLUSION

The purpose of this chapter was to explain the strategies and methods used by coaches of high performance athletes. Until recently, coaching science researchers have found it challenging to define the nature of effective coaching. Côté and Gilbert (2009), who have years of experience as researchers and practitioners, determined that effective coaching is a combination of coaches' knowledge (i.e., professional, interpersonal, and intrapersonal) and athletes' outcomes (competence, confidence, connectedness, and character/caring), ultimately influenced by the context in which they coach. Building on their definition, the authors of this chapter advanced a diagram of coaching effectiveness (Figure 1), which helped frame the discussion on coaches of high performance athletes. Research and conceptual frameworks specific to the contexts of coaching Intercollegiate, Olympic/Paralympic, Professional, and Masters athletes were described. In sum, coaches across all these levels ascribed to similar pedagogic knowledge and strategies which involved a holistic coaching style. Our research suggests that coaches who follow the recommendations outlined in this chapter will stand a better chance of developing their athletes both on and off the playing field.

REFERENCES

Baker, J., & Schorer, J. (2010). Maintenance of skilled performance with age: Lessons from the Masters. In J. Baker, S. Horton, & P. Weir (Eds.), *The Master athlete: Understanding the role of sport and exercise in optimizing aging* (pp. 66–78). New York: Routledge.

Banack, H. R., Sabiston, C. M., & Bloom, G. A. (2011). Coach autonomy support, basic need satisfaction and intrinsic motivation of Paralympic athletes. *Research Quarterly for Exercise & Sport, 82,* 722–730. doi:10.1080/02701367.2011.10599809.

Barnett, G. (1996). *High hopes: Taking the purple to Pasadena.* New York: Warner.

Bennie, A., & O'Connor, D. (2010). Coaching philosophies: Perceptions from professional cricket, rugby league and rugby union players and coaches in Australia. *International Journal of Sports Science & Coaching, 5,* 309–320. doi:10.1260/1747-9541.5.2.309.

Bloom, B. S. (Ed.) (1985). *Developing talent in young people.* New York: Ballantine.

Bloom, G. A. (2007). Coaching psychology. In P. R. E. Crocker (Ed.), *Sport psychology: A Canadian perspective* (pp. 239–265). Toronto, ON: Pearson.

Bloom, G. A., Durand-Bush, N., Schinke, R. J., & Salmela, J. H. (1998). The importance of mentoring in the development of coaches and athletes. *International Journal of Sport Psychology, 29,* 267–281.

Bloom, G. A., & Salmela, J. H. (2000). Personal characteristics of expert team sport coaches. *Journal of Sport Pedagogy, 6,* 56–76.

Burkett, B. (2013). Coaching athletes with a disability. In P. Potrac, W. Gilbert, & J. Denison (Eds.), *Routledge handbook of sports coaching* (pp. 196–209). Abingdon, Oxon: Routledge.

Burkett, B. J., & Mellifont, R. B. (2008a). Sport science and coaching in Paralympic cycling. *International Journal of Sports Science & Coaching, 3,* 95–104. doi:10.1260/174795408784089360.

Burkett, B. J., & Mellifont, R. B. (2008b). Sport science and coaching in Paralympic swimming. *International Journal of Sports Science & Coaching, 3,* 105–112. doi:10.1260/174795408784089360.

Cassidy, T. (2010). Holism in sports coaching: Beyond humanistic psychology. *International Journal of Sports Science & Coaching, 5,* 439–443. doi:10.1260/1747-9541.5.4.439.

Cassidy, T. (2013). Holistic sports coaching: A critical essay. In P. Potrac, W. Gilbert, & J. Denison (Eds.), *Routledge handbook of sports coaching* (pp. 172–183). New York: Routledge.

Chelladurai, P. (1990). Leadership in sports: A review. *International Journal of Sport Psychology, 21,* 328–354.

Coaching Association of Canada (2013). *Coach training in Canada.* Retrieved June 21, 2013, from http://www.coach.ca/coach-training-in-canada-s15408.

Collinson, V. (1996). *Becoming an exemplary teacher: Integrating professional, interpersonal, and intrapersonal knowledge.* Paper presented at the JUSTEC Annual Conference, Naruto University of Education, Naruto, Japan. *ERIC Document Reproduction Service No.* ED 401 227.

Côté, J., Bruner, M., Erickson, K., Strachan, L., & Fraser-Thomas, J. (2010). Athlete development and coaching. In J. Lyle and C. Cushion (Eds.), *Sports coaching: Professionalization and practice* (pp. 63–84). Edinburgh: Elsevier.

Côté, J., & Gilbert, W. D. (2009). An integrative definition of coaching effectiveness and expertise. *International Journal of Sports Science & Coaching, 4,* 307–323. doi:10.1260/174795409789623892.

Côté, J., Salmela, J. H., Trudel, P., Baria, A., & Russell, S. J. (1995). The coaching model: A grounded assessment of expert gymnastic coaches' knowledge. *Journal of Sport & Exercise Psychology, 17,* 1–17.

Côté, J., Young, B., North, J., & Duffy, P. (2007). Towards a definition of excellence in sport coaching. *International Journal of Coaching Science, 1,* 3–17.

Cregan, K., Bloom, G. A., & Reid, G. (2007). Career evolution and knowledge of elite coaches of swimmers with a physical disability. *Research Quarterly for Exercise & Sport, 78,* 339–350. doi:10.1080/02701367.2007.10599431.

Davies, M. J., Bloom, G. A., & Salmela, J. H. (2005). Job satisfaction of accomplished male university basketball coaches: The Canadian context. *International Journal of Sport Psychology, 36,* 173–192.

Deci, E. L., & Ryan, R. M. (1985). *Intrinsic motivation and self-determination in human behavior.* New York: Plenum Press.

Deci, E. L., & Ryan, R. M. (2000). The "what" and "why" of goal pursuits: Human needs and the self-determination of behavior. *Psychological Inquiry, 11,* 227–268. doi:10.1207/S15327965PLI1104_01

DePauw, K., & Gavron, S. (2005). *Disability sport.* Champaign, IL: Human Kinetics.

Dieffenbach, K. D., Murray, M., & Zakrajsek, R. (2011). The coach education internship experience: An exploratory study. *International Journal of Coaching Science, 5,* 3–25.

Dixon, M., Lee, S., & Ghaye T. (2012). Coaching for performance: Reflections of Olympic diving coach, Andy Banks. *Reflective Practice, 13,* 355–358. doi:10.1080/04419057. 2002.9674274.

Draper, S. P. (1996). Coaching contexts. In J. H. Salmela (Ed.), *Great job coach! Getting the edge from proven winners* (pp. 181–205). Ottawa, ON: Potentium.

Duchesne, C., Bloom, G. A., & Sabiston, C. M. (2011). Intercollegiate coaches' experiences with elite international athletes in an American sport context. *International Journal of Coaching Science, 5,* 49–68.

Ericsson, K. A., & Charness, N. (1994). Expert performance. *American Psychologist, 49,* 725–747.

Ericsson, K. A., Krampe, R. T., & Tesch-Römer, C. (1993). The role of deliberate practice in the acquisition of expert performance. *Psychological Review, 100,* 363–406.

Ericsson, K. A., & Lehmann, A. C. (1996). Expert and exceptional performance: Evidence of maximal adaptation to task constraints. *Annual Review of Psychology, 47,* 273–305.

Fasting, K., & Pfister, G. (2000). Female and male coaches in the eyes of female elite soccer players. *European Physical Education Review, 6,* 91–110. doi:10.1177/1356336X 000061001.

Fell, J., & Williams, A. (2010). Aging and recovery. In J. Baker, S. Horton, & P. Weir (Eds.), *The Master athlete: Understanding the role of sport and exercise in optimizing aging* (pp. 79–102). New York: Routledge.

Gearity, B. T., & Murray, M. A. (2011). Athletes' experiences of the psychological effects of poor coaching. *Psychology of Sport and Exercise, 12,* 213–221. doi:10.1016/j.psychsport.2010.11.004.

Gilbert, W. D. (2010). The passing of a legend: Coach John Wooden. *International Journal of Sports Science & Coaching, 5,* 339–342. doi: 10.1260/1747-9541.5.3.339.

Gilbert, W. D., & Rangeon, S. (2012). Current directions in coaching research. *Revista de Iberoamericana de Psicologia del Ejercicio y el Deporte, 6,* 217–236.

Gilbert, W. D., & Trudel, P. (2004). Analysis of coaching science research published from 1970-2001. *Research Quarterly for Exercise & Sport, 75,* 388–399. doi:10.1080/02701367.2004.10609172.

Gould, D., & Carson, S. (2008). Life skills development though sport: Current status and future directions. *International Review of Sport and Exercise Psychology, 1,* 58–78. doi:10.1080/17509840701834573.

Greenleaf, C., Gould, D., & Dieffenbach, K. (2001). Factors influencing Olympic performance: Interviews with Atlanta and Nagano US Olympians. *Journal of Applied Sport Psychology, 13,* 154–184. doi:10.1080/104132001753149874.

Hodge, K., Allen, J. B., & Smellie, L. (2008). Motivation in masters sport: Achievement and social goals. *Psychology of Sport and Exercise, 9,* 157–176. doi:10.1016/j.psychsport. 2007.03.002.

Horn, T. S. (2008). Coaching effectiveness in the sport domain. In T. S. Horn (Ed.), *Advances in sport psychology* (3rd ed., pp. 239–267). Champaign, IL: Human Kinetics.

Horn, T. S., Bloom, P., Berglund, K. M., & Packard, S. (2011). Relationship between collegiate athletes' psychological characteristics and their preferences for different types of coaching behavior. *The Sport Psychologist, 25,* 190–211.

Jackson, P., & Delehanty, H. (1995). *Sacred hoops*. New York: Hyperion.

Jowett, S. (2003). When the "honeymoon" is over: A case study of a coach-athlete dyad in crisis. *The Sport Psychologist, 17,* 444–460.

Jowett, S., & Cockerill, I. M. (2003). Olympic medalists' perspective of the athlete-coach relationship. *Psychology of Sport and Exercise, 4,* 313–331. doi:10.1016/S14690292(02)00011-0.

Jowett, S., & Lavallee, D. (2007). *Social psychology in sport*. Windsor, ON: Human Kinetics.

Jowett, S., & Meek, G. A. (2000). The coach-athlete relationship in married couples: An exploratory content analysis. *The Sport Psychologist, 14,* 157–175.

Keshtan, M. H., Ramzaninezhad, R., Kordshooli, S. S., & Panahi, P. M. (2010). The relationships between collective efficacy and coaching behaviours in professional volleyball league of Iran clubs. *World Journal of Sport Sciences, 3,* 1–6.

Kimiecik, J., & Gould, D. (1987). Coaching psychology: The case of James "Doc" Counsilman. *The Sport Psychologist, 1,* 350–358.

Krampe, K. T., & Ericsson, K. A., (1996). Maintaining excellence: Deliberate practice and elite performance in young and older pianists. *Journal of Experimental Psychology: General, 125,* 331–359. doi:10.1037/0096-3445.125.4.331

Kristiansen, E., Roberts, G. C., & Sisjord, M. K. (2012). Coping with negative media content: The experiences of professional football goalkeepers. *International Journal of Sport and Exercise Psychology, 9,* 295–307. doi:10.1080/1612197X.2011.623451.

Lyle, J. (2002). *Sports coaching concepts: A framework for coaches' behavior.* London, England: Routledge.

Mechikoff, R. A., & Kozar, B. (1983). *Sport psychology: The coaches' perspective.* Springfield, IL: Charles C. Thomas.

Medic, N. (2010). Understanding masters athletes' motivation for sport. In J. Baker, S. Horton, & P. Weir (Eds.), *The Master athlete: Understanding the role of sport and exercise in optimizing aging* (pp. 105–121). New York: Routledge.

Medic, N., Young, B. W., Starkes, J. L., & Weir, P. L. (2012). Relationship between having a coach and master athletes' motivational regulations for sport and achievement goal orientations. *International Journal of Coaching Science, 6,* 65–79.

Mielke, D. (2007). Coaching experience, playing experience and coaching tenure. *International Journal of Sports Science & Coaching, 2,* 105–108. doi:10.1260/174795407781394293.

Moskal, B. S. (1997). Coaching a turnaround. *Industry Week, 246,* 48–54.

Nater, S., & Gallimore, R. (2006). *You haven't taught until they have learned.* Morgantown, WV: Fitness Information Technology.

Nicholls, A. R., Holt, N. L., Polman, R. C., & Bloomfield, J. (2006). Stressors, coping, and coping effectiveness among professional rugby union players. *The Sport Psychologist, 20,* 314–329.

Nicholls, J. G. (1989). *The competitive ethos and democratic education.* Cambridge, MA: Harvard University Press.

Noblet, A. J., & Gifford, S. M. (2002). The sources of stress experienced by professional Australian footballers. *Journal of Applied Sport Psychology, 14,* 1–13. doi:10.1080/10413200209339007.

Ogles, B. M., & Masters, K. S. (2000). Older vs. younger adult male marathon runners: Participative motives and training habits. *Journal of Sport Behavior, 23,* 130–142.

Packer, B., & Lazenby, R. (1998). *Why we win.* Chicago, IL: Master Press.

Papacharisis, V., Goudas, M., Danish, S. J., & Theodorakis, Y. (2005). The effectiveness of teaching a life skills program in a sport context. *Journal of Applied Sport Psychology, 12,* 247–254. doi:10.1080/10413200591010139.

Philippe, R. A., & Seiler, R. (2006). Closeness, co-orientation and complementarity in coach-athlete relationship: What male swimmers say about their male coaches. *Psychology of Sport and Exercise, 7,* 159–171. doi: 10.1016/jpsychsport.2005.08.004.

Porter, M. M., Vandervoort, A. A., & Lexell, J. (1995). Aging of human muscle: Structure, function and adaptability. *Scandinavian Journal of Medicine and Science in Sports, 5,* 129–142. doi:10.1111/j.1600-0838.1995.tb00026.x.

Potrac, P., Brewer, C., Jones, R., Armour, K., & Hoff, J. (2000). Toward a holistic understanding of the coaching process. *Quest, 52,* 186–199. doi:10.1080/00336297.2000.10491709.

Potrac, P., Jones, R., & Armour, K. (2002). It's all about getting respect: The coaching behaviours of an expert English soccer coach. *Sport, Education and Society, 7,* 183–202. doi:10.1080/1357332022000018869.

Potrac, P., Jones, R., & Cushion, C. (2007). Understanding power and the coach's role in professional English soccer. *Soccer & Society, 8,* 33–49. doi:10.1080/14660970600989509.

Riemer, H. A., & Chelladurai, P. (1995). Leadership and satisfaction in sport. *Journal of Sport & Exercise Psychology, 17,* 276–293.

Riley, P. (1993). *The winner within: A life plan for team players.* New York: Berkley.

Ryan, R. M., & Deci, E. L. (2000). Self-determination theory and the facilitation of intrinsic motivation, social development, and well-being. *American Psychologist, 55,* 68–78. doi:10.1037110003-066X.55.1.68

Smith, D. (2002). *A coach's life.* New York: Random House.

Sport Canada. (2006). *Policy on sport for persons with a disability* (Publication No. CH24-14/2006). Ottawa: Canadian Heritage.

Statistics Canada. (2002, December 3). Participation and activity limitation survey: A profile of disability in Canada. *Statistics Canada Press Release.* Retrieved April 23, 2008, from http://www.canadianheritage.gc.ca/progs/sc/pol/pwad/3_e.cfm.

Statistics Canada. (2007, December 3). Physical activity limitation survey. *Statistics Canada Press Release.* Retrieved April 23, 2008, from http://www.statcan.ca/english/freepub/89-628-XIE/2007003/series1-en.htm.

Stevenson, C. L. (2002). Seeking identities: Toward an understanding of the athletic careers of master swimmers. *International Review for the Sociology of Sport, 37,* 131–146. doi: 10.1177/1012690202037002001.

Sullivan, P. J., & Kent, A. (2003). Coaching efficacy as a predictor of leadership style in intercollegiate athletics. *Journal of Applied Sport Psychology, 15,* 1–11. doi:10.1080/10413200305404.

Tarpenning, K. M., Hamilton-Wessler, M., Wiswell, R. A., & Hawkins, S. A. (2004). Endurance training delays age of decline in leg strength and muscle morphology. *Medicine and Science in Sports and Exercise, 36,* 74–78. doi:10.1249/01.MSS. 0000106179.73735.A6.

Tawse, H., Bloom, G. A., Sabiston, C. M., & Reid, G. (2012). The role of coaches of wheelchair rugby in the development of athletes with a spinal cord injury. *Qualitative Research in Sport, Exercise and Health, 4,* 206–225. doi:10.1080/2159676X.2012. 685104.

Thelwell, R. C., Weston, N. J. V., Greenlees, I. A., & Hutchings, N. V. (2008). A qualitative exploration of psychological-skills use in coaches. *The Sport Psychologist, 22,* 38–53.

Torre, J., & Verducci, T. (2009). *The Yankee years.* New York: Random House.

Trudel, P., & Gilbert, W. D. (2004). Communities of practice as an approach to foster ice hockey coach development. In D. J. Pearsall & A. B. Ashare (Eds.), *Safety in ice hockey* (4th ed., pp. 167–179). West Conshohocken, PA: ASTM International.

Vallée, C. N., & Bloom, G. A. (2005). Building a successful university program: Key and common elements of expert coaches. *Journal of Applied Sport Psychology, 17,* 179–196. doi:10.1080/10413200591010021.

Vandervoort, A. A. (2002). Aging of the human neuromuscular system. *Muscle Nerve, 25,* 17–25.

Walton, G. M. (1992). *Beyond winning: The timeless wisdom of great philosopher coaches.* Champaign, IL: Human Kinetics.

Wang, J., & Straub, W. F. (2012). An investigation into the coaching approach of a successful world class soccer coach: Anson Dorrance. *International Journal of Sports Science & Coaching, 7,* 431–447. doi:10.1260/1747-9541.7.3.431

Warburton, J. C., Ashe, M. C., Miller, W. C., Shi, P., & Marra, C. A. (2009). Does physical activity reduce seniors' need for healthcare? A study of 24 281 Canadians. *British Journal of Sports Medicine, 44,* 902–904. doi:10.1136/bjsm.2008.057216.

White, P., Persad, S., & Gee, C. J. (2007). The effect of mid-season coach turnover on team performance: The case of the national hockey league (1989-2003). *International Journal of Sports Science & Coaching, 2,* 143–152. doi:10.1260/174795407781394275.

Wilson, L. M, Bloom, G. A., & Harvey, W. J. (2010). Sources of knowledge acquisition: Perspectives of the high school teacher/coach. *Physical Education and Sport Pedagogy, 15,* 383–399. doi:10.1080/17408980903273154.

Wooden, J. (1988). *They call me coach.* New York: Contemporary Books.

World Master Athletics. (2013). *World masters athletics history.* Retrieved from: http:// www.world-masters athletics.org/files/history/WMA_Handbook_Short_History.pdf.

Wrisberg, C. A. (1990). An interview with Pat Head Summit. *The Sport Psychologist, 4,* 181–191.

In: Positive Human Functioning ...   ISBN: 978-1-62948-974-2
Editors: A. R. Gomes, R. Resende & A. Albuquerque   © 2014 Nova Science Publishers, Inc.

Chapter 7

LEADERSHIP IN A TEAM SPORT CONTEXT: IMPLICATIONS FOR COACHES

Harold A. Riemer and Sebastian Harenberg

Faculty of Kinesiology and Health Studies, University of Regina, Canada

ABSTRACT

Leadership continues to be a hot topic in sport psychology. Researchers and practitioners have been interested in the impact a coach's behaviors have on athletic performance and other team processes. This chapter provides an overview of our current understandings of athletic leadership as well as future directions. It is structured in three parts: (a) defining leadership, (b) the origins and structure of the Multidimensional Model of Leadership (Chelladurai, 1990) and (c) recent directions in leadership (i.e., transforming) are discussed.

INTRODUCTION

Leadership is of interest to most people. Those interested in team sports (e.g., football/soccer, ice hockey, rugby, etc.) see the primary leader of the team (i.e., head coach/trainer) as playing a key role in how successful the individual players and the team are. Examine the sport section of any newspaper, sport related magazine, or sport broadcast website to see evidence of this fundamentally held belief. Fans, broadcasters/journalists, administrators/owners, and athletes often tie a team's on-field performance, whether good or bad, directly to the effectiveness of the head coach's leadership. Highly successful coaches are often deified (e.g., Sir Alex Ferguson – soccer, Mike Babcock - hockey). Unsuccessful teams tend to replace the head coach. Every season sees coaches fired and hired on the belief that good leadership should result in success. For most, there is a link between team performance and the coach's leadership. Few would suggest that leadership is not important.

This chapter examines the academic/scholarly literature about leadership in general, and coaching leadership in particular. Our goal is to provide you with an appreciation for the complexity of leadership, what we know about leadership in a sport context, and what needs to be explored. We provide insights into what a coach should consider in his/her own leadership to be effective.

Definition of Leadership

We begin by defining leadership. There are thousands of definitions of leadership. We have chosen two to illustrate: the "behavioral process of influencing individuals or groups toward set goals" (Barrow, 1977, p. 232); "Leadership is a process whereby an individual influences a group of individuals to achieve a common goal" (Northouse, 2007, p. 3). Most definitions highlight five key ideas: organization, influencing/motivating, goal achievement, behavior, and social context.

Organization
Leadership typically occurs in an *organizational* (group) context. Athletic teams may be classified as a type of organization. Understanding what an organization is provides insights into key functions associated with leadership. An organization is "a social entity created to coordinate the efforts of individuals with the intent to achieve goals" (Parks, Thibault, & Quarterman, 2007, p. 316). All organizations require at least two individuals (e.g., players), who together are pursuing some kind of common goal (e.g., a championship), where the individual members have specialized functions/roles (e.g., goalie, forward, midfielder, etc.), and the individual efforts are coordinated in some way (e.g., how the different positions will play together to achieve the goal) (Chelladurai, 2005).

Researchers (e.g., Chelladurai, 2005; Waring, 1996; Katz & Kahn, 1966) have argued that organizations are best understood as *open systems*. A *system* is an "interconnected set of elements that have orderly interactions that form a unitary whole" (Black & Porter, 2000, p. 57). A key idea is that change in one element of the organization (e.g., a player is injured, one player is replaced by another, etc.) results/requires further change(s) in other elements of the organization (Morecroft, Sanchez, & Heene, 2002). An *open* system is one that is influenced by, and influences, the environment in which it functions. *Environment* is simply a "set of forces surrounding an organization that have the potential to affect the way it operates and its access to resources" (Jones, 2004, p. 60). All organizations must function in two basic environments: the *general environment* and the *task environment*.

Parks et al. (2007) note that the general or distal environment affects all organizations and includes (a) the economic conditions, (b) technology, (c) politics, and (d) social and cultural forces (i.e., the society in which the organization operates). The task or proximal environment can be thought of those factors that have a "direct and immediate effect on the organization" (Chelladurai, 2005, p. 77) and may include key stakeholders. In a sport team context, the task environment would typically include the team's competitors, its fans, the families of the players, the general availability of athletic talent, and the team's suppliers.

Finally, all organizations must fulfill two basic functions. The first is to *adapt* to changes in the external environment. For example, changes in technology (e.g., video, equipment) have changed how coaches assess the team's performance and teach important concepts to athletes. The second function is to provide *stability* in the internal environment. For example, coaches formulate expectations and hold players accountable to established routines (e.g., sticking to a time schedule for games and practices).

Organizations are complex – even organizations as 'simple' as a youth league team have complex dynamics at play. All key elements of an organization are influenced by the leader/coach. Leaders are typically responsible for setting the group's direction (i.e., goals), assigning roles and functions to team members, and ensuring team members' work is coordinated.

Influencing/Motivating

Coaches understand that motivating athletes to improve and perform is a central feature of what he/she must do. I (H.A.R.) once had a player say to me during a game: "You need to motivate me". Much of what leaders do requires persuading or encouraging group members to move in a particular direction. A coach's role includes ensuring his/her athletes demonstrate characteristics of motivated behavior in the pursuit of the team's goal(s) (i.e., direction, intensity, persistence). A sound understanding of human motivation is necessary if we are to be effective leaders. Ideas and assumptions about motivation are foundational to most leadership theories (see Latham & Ernst, 2006, for an overview of key motivation theories).

Goal Achievement

Setting, pursuing, and reaching goals are central to all leadership since organizations exist primarily to achieve goals. Ineffective organizations are those that fail to achieve their goals. Coaches are often dismissed for the team's failure to reach its competitive goals (e.g., wins and losses). In some leadership theories, the word 'vision' or 'visionary' replaces goal, but the principle is the same; a vision is a statement about a preferred future state. For example, Nanus (1992, p. 7) defined vision as a "realistic, credible, attractive future for an organization". Many contemporary leadership approaches suggest vision creation, or being visionary, is a key to leadership effectiveness.

Behavior

What really matters is what the leader does. Behaviors are an extension of our thoughts, beliefs, values, and attitudes. Moreover, most of us draw conclusions about a leader's style from his/her actions. Most instruments/tools that evaluate a person's leadership are collections of 'behavioral descriptors'; completing the questionnaire, the participant indicates the extent to which the leader has been observed engaging in particular behaviors.

Social Context

Finally, leadership is a social function since it requires interaction with people as individuals, and within a group setting. The complexity of leadership stems, in part, from the fact that human beings are complicated social creatures. Even in small groups (or dyads/couples) we find a range of experiences, skills, abilities, traditions, values, ideas, preferences, and personalities. One reason why human beings tend to create groups is tied to this complexity – the potential of what we might accomplish together is quite great because of this large variation in humanness. It is also one of the reasons why leadership is difficult and challenging (cf., Benjamin & O'Reilly, 2011).

MULTIDIMENSIONAL MODEL OF LEADERSHIP

A discussion of leadership in a sport context must include the Multidimensional Model of Leadership (Chelladurai, 1993). Chelladurai's leadership ideas, along with his measurement tool, the Leadership Scale for Sports (Chelladurai & Saleh, 1980), have dominated the academic/research literature since they were first introduced.

Building Blocks of the MML

The MML has its foundation in the rich history of leadership research in management/business (or organizational psychology). The MML has integrated important themes and/or understandings of leadership from this tradition. It is worth reviewing the key works shaped the MML's ideas. Many of these same themes/concepts/ideas are present in the other approaches to understanding sport leadership (e.g., Mediational Model, Peer Leadership, and Leadership Dyads).

Personal Traits/Characteristics

Early work in the area of leadership focused on the traits or characteristics required to make a leader successful. This approach suggests that leaders have different characteristics than non-leaders. Work on traits largely stopped after Stogdill (1948) concluded, "a person does not become a leader by virtue of the possession of some combination of traits" (p. 64). Early trait research had other problems. For example, a focus on simple bi-variate relationships between a particular trait and leadership effectiveness (Lord & Hall, 1992) and no real understanding as to why certain traits might predict leadership (Yukl, 1999).

However, work on traits has recently been revived. Kirkpatick and Locke (1991) suggest six general categories of traits/characteristics that may increase the likelihood that leaders will be successful: (a) Drive (which includes achievement, ambition, energy, tenacity, initiative), (b) Motivation to lead, (c) Honesty and integrity, (d) Self-confidence, (e) Cognitive ability, and (f) Task-related knowledge.

Judge, Bono, Ilies, and Gerhardt's (2002) meta-analysis reported the personality traits of agreeableness, conscientiousness, emotional stability, extraversion, and openness to experience together influenced leadership effectiveness. Building on this work, Hendricks and Payne (2007) hypothesized how these personality traits, along with goal orientation (both performance and learning orientations; Dweck, 1986), a person's motivation to lead (i.e., tendency and reasons for a person to seek out leadership roles; cf., Chan & Drasgow, 2001), and leadership self-efficacy ("capability to perform cognitive and behavioral functions required to effectively perform a specific leadership task" – Kane, 1999, p. 5), interact to influence a leader's effectiveness.

Work in this area continues. Kirkpatrick and Locke (1991) provide good advice: "*Traits alone* are not sufficient for successful leadership – they are only a precondition. Leaders who possess the requisite traits must take certain *actions* to be successful (e.g., formulating a vision, role modeling, setting goals). Possessing certain traits only makes it more likely that such actions will be taken and be successful" (p. 49).

Approaches to Decision Making

All leaders make decisions. Ground breaking work in decision making was carried out by Kurt Lewin and colleagues (Lewin, Lippitt, & White, 1939). Lewin was interested in understanding whether autocratic or democratic style leaders would be more successful. In his early experimental work, graduate students were trained to lead groups of boys either democratically or autocratically. For a control group, the graduate student provided no leadership (i.e., laizze-faire leadership). Results suggested the democratic style of leadership lead to greater satisfaction from the boys, and these groups were seen as operating in a positive and orderly fashion. The autocratically lead groups were observed to exhibit greater levels of aggressive behavior (Lewin et al., 1939). Subsequent work by Lippitt and White (1943), however, indicated that productivity was greatest when leadership was more autocratic, but only when leader was physically present (i.e., directly supervising). Other researchers, most notably Victor Vroom continued this line of work. Vroom's work suggested that either democratic or autocratic (or variations thereof) could be effective depending on the nature of the decision that needs to be made.

Leadership Styles

What a leader does or the behaviors he/she engages in (i.e., how that person leads) determine the effectiveness of leadership. Important work in understanding key behaviors (often referred to as styles) happened during the 1950's and involved a variety of research groups (e.g., Ohio State University - Hemphill, 1950) and focused on specific observable behaviors that effective leaders engage in. Using different methods (e.g., questionnaires, interviews, and observation), the same conclusions were drawn: two key behaviors largely determine whether a leader will be effective. *Consideration behaviors* are those in which the leader considers the group members as individuals and their "comfort, well-being, status, and contribution" in/to the group (Stogdill, 1963, p. 3). Examples of phrases that describe/operationalize consideration behavior include: "friendly and approachable... (does) little things to make it pleasant to be a (team member)... put(s) suggestions made by group into operation... (treat) group members as equals... (gives) advance notice of changes... (looks) out for the personal welfare of group members... (and) willing to make changes" (Fisher College of Business, 1962, pp. 2-5). Consideration also includes the notion of a more democratic or consultative approach to decision making. *Initiation of Structure* are behaviors through which the leader "clearly defines own role, and lets followers know what is expected" (Stogdill, 1963, p. 3). Examples of phrases that describe/operationalize initiating of structure include: "let group members know what is expected of them... (encourages) the use of uniform procedures... (tries out) ideas in the group... (makes his/her) attitudes clear to the group... (decides) what shall be done and how it shall be done... assign group members to particular tasks... (makes certain his/her role) in the group is understood by the group... schedule work to be done... maintain definite standards of performance... (asks that group) follow standard rules and regulations" (Fisher College of Business, 1962, pp. 2-5).

However, as Stoghill (1963) noted, it is not "reasonable to believe that two factors are sufficient to account for all the observable variance in leader behavior" (p. 2); there are other behaviors that leaders engage in, and necessary, for effective group functioning. The Leader Behavior Description Questionnaire went on to propose other important dimensions: representing the group to others; reconciling conflicting demands and system disorder; ability to tolerate uncertainty; has conviction and uses persuasion and argument effectively; allows for initiative, decision, and action from members; actively exercises leadership; applies pressure for production; able to anticipate outcomes; creates a close knit group where conflict is resolved; and fosters relationships with superiors. Many of these concepts have been re-emphasized in more recent approaches to effective leadership.

Contingency Theories

Four basic contingency theories form the foundation for much of the MML and other contemporary theories: (a) Fiedler's (1967) model of leadership effectiveness, (b) Evan's (1970) and House's (1971; House & Dressler, 1974) path-goal theory of leadership, (c) Osborne and Hunt's (1975) adaptive-reactive theory of leadership, and (d) Yukl's (1971) discrepancy model of leadership. These theories tend to see leadership from one or more of the following perspectives: (a) the *leader*, (b) the *member* (follower/subordinate/athlete), and/or (c) the *situational context* in which the leadership takes place.

One of Fiedler's (1967) key assumptions was that leaders have a dominant style of leading and it is difficult for leaders to lead using a non-dominant style. In his conceptualization, dominant leadership styles included (a) accomplishing the group's task/goal(s) (i.e., initiates structure), or (b) ensuring a good relationship with the employee or follower (i.e., consideration). Whether a leader is effective is determined largely by whether the particular 'situation' is 'favourable' toward the particular dominant style. Fiedler defined favourableness in a particular way, with key considerations including: (a) what is the relationship like between the leader and the team members? (b) what kind of power is tied to the leader's role (i.e., position power)? (c) how clear is it what the team needs to accomplish (i.e., task goal clarity)? (d) how complex is (are) the team's task(s), and (e) is it easy to determine whether a leader's decisions are good/bad?

Fiedler made three important contributions. First, any leadership style (or combination of leadership styles) may be effective if it is matched with an appropriate situation. Second, leaders can alter the situation to better suit their particular style(s) of leading. For example, coaches can release athletes with whom they have difficulty; recruit athletes who prefer a particular way of leading; clarify goals; increase or decrease task complexity, etc. Finally, Fiedler identified what elements of the situation impact leadership (and needs to be considered).

Building on Vroom's (1964) *expectancy theory*, House's (1971) *path-goal theory of leadership* argues individuals will be motivated to engage in goal directed behaviors (e.g., off season training) because he/she believes ('expects') they will lead to a personally valued outcome. A fundamental proposition is that group/team goal accomplishment must connect to the individual's personal goals in some way. From House's perspective, a leader is able to influence all the determinants of an individual's motivation proposed by expectancy theory (i.e., valence, instrumentality, and expectancy).

Two things really separate House from Fiedler's view on effective leadership. First, House operates on the assumption that leaders are able to, and should, adapt their leadership style (or combination of styles) to a given situation. Second, Fielder focused on the leader, House focuses on those being lead and argued that a leader's primary role is to motivate team members to engage in team tasks. To do this, the leader must ensure team members understand the connection between team related tasks and personal goal attainment. House (1971, p. 324) believes the leaders job is to: "increase personal pay-offs to subordinates for work-goal attainment, and making the path to these pay-offs easier to travel by clarifying it, reducing road blocks and pitfalls, and increasing the opportunities for personal satisfaction en route". To accomplish this, different team members might require different leadership styles or approaches. House's theory is relevant since many athletes are goal oriented and team membership allows them to pursue their personal goals. So, if an amateur athlete values a personal goal of playing professional hockey, a coach needs to ensure the athlete sees the connection between working hard to accomplish team related tasks (and/or goals) and the reaching of their personal goals.

The *adaptive-reactive theory of leadership* (Osborn & Hunt, 1975) introduces the larger organizational environment (e.g., athletic department, sport club, sport league, community association, etc.) in which the group/team functions (or is connected to) as a leadership consideration. This environment has an impact on team members and leaders. The theory notes that leaders do not operate in a vacuum; just as coaches place expectations upon athletes, coaches have expectations placed upon them by elements of the organizational system. For example, Canadian universities require that coaches, and the teams they lead, adhere to the same policies and procedures that apply to academic units. In the United States, when coaches are recruiting athletes, they must follow the policies set out by the NCAA, an administrative body which governs university sport in the US. Even coaches of minor league teams must adhere to a variety of policies that may govern coach-athlete relationships, coach-parent relationships, use of funds raised, and even how playing time needs to be allocated. Leaders/coaches must '*adapt*' their leadership to the requirements of the organization. These expectations will vary and are a function of such things as unit size, level of technology, formal structure, broader organizational culture, etc.

Osborne and Hunt also highlight that leaders/coaches have expectations placed upon them by those being lead. For example, as a coach of a variety of different teams, I (H.A.R.) have had athletes who expect me to make all the decisions, others want to participate in the decision making. How I treat and coach younger athletes tends to be different than how I treat older athletes. I have had some athletes who prefer that I yell at them to 'get them going' (i.e., motivate them to play better), while others, on the same team would respond negatively to such an approach. Players also have expectations (and these will vary from player to player) with regard to the tactics and strategies that I might employ. From a theoretical perspective, leaders/coaches must also '*react*' to the needs and desires of the group as a whole, as well as the individual. These expectations will often vary with the nature of the task, individual differences, and previous experiences.

In the case of minor sports, an athlete's expectations are also influenced by his/her parent(s). Depending on the nature of the organization, parents may also influence the shaping policies that govern expectations of coaches (e.g., through annual meetings, contacting board members directly, sitting on boards, etc.). Arguably, youth sport coaches need to consider a child's parent(s) as a third 'factor' or source of expectations.

Yukl (1971) made several important contributions leadership theory development. First, he saw the leadership behaviors of *consideration, initiating structure,* and *decision-making style* as three important, independent (yet connected), dimensions of leadership. He argued that decision-making style should be treated as a single dimension (*decision-centralization*). When measured, a high score would mean a lack of group/team member involvement in decision making (i.e., autocratic) and a low score indicate members play a key role in the decision making (i.e., consultative, participative or democratic). More importantly, Yukl suggested that having a style dominated by either *consideration* or *initiating structure* types of behaviors does not presume that one's approach to decision making will necessarily be one way or the other (i.e., high or low score on decision centralization). In Yukl's own words, "benevolent autocrats" and "malevolent democrats" (p. 419) are both possible. What makes this important is that there is a continued realization that multiple approaches to leading are possible, and may be successful (i.e., there may not be one 'best' way).

Second, Yukl proposed a *discrepancy model* that explained the connection between leadership and the group members' level of satisfaction. Specifically, a team member's satisfaction is a function of the *discrepancy* (if any) between that individual's preferences for a particular combination of leadership behaviors and their actual experiences. A person's particular preferences were thought to be influenced by an individual's personality (i.e., Yukl focused particularly on the constructs/traits of *authoritarianism* - cf., Vroom, 1959 and *need for independence* – cf., Trow, 1957, Ross & Zander, 1957) and his/her relationship to that particular group or team (e.g., importance of a particular decision, his/her commitment to the group).

Finally, Yukl outlined the connection between leadership and three necessary group components that directly impact a group's performance. If a group's (and individual's) performance are to increase then (a) they/he/she must be *motivated* to engage in the necessary tasks (e.g., preparing for competition, playing games, etc.), (b) the individual and collective level of task related skill must increase (i.e., through replacement/recruitment, training, etc.), and (c) decision making with respect to the technical aspects of the task(s) be sound (e.g., how to structure practice, capitalizing on player's strengths/weaknesses in strategy, etc.). Yukl argued that leadership may influence a group's performance only indirectly through these three components. From this perspective, leaders facilitate a team's performance.

Transactional and Transformational Leadership

Much of the academic discussion regarding transactional and transformational leadership appears after the MML was first introduced. However, these elements are either implicit in the model (i.e., transactional) or were added to the model in a later modification (i.e., transformational, cf. Chelladurai, 1990). Therefore, some mention of them is important. We will look at transformational leadership in greater depth later in the chapter.

Kuhnert and Lewis (1987) note: "*transactional* leaders give followers something they want in exchange for something the leaders want" (p. 649). The relationship between leaders and individuals/group/team is an *exchange* relationship. In an athletic context, an athlete may exchange their commitment to a team for an athletic scholarship (economic transaction), or work hard at practice in exchange for the coach providing a supportive environment (intangible attitudinal transaction). Transactional theories/models highlight that leaders/coaches and group/team members have a mutually dependent relationship – one cannot be effective without the other. Similar to some previously discussed theories, members/athletes have needs and also bring expectations to the relationships (as do the leaders). If a leader is to be effective, he/she must be able to address various (often changing) and differing expectations and needs that group/teams members have (Kellerman, 1984). Transactional leadership also builds on Vroom's ideas about how expectancies motivate individuals. If a leader can tie a particular behavior to a future desirable state (often tied to a need the individual has), then motivation is enhanced (e.g., if you accomplish 'X', then you will gain a starting position on the roster). Transactional leadership has been used by leaders for a long time and may be used effectively and, often very efficiently, to accomplish the group's goals.

Transformational leadership, (Bass, 1985) (*new leadership* - Bryman, 1992; *visionary* - Sashkin, 1988; *charismatic* – Conger, 1989) is often seen as standing in contrast to transactional forms of leadership. It describes leaders who connect with their group/team members in ways that lead to extraordinary individual and group performance(s) (Yammarino, Dubinsky, Comer, & Jolson, 1997). Transformational leaders are able to create an environment where individuals (a) buy into organization's (or often leader's) vision, (b) are interested in fulfilling higher order needs (e.g., those typically related to Maslow's [1943] higher order needs such as Esteem and Actualization), and as a result (c) exceed performance expectations. Bass (1985) notes that a leader can, and often will, exhibit varying degrees of both transformational and transactional leadership. As Doherty and Danylchuk (1996) note, "all leaders are transactional to some extent, exchanging rewards for performance, but some leaders are also transformational, going beyond simple leader-subordinate exchange relations" (p. 294).

The Multidimensional Model of Leadership

The Multidimensional Model of Leadership (MML) indicates that effective leadership is a process influenced by multiple factors. The MML (refer to Figure 1) has three basic parts. First and foremost, the *outcomes of leadership* are defined (*Athlete Satisfaction* and *Individual and Team Performance*). Leadership is always evaluated in terms of outcomes. Second, a central role in the model is assigned to the leader's *Actual Behavior*. How a person leads (what is done, what is said, how it is done) is of singular importance in determining what individual and group outcomes will be. Finally, the model identifies factors that play a role in influencing what a leader's actual behavior will be. Some of these will be more influential than others. More direct influencers include the *leader characteristics*, the *preferred behaviors* from athletes/group members, and *required behaviors* typically stemming from the organization. The indirect influences include whether or not the leader exhibits *transformational leadership,* as well as the individual and collective *athlete characteristics* along with the *situational characteristics*. Clearly, the MML proposes that leadership is a complex process.

The MML's has several key propositions. First, performance and satisfaction are tied directly to whether a leader's actual behavior is consistent (*congruent*) with the leadership preferences of the athlete(s) and the requirements and constraints (or expectations) placed on leader behavior (arrows # 1, 2, & 3). This particular relationship is hypothesized to be positive; the more a leader's actual behavior matches the preferences of group members, and is consistent with requirements for a given situation, the greater performance and satisfaction should be.

Second, the MML argues that how a leader leads will be determined, at least in part, by the leader's level of familiarity/knowledge he/she will have about the people making up the team and the context in which the team must operate (arrows # 4 & 5). Knowing team members' preferences for leadership may result in the leader adjusting his/her behavior to match those preferences. For example, a coach who is aware that his starting quarterback prefers to call her own plays (and has the ability to do so) is likely to give more latitude to this player either by letting the player actually call her own plays or allowing more input when developing the week's game plan. However, this knowledge may also result, as Fiedler has suggested, in the coach finding a replacement for that player and ensuring the replacement has preferences that are more consistent with the coach's own behaviors. A third possibility is that a coach tries to modify the athlete's preferences. For example, he or she may make it very clear at the beginning of the season that athletes will not have a say in determining strategy. Regardless, the result is the same (i.e., greater consistency between preferences and a coach's behavior). We must, however, be aware that knowledge does not necessarily result in any action; the coach could ignore the information.

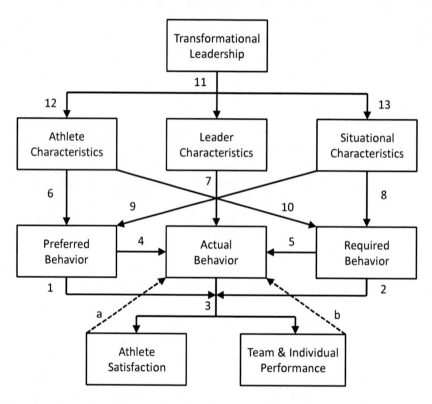

Figure 1. The Multidimensional Model of Leadership (Adapted from Riemer, 2007).

Understanding of the context in which a leader must lead will also likely, but not necessarily, influence his or her leadership. For example, a women's basketball coach who receives pressure from an athletic director or club director to reduce the amount of personal contact he/she has with his/her athletes away from the gym is likely to modify that aspect of his/her leadership. Some elements of the context (situation) may be more influential than others in determining whether a coach will modify behavior. So, while parental expectations may be salient for a volunteer coach in Little League, they may not be as important for a professional coach working in a professional soccer clubs developmental program. In the latter instance, management and/or shareholder expectations will be more influential.

Third, the MML proposes that coaches receive feedback about (a) satisfaction levels, and (b) individual and collective performance. Some of this feedback may be formally collected or provided (e.g., a survey at the end of the season, game/season statistics), but much of this 'data' is provided by doing, as Hackman and Oldham (1976) have suggested, the job itself. For example, sensing the reactions of players to decisions or how they are interacted with, or noting improvement in team commitment to winning, etc. Any feedback a coach receives in this regard has the potential to determine or influence future behaviors the coach engages in (i.e., may or may not result in modifications to leadership) (arrows # a & b). As Chelladurai (2001) notes, leaders are flexible and are able to modify their own behavior to ensure particular outcomes. Building on a previous example, the same coach who allowed athletes more input into game strategy because of his/her understanding of the athlete's preferences, may revert to a less consultative or democratic approach if the team's performance is perceived to be negatively impacted.

Fourth, there are a variety of hypotheses related to what influences a coach's *actual leadership,* an athlete's or group's *preferred behavior* from the coach, and the *required behavior* from the coach. Specifically, the characteristics of the athlete(s), the situation, and the coach all play a role (arrows 6, 7, 8, 9, & 10). Chelladurai includes an athlete's abilities, traits (including personality and cultural influences) in the realm of athlete characteristics. Logically, it would also include a person's life experiences, previous influences, values, and really anything that plays a role in shaping a human being to be who they are. The human motivation literature plays an important role in helping us understand how athlete characteristics influence preferences; it provides information about what makes individuals respond more positively to one type of leadership behavior over the other.

Required behavior (expectations and/or limitations a leader must deal with) is influenced by characteristics of the situation (which influence required behavior – arrow #8) (tied to the greater organization the team functions within). These situational characteristics include rules, policies and procedures, the strategic plan and vision of the organization. It also includes the organization's philosophy and culture, along with the characteristics of those leading the broader organization since these individuals have a tremendous impact on key characteristics of the organization (e.g., mission, vision, direction, etc.). Situational characteristics extend to the characteristics of the operating environment beyond the immediate organization the team might be associated with. This might include other governing bodies (e.g., regional, provincial, national, international, parent associations, lobbying groups) and even the broader culture and political environment the team operates in. It should be clear that there are a considerable number of factors to consider in this particular realm.

While it is obvious that athlete characteristics influence athlete preferences (Arrow #6), and the characteristics of the situation influence the requirement of the required behavior (Arrow #8), it is important to note that Chelladurai also suggests athlete characteristics (particularly as a collective or a group) may have an impact on required behavior (Arrow #10) and situational characteristics may influence athlete preferences (Arrow #9). Chelladurai has noted that the team's general ability level, sex, and age influence behaviors required or expected of the leader. For example, over the past number of years there have been numerous newspaper stories that suggest that traditional ways of coaching today's professional athlete no longer work and coaches need to change. Athlete characteristics are now influencing general managers and team owners to adjust their demands how coaches work. Similarly, if an athlete who is aware that the league in which she plays has an 'equal play' policy governing a coach's decisions in allocating playing time, she may allow her preferences to be influenced by this knowledge. Chelladurai notes that athletes sometimes lack understanding about what appropriate leadership behaviors for their situation are (i.e., do not know what they should actually prefer) and the leader "may be required to decide for the member" (1993, p. 649). For example, three and four year old soccer players would not know that it is inappropriate to punish players for losing the game. The coach is expected to take the age and motivations of these children into account when making decisions about leadership he/she will engage in. Those expectations would likely be tied to league rules or the parents involved.

The leader's characteristics are thought to directly influence how a leader leads or the actual behaviors he or she will exhibit (Arrow #7). As in the case of the athlete, leader characteristics include such things as ability, personality, experience(s), education, philosophy, values, and background. Moreover, since people are forever changing, as the characteristics of a coach change, the leadership behaviors he/she chooses to engage will necessarily change as well. By way of example, a coach who takes a course on sport psychology and learns (and is convinced of) the value of providing feedback during practice will likely look for ways to increase the feedback being provided to athletes (thus modifying his/her 'actual behavior').

Based on the preceding discussion, what should be evident is that there is considerable interaction between athlete characteristics, situational characteristics, and the leader characteristics. While not necessarily illustrated well in the model, those interactions exist.

Finally, there are important propositions related to *transformational leadership*. The model proposes that transformational leadership will affect the characteristics of the leader (arrow # 11). Although it has been demonstrated that transformational leadership may be taught (e.g., Barling, Weber, & Kelloway, 1996; Dvir, Eden, Avolio, & Shamir, 2002), there has always been the suggestion that transformational leaders exhibit different characteristics than non-transformational leaders. Moreover, transformational leadership will also influence the group/team members (arrow #12) as well as the situation and/or organization (arrow #13). This part of the model "links the notion of transformational leadership to the elements of transactional leadership within the model" (Chelladurai, p. 319). Transformational leaders may influence the *situational characteristics* by introducing a new vision for the organization, which in turn may result in changes to the organizations values, goals, traditions, and even culture. Such leaders are also thought to influence an *athlete's characteristics* (or the characteristics of the group of athletes) by demonstrating confidence in the player's ability to help the team achieve the new vision (generally the leader's vision) and the goals tied to the vision. When the leader is transformational, it is thought that players adjust their personal values and goals to match those of the team, and also believe that they are able to accomplish the tasks/goals required of them (i.e., efficacy).

It is important to note that not all leaders are seen to be transformational. The construct is typically measured using an interval scale (see Multifactor Leadership Questionnaire-MLQ) and therefore suggests that some leaders may exhibit some or all of the characteristics/dimensions of transformational leadership at some level of regularity (e.g., 'not at all' to 'all the time'). The MML proposes that transformational leadership may result in a more effective leader (greater performance, greater satisfaction), but it is not a prerequisite for effective leadership. In the model, transformational leadership plays an indirect role; it influences the antecedents of preferred, actual and required leadership. According to the model, coaches who are not transformational, can (and have been) very effective.

MOVING LEADERSHIP RESEARCH FORWARD

There have been considerable developments in the understanding of leadership in non-sport contexts in the past twenty years. It is worth our while to look at them in a more systematic way within a sport context. Three specific areas are worth examining.

Transformational Leadership

Although incorporated into the MML framework, the view of transformational leadership as a stand-alone model of leadership has been around for some time. This particular view of leadership has dominated the leadership literature for over a quarter century. Recently Hoption, Phelan, and Barling (2007) argued that transformational leadership, as described in the organizational literature, focuses on "the very behaviors that have been observed in sport teams and among the empirical research supporting the effectiveness of transformational leadership" (p. 46) hence, transformational leadership may be an important framework to help us understand leadership in the sport context.

Transformational leadership has always been closely linked with the idea of *charismatic* leadership; a concept first noted by Max Weber. He suggested that charismatic leadership rests on the follower's devotion to "the exceptional sanctity, heroism or exemplary character of an individual person, and of the normative patterns or order revealed or ordained by him" (1925, quoted from Appelrouth & Edles, 2008, p. 175). There exists the idea that followers are attracted to such individuals or the ideas they espouse. What many people consider 'charismatic leaders' exist in sport. For example, Vince Lombardi in American Football, Franz Beckenbauer in German Soccer/Football, and Scotty Bowman in North American Hockey. People (and coaches) are still very attracted to these individuals and the ideals/ideas they espoused.

The modern idea of transformational leadership was first proposed by Burns (1978) but has been largely developed by Bass and his colleagues (e.g., Bass, 1985, 1998; Bass & Avolio, 1994; Bass & Riggio, 2006). It is a popular approach to leadership (i.e., *Full Range Leadership Theory* - Bass & Avolio, 1994). Three basic leadership forms exist: transformational leadership, transactional leadership (leader provides or withholds something of value in exchange for increased performance, etc.), and non-transactional laissez-faire leadership (non-leadership or the absence of leadership).

Transformational leaders are believed to be "proactive, raise follower awareness for transcendent collective interests, and help followers achieve extraordinary goals" (Antonakis, Avolio, & Sivasubramaniam, 2003, p. 264). Rafferty and Griffin (2004) suggest such leaders "motivate followers to achieve performance beyond expectations by transforming follower's attitudes, beliefs, and values as opposed to simply gaining compliance" (p. 330). Bass (1985) suggested that previous leadership theories tended to ignore how leaders might convince those being lead to shift their focus from their own self-interests to the greater good of the organization. Bass' ideas are grounded in the belief that collectively a group can achieve more than the sum of its individual parts. In many ways, what Bass proposed is what coaches constantly do: have individual athletes set aside or align their personal goals and ambitions with those of the team.

When trying to understand what transformational leadership is – or the processes/behaviors that might achieve this 'transformation', it is often best to examine the manner in which transformational leadership has been measured. Bass' instrument (the MLQ – Bass & Avolio, 1995) measures five different dimensions of transformational leadership. *Idealized influence (attributed)* measures whether the leader is seen as confident, powerful, and focused on higher-order ideals and ethics (that leaders is seen as having charisma). *Idealized influence (behavior)* refers to behaviors or actions in which the leader promotes his/her and/or the organization's values, beliefs, mission. These ideals are often seen as being charismatic or attractive.

Inspirational motivation refers to how a leader might use an optimistic view of the future, ambitious goals, a desirable future state, and a belief in the individual(s) or group to achieve the future state in an effort to motivate the group members. By way of example, I (H.A.R.) can still recall how motivating and energized I was as an athlete, when after a particularly devastating loss, one of our coaches came and expressed confidence in our collective ability to still achieve the team's lofty goals, in spite of the uphill battle we would face. I still have warm feelings when I think back to that experience. The team became even more determined to achieve our goal of making the playoffs and this was manifested in greater intensity in practice, training, and games, along with a renewed commitment to work as a single unit. Although we ultimately did not achieve that performance goal it was a significant building block upon which the remainder of that season, along with the following season (a very successful season) was built.

Intellectual stimulation is a transformational behavior in which the leader encourages problem solving in ways that are creative and logical; proactive rather than reactive. Sometimes referred to 'thinking outside of the box', these activities are tied to transformational leadership since such activities transform organizations and individuals over the long term. Finally, *individualized consideration* is not unlike the leadership behavior of *consideration* that grew out of the work at Ohio State in the 1950s. It is tied closely to a person's individual satisfaction because the leader is concerned about members of the team developing as persons and/or their self-actualization. Leaders do this by providing advice and support, and paying attention to or trying to understand what the member's personal goals or ambitions might be.

Although this perspective on leadership is intuitively appealing, it has not been without its critics (cf., Barbuto, 1997; Beyer, 1999). Yet others have proposed alternate ways of defining and measuring the construct. These critics are not suggesting that transformational leadership is not relevant, but rather that our understanding of what transformational leadership is may not be well defined, or even fully realized yet.

Rafferty and Griffin (2004) have suggested that transformational leadership is better defined as including the dimensions of: *vision, inspirational communication, supportive leadership, intellectual stimulation,* and *personal recognition. Vision* is seen as "an expression of an idealized picture of the future based around organizational values" (p. 332). In contrast to charisma, the focus here is on the attractiveness of the goals and the values upon which the goals are built, rather than on the attraction one might have to the leader per se. The concept of vision being an important is not new. There is an Old Testament reference to its role: "Where there is no vision, the people perish" (Proverbs 29: 18 KJ). Giving those we lead an optimistic and ideal view of what the future could be like is important because it encourages group members to continue to move forward and press on. In many respects, a vision is a type of goal and there is considerable evidence of the motivational power that goals (and goal setting) have (has) (Locke & Latham, 2013). While vision certainly has conceptual overlap with some of Bass' proposed constructs, there is value in considering it as an important element of transformational leadership on its own. There is considerable anecdotal evidence of the power that this element of leadership has on people. The famous "I have a dream" speech of Rev. Martin Luther King, Jr. presented a vision for race relations in the United States and helped mobilize an entire generation of people to work toward change.

Inspirational Communication builds on Bass' work that suggests that transformational leaders need to provide inspirational motivation (see previous section). However, in Bass' conceptualization the construct has been defined in various ways (Barbuto, 1997) and there is considerable overlap between vision and inspiration. Rafferty and Griffin argue that there is value in treating these two constructs as unique. Building on the work of Downton (1973), Bass (1985), and Yukl (1981), they note that a recurring theme in definitions of inspiration is "the use of oral communication to motivate and arouse follower's emotions" (p. 332). In a sport context, this element of leadership has been documented in many ways. Certainly the famous 'half-time speech' (that fans are now even able to witness through television broadcasts or similar documentaries – e.g., HBO's 24/7) that result in increased efforts in the second half are part of the sport vocabulary. Every athlete has, at one time or another, been inspired through this form of oral communication. Rafferty and Griffin define this element of leadership as: "the expression of positive and encouraging messages about the organization, and statements that build motivation and confidence" (p. 332). It is worth noting that this definition focuses on 'positive and encouraging' messages. Yet, there may be some evidence that harsh words can provide, at least some short term, changes in behavior as well. I (H.A.R.) recall one athlete telling me she needs to be yelled at in order to motivate her to play better. Regardless, there can be no doubt that this element of leadership is likely a critical one in an athletic leadership context.

Supportive Leadership is defined as "expressing concern for followers and taking account of their individual needs. This element of transformational leadership is essentially the same as Bass' concept of *Individualized Consideration*. This concept has been recognized as an important aspect of leadership over the past 60 years. An organization is really a collection of individuals and while the collective (and collective good) is certainly the focus, there is considerable evidence that effective leaders need to focus on all the individuals that make up that team/group. Given the organic and interdependent nature of teams/groups, when one element of the team is doing poorly, not contributing, or unmotivated, the rest of the group is likely to suffer. One example of this concept is the 'cancer' in the locker-room. That is, one or two team members are in some way dissatisfied and this begins to impact overall performance.

Rafferty and Griffin attempt to better define Bass' original conceptualization of what *Intellectual stimulation* actually is. Lowe, Kroeck, and Sivasubramaniam (1996) see this as an underdeveloped aspect of transformational leadership theory. Rafferty and Griffin build on Bass (1985) and define this element of leadership as: "enhancing employee's interest in, and awareness of problems, and increasing their ability to think about problems in new ways" (p. 333). While the MLQ items focus largely on whether the leader challenges people to think differently about the problem and potential solutions, we would argue that this element of being a transformational leadership also requires a willingness to be more democratic, or at least consultative in the approach to decision making. This requires a certain level of transparency on the part of the leader (i.e., a willingness to share what the problems or challenges might be).

Finally, Rafferty and Griffin attempt to reconcile previous evidence from the transformational leadership literature that suggests a strong connection between the very transactional behaviors of giving praise as a reward in exchange for good performance and transformational leadership (e.g., Hartog, Muijen, & Koopman, 1997; Tepper & Percy, 1994). The act of providing praise for performance, while being a type of transaction, also encompasses elements tied to transforming leadership; rewards are tied to performance or achievement of goals that are connected to the vision of the organization (Goodwin, Wofford, & Whittington, 2001). Achieving or making progress toward the desire future state, and being recognized for it would certainly meet some fundamental needs we all have at the individual level (e.g., Maslow's esteem), and also demonstrate, in a tangible way, the group members important role in helping the team achieving its vision. *Personal Recognition* (defined as "the provision of rewards such as praise and acknowledgement of effort for achievement of specified goals", Rafferty & Griffin, 2004, p. 334) as an element of what is transforming leadership is an important contribution. In a sport context there is certainly evidence that this form of behavior (the LSS calls it *Positive Feedback*) is linked to individual player satisfaction and team satisfaction (e.g., Karreman, Dorsch, & Riemer, 2009) as well as performance.

In either approach to measuring transformational leadership, what should be clear is the relevance and power of transforming leadership in the coaching context. Hoption et al. (2007) provided additional evidence of the intricate connection between transforming leadership and coaching and/or sport leadership by citing relevant examples from the world of professional sport. They also provide compelling arguments for why such behaviors increase the likelihood of desirable individual and organizational outcomes occurring (e.g., performance, attitudes, commitment, cooperation, efficacy, cohesion, satisfaction, etc.). Given what we already know from the organizational context, and what we will find in a sport context as work in this area of leadership progresses, coaches need to look to become more transformational.

Servant Leadership

Potential dangers of transformational leadership have been raised over time. Transformational leaders, in an effort to promote self-interests, may ignore the contributions of team member (Kelley, 1992), result in overly dependent group members (Johnson, 2001), or provide only pseudo empowerment to group members (Ciulla, 1998). Even Bass (1995) noted that it is possible for pseudo-transformational leadership to exist and true transformational leadership must be rooted in altruism, not self-interest. Whetstone (2002) argues that the most "serious weakness of transformational leadership theory, and the danger of its practice, is that it can be so effectively used for immoral ends" (p. 387). Roberts (1987) suggested that Hilter, Napolean, and Atilla the Hun all demonstrated transformational leadership. Whetstone (2002) and others (e.g., Rasmussen, 1995; Sendjaya, Sarros, & Santora, 2008) have suggested a flawed vision, or no concern as to how the vision is achieved, leads to catastrophic outcomes.

In general, Sendjaya et al. (2008) and others (e.g., Einarsen, 1999; Thornthwaite, 2004) have noted that leadership may often result in organizational problems (e.g., abuse of power, unethical or corrupt practices, alienation of individuals, etc.). Sport and athletics has not been immune from these failures of leadership. In the Canadian context, the general manager and coach of an elite hockey team, the Swift Current Broncos of the Western Hockey League, abused his position of leadership and influence to sexually abuse and control young men on this team. More recently, the Penn State football scandal was in the news (Chappell, 2012). These sorts of failures of leadership have resulted in increased interested in more value based approaches to leadership (e.g., Authentic Leadership – Avolio & Gardner, 2005; Spiritual Leadership – Fry, 2003). Whetstone (2002) made a compelling argument that leadership needs to be grounded in the ideology of personalism and that the leadership model that best fits this ideology is Servant Leadership.

Servant leadership, in its modern form, was first proposed by Greenleaf (1977) who was strongly influenced by his reading of Hesse's (1956) *Journey to the East.* A story of how the servant of a group of religious pilgrims becomes their leader. It highlights the paradox of servant-hood and leadership. Greenleaf suggested that leadership "begins with the natural feeling that one wants to serve, to serve first. Then the conscious choice brings one to aspire to lead" (p. 13). Daft and Lengel (2000) note that for such leaders "the desire to serve others takes precedence over the desire to be in a formal leadership position" (p. 176). The Greenleaf Center for Servant Leadership suggests that servant leaders are characterized by listening, empathy, healing, persuasion, self-awareness, foresight, stewardship, commitment to people's development, community building. It is worth noting that the concept of servant leadership is not original to Greenleaf and has often been tied to religious thought (e.g., Eastern traditions such as Hinduism, Judeo-Christian theology, etc.) (Getz, 1984).

Conceptually, Sendjaya et al. (2008) argue there are some key ideas that set servant leadership apart from other forms of transforming leadership models. First, the primary intent of the leader and the leader's self-identity are tied to servant-hood. Second, there is the view that a team's long-term goals (i.e., the vision) will only be realized when the individual group member's growth, development, and needs are looked after. Third, leadership should elevate the ethics and morals of the group member(s). Finally, and most problematic for many who are introduced to the theory, spirituality is an important source of motivation for the servant leader.

While the notion of servant leadership is compelling, it is important to begin to operationalize what such leadership actually looks like in terms of behaviors a servant leader might engage in. This is important for two reasons. First, if we are to evaluate whether servant leadership is as effective as its proponents suggest, then we need some way of measuring the presence of servant leadership in a more objective way. Second, a measurement tool also provides examples (through the items) of specific examples of behaviors that characterize servant leaders. These may be used as the basis for adjusting one's own leadership to become more servant-like.

Recently, Sendjaya et al. (2008) developed just such an instrument (although others have been proposed as well, e.g., Barbuto & Wheeler, 2006; Laub, 2003). They propose that servant leadership consists of six different dimensions: *voluntary submission, authentic self, covenantal relationship, responsible morality, transcendental spirituality,* and *transforming influence.*

Voluntary submission evaluates whether the leader being observed has the attitude of a servant (thinks like a servant) and demonstrates service (acts like a servant). The sub-scale *authentic self* is interested in knowing whether the leader is characterized by integrity and accountability, and demonstrates willingness to be vulnerable (which requires transparency).

Covenantal Relationship is linked to the differences that exist between a covenant and a contract. The basic difference between the two is that in a covenantal relationship one party is committed to the second party regardless of whether the second party reciprocates or is deserving of the commitment. Some marriage vows, for example, have each partner indicate they are committed to the other even if the other is sick, or becomes poor, etc. A contract, allows for a relationship to be dissolved should one party fail to hold up their obligations (e.g., a prenuptial agreement). In the context of leadership it suggests that servant leaders demonstrate acceptance of their team members, are available to them, treat people equally, and collaborate with them even if this behavior is not reciprocated.

Responsible Morality assesses whether a leader's or coach's reasoning, as well as demonstrated actions, may be characterized as moral in nature. That is, does the leader think and do what is right. *Transcendental spirituality* looks at whether the leader has a sense of religiousness, interconnectedness, as well as a sense of mission beyond the immediate goals or objectives. Finally, *transforming influence* includes items that evaluate the leader's vision, modeling and mentoring behavior, the trust they extend to those being lead, and how much the leader actually empowers group members.

The discussion of the role of servant leadership in a sport and athletic context has been essentially non-existent. There is value in the application of this model or framework for coaches, not only for athletes, for sport in general.

Collective Leadership

The most recent discourse in the area of leadership concerns the idea of collectivist leadership (Yammarino, Salas, Serban, Shirreffs, & Shuffler, 2012). Simply put, it is the notion of 'we' leadership versus 'I' leadership. These ideas may be particularly relevant in a sport context since many teams do not have a single leader, but rather a group of leaders who work together to help the team achieve its goals (e.g., a coaching staff). It is defined as "multiple individuals assuming (and perhaps divesting themselves) of leadership roles over time in both formal and informal relationships" (Yammarino et al., 2012, p. 382). Formal relationships here refer to large and small groups, dyads, or even multi-team systems while informal relationships include personal networks within and outside of the group or team. One of the characteristics of this form of leadership is that more traditional power structures (e.g., hierarchical) are be redefined or avoided. Yammarino et al. argue that there are many positive outcomes tied to such leadership (e.g., increased satisfaction, commitment, loyalty, cohesion, performance, etc.) and that leadership must necessarily move in this direction because of the increasing complexity and competitive demands of the operating environment. Such leadership helps minimize the risk of making poor decisions within our ever-changing environment. In fact, professional sport teams have recognized this complexity (and increase in competition) and have moved in collectivist direction. In hockey for example, the coaching staff now includes on ice specialists (e.g., goal tender coach; power-play coach) as well as video coaches.

Different approaches to collectivist leadership include: *Team Leadership* (Day, Gronn, & Salas, 2004), *Network Leadership* (Balkundi & Kilduff, 2005), *Shared Leadership,* and *Complexity Leadership* (Uhl-Bien, Marion, & McKelvey, 2007). This is the new frontier in leadership research and we would suggest are not inconsistent with both transformational leadership and/or servant leadership. Above all, those interested in leadership in a sport context should not ignore this new paradigm shift in the organizational literature.

IMPLICATIONS FOR PRACTICE AND CONCLUSION

Leadership is complex. Leadership is central to sport. Despite its long research history, there are still more questions than answers. Yet, there are things we do know that can help all of us become better coaches or train better coaches. In this chapter, we provided you with an outline of historical and more recent approaches to understanding leadership in an athletic setting. The models/theories we reviewed provide insights that will enhance coaching effectiveness since, as Kurt Lewin (1952, p. 169) suggested, "there is nothing more practical than a good theory".

The MML, and most of its historical foundations, tells us that an effective coach will take into account the individual, the group, the situation, and one's own characteristics. In the chapter we outlined some of the practical implications of considering these various parameters. However, there are some key actions coaches need to take. First, coaches need to understand themselves: what are my leadership strengths, what areas do I struggle with, how do I like to lead, what sorts of qualities/traits do I possess? Taking such a 'self-inventory' is really the first step since much of the literature suggests that some traits/styles/behaviors/ approaches are more effective than others. The question is, how do I do this. While self-reflection is useful, there are many good tools that exist that can provide the coach with information about what sort of leader they are. Rarely do we make use of these for purposes other than research (e.g., training leaders, self-assessment, etc.).

Second, leaders also need to take into account the person(s) they are leading. Practically speaking, in sport we know that most people prefer coaches to focus on providing tools that will assist them in becoming better athletes (or teams), and that we provide them with considerable positive feedback. From the research into transformational theories, we also know that people generally like to have a good view of where it is they are being lead, are motivated when leaders believe in a future that is bright, and want a goal they can identify with or connect to personally. To do this, we must communicate directly with people. While many new methods of communication exist, nothing is as effective and speaking with people face to face. Much can be accomplished, by way of persuasion, if coaches demonstrate interest in the individual this communication. Servant leadership has also suggested that our focus must be on the individual, rather than ourselves.

Finally, coaches must always remember to consider the greater good of the larger organization in which they function. Generally coaches have been placed in the position by some sort of larger organization. Servant leadership suggests that coaches are stewards of the teams and athletes they have been entrusted with. As such, they need to accountable to someone other than themselves. Coaches must always consider whether they, through their work with their particular collections of athletes, are helping the organization accomplish its larger mission.

In conclusion, good and effective coaching really begins with the individual acknowledging that he or she actually knows very little. Like most things in life, it begins with our attitude toward coaching. The best coaches we know are always looking to learn more about how to best lead their group of athletes. They do not believe they know it all. They spend considerable time in self-reflection and use the work of others to inform their own practice. The good news is, in the field of leadership, we already have a lot of information that will make us better coaches. We just need to choose to use it. We trust the chapter provided you with a starting point for key areas to consider working on in your own coaching development.

REFERENCES

Antonakis, J., Avolio, B. J. & Sivasubramaniam, N. (2003). Context and leadership: An examination of the nine-factor full-range leadership theory using the Multifactor Leadership Questionnaire. *The Leadership Quarterly, 14*(3), 261-295.

Appelrouth, S. & Edles, L. D. (2008). *Classical and contemporary sociological theory: Text and readings*. New York: Pine Forge Press.

Avolio, B. J. & Gardner, W. L. (2005). Authentic leadership development: Getting to the root of positive forms of leadership. *The Leadership Quarterly, 16*(3), 315-338.

Balkundi, P. & Kilduff, M. (2006). The ties that lead: A social network approach to leadership. *The Leadership Quarterly, 17*(4), 419-439.

Barbuto, J. E. (1997). Taking the charisma out of transformational leadership. *Journal of Social Behavior and Personality, 12*(3), 689-697.

Barbuto, J. E. & Wheeler, D. W. (2006). Scale development and construct clarification of servant leadership. *Group & Organization Management, 31*, 300-26.

Barling, J., Weber, T. & Kelloway, K. E. (1996). Effects of transformational leadership training on attitudinal and financial outcomes: A field experiment. *Journal of Applied Psychology, 81*, 827-832.

Barrow, J. C. (1977). The variables of leadership: A review and conceptual framework. *Academy of Management Review, 2*, 231-251.

Bass, B. M. (1985). *Leadership and performance beyond expectations*. New York: The Free Press.

Bass, B. M. (1998). *Transformational Leadership: Industrial, military and educational impact*. Mahwah, NJ: Lawrence Erlbaum.

Bass, B. M. & Avolio, B. J. (1994). *Improving organizational effectiveness through transformational leadership*. Thousand Oaks, CA: Sage.

Bass, B. M. & Avolio, B. J. (1995). *MLQ Multifactor leadership questionnaire*. Redwood City, CA: Mind Garden.

Bass, B. M. & Riggio, R. E. (2006). *Transformational leadership*. Mahwah, NJ: Lawrence Erlbaum.

Benjamin, B. & O'Reilly, C. (2011). Becoming a leader: Early career challenges faced by MBA graduates. *Academy of Management Learning & Education, 10*(3), 452-472.

Beyer, J. M. (1999). Taming and promoting charisma to change organizations. *The Leadership Quarterly, 10*(2), 307-330.

Black, J. S. & Porter, L. W. (2000). *Management: Meeting new challenges.* Upper Saddle River, NJ: Prentice-Hall International.

Bryman, A. (1992). *Charisma and leadership in organizations.* London: Sage.

Burns, J. M. (1978). *Leadership.* New York: Harper & Row.

Chan, K. Y. & Drasgow, F. (2001). Toward a theory of individual differences and leadership: understanding the motivation to lead. *Journal of Applied Psychology, 86*(3), 481-498.

Chappell, B. (June 21, 2012). Penn State abuse scandal: *A guide and timeline. National Public Radio.* Retrieved from: http://www.npr.org/2011/11/08/142111804/penn-state-abuse-scandal-a-guide-and-timeline.

Chelladurai, P. (1990). Leadership in sports: A review. *International Journal of Sport Psychology, 21*, 328-354.

Chelladurai, P. (1993). Leadership. In R. N. Singer, M. Murphey, & L. K. Tennant (Eds.), *Handbook on research in sport psychology* (647-671). New York: MacMillan.

Chelladurai, P. (2001). *Managing organizations for sport and physical activity: A systems perspective.* Holcomb Hathaway.

Chelladurai, P. (2005). *Managing organizations for sport and physical activity: A systems perspective.* Scottsdale, AZ: Holcomb Hathaway, Publishers.

Chelladurai, P. & Saleh, S. D. (1980). Dimensions of leader behavior in sports: Development of a leadership scale. *Journal of Sport Psychology, 2*, 34-45.

Ciulla, J. B. (1998). Leadership and the problem of bogus empowerment. In J. B. Ciulla (ed.), *Ethics, the heart of leadership* (63-86). Westpont, CT: Praeger.

Conger, J. A. (1989). *The charismatic leader: Behind the mystique of exceptional leadership.* San Francisco: Jossey-Bass.

Daft, R. L. & Lengel, R. H. (2000). *Fusion leadership: Unlocking the subtle forces that change people and organizations.* San Francisco, CA: Berrett-Koehler.

Day, D. V., Gronn, P. & Salas, E. (2004). Leadership capacity in teams. *The Leadership Quarterly, 15*(6), 857-880.

Doherty, A. J. & Danylchuk, K. E. (1996). Transformational and transactional leadership in interuniversity athletics management. *Journal of Sport Management, 10*(3), 292-309.

Downton, J. V. (1973). *Rebel leadership: Commitment and charisma in revolutionary processes.* New York: The Free Press.

Dvir, T., Eden, D., Avolio, B. J. & Shamir, B. (2002). Impact of transformational leadership on follower development and performance: A field experiment. *Academy of Management Journal, 45*(4), 735-744.

Dweck, C. S. (1986). Motivational processes affecting learning. *American Psychologist, 41*(10), 1040-1048.

Einarsen, S. (1999). The nature and causes of bullying at work. *International Journal of Manpower, 20*, 16-27.

Evans, M. G. (1970). The effects of supervisory behavior on the path-goal relationship. *Organizational behavior and human performance, 5*(3), 277-298.

Fiedler, F. E. (1967). *A theory of leader effectiveness.* New York: McGraw-Hill.

Fisher College of Business. (1962). *Leadership Behavior Description Questionnaire-Form XII Self.* Columbus, OH: Ohio State University.

Fry, L. W. (2003). Toward a theory of spiritual leadership. *The Leadership Quarterly*, *14*(6), 693-727.

Getz, G. A. (1984). *Serving one another*. Wheaton, IL: Victor.

Goodwin, V. L., Wofford, J. C. & Whittington, J. L. (2001). A theoretical and empirical extension to the transformational leadership construct. *Journal of Organizational Behavior*, *22*, 759-774.

Greenleaf, R. K. (1977). *Servant leadership: A journey into the nature of legitimate power and greatness*. NewYork: Paulist Press.

Hackman, J. R. & Oldham, G. (1976). Motivation through the design of work: Test of a theory. *Organizational Behavior and Human Performance*, *16*, 250-279.

Hartog, D. N., Muijen, J. J. & Koopman, P. L. (1997). Transactional versus transformational leadership: An analysis of the MLQ. *Journal of Occupational and Organizational Psychology*, *70*(1), 19-34.

Hemphill, J. K. (1950). *Leader behavior description*. Ohio State University.

Hendricks, J. W. & Payne, S. C. (2007). Beyond the Big Five: Leader goal orientation as a predictor of leadership effectiveness. *Human Performance*, *20*(4), 317-343.

Hesse, H. (1956). *The Journey to the East*. New York: Noonday.

Hoption, C., Phelan, J. & Barling, J. (2007). Transformational leadership in sport. In M. R. Beauchamp & M. A. Eys (eds.), *Group dynamics in exercise and sport psychology: Contemporary themes* (45-60). Champaign, IL: Human Kinetics.

House, R. J. (1971). A path goal theory of leader effectiveness. *Administrative Science Quarterly*, 321-339.

House, R. J. & Dressler, G. (1974). Perceived leadership behavior scales. In W. O. Beardon & R. G. Netemeyer (Eds.), *Handbook of marketing scales* (305-306). Newbury Park: Sage.

Johnson, C. (2001). *Meeting the ethical challenges of leadership*. Thousand Oaks, CA: Sage.

Jones, G. R. (2004). *Organizational theory, design, and change. Text and cases*. Upper Saddle River, NJ: Pearson Prentice Hall.

Judge, T. A., Bono, J. E., Ilies, R. & Gerhardt, M. W. (2002). Personality and leadership: A qualitative and quantitative review. *Journal of Applied Psychology*, *87*(4), 765-780.

Kane, T. (1999). *An examination of the leader's regulation of groups*. Unpublished doctoral dissertation. George Mason University, Fairfax, VA.

Karreman, E., Dorsch, K. & Riemer, H. (2009). Athlete satisfaction and leadership: Assessing group-level effects. *Small Group Research*, *40*(6), 720-737.

Katz, D. & Kahn, R. L. (1966). Organizations and the system concept. *The Social Psychology of Organizations*, *1*, 14-29.

Kellerman, B. (1984). *Leadership: Multidisciplinary perspectives*. Englewood Cliffs, NJ: Prentice-Hall.

Kelley, R. (1992). *The power of followership*. New York: Doubleday/Currency.

Kirkpatick, S. A. & Locke, E. A. (1991). Leadership: Do traits matter?. *The Executive*, *5*(2), 48-60.

Kuhnert, K. W. & Lewis, P. (1987). Transactional and transformational leadership: A constructive/developmental analysis. *Academy of Management Review*, *12*(4), 648-657.

Latham, G. P. & Ernst, C. T. (2006). Keys to motivating tomorrow's workforce. *Human Resource Management Review*, *16*(2), 181-198.

Laub, J. (2003). *From paternalism to the servant organization*. Servant Leadership Research Roundtable, Virginia Beach, VA.

Lewin, K., Lippitt, R. & White, R. K. (1939). Patterns of aggressive behavior in experimentally created "social climates". *The Journal of Social Psychology, 10*(2), 269-299.

Lewin, K. (1952). *Field theory in social science: Selected theoretical papers by Kurt Lewin.* London: Tavistock.

Lippitt, R. & White, R. (1943). The 'social climate' of children's groups. In R. G. Barker, J. Kounin, & H. Wright (Eds.), *Child Behavior and Development* (485–508). New York: McGraw-Hill.

Locke, E. A. & Latham, G. P. (Eds.). (2013). *New developments in goal setting and task performance.* New York: Routledge.

Lord, R. G. & Hall, R. J. (1992). Contemporary views of leadership and individual differences. *The Leadership Quarterly, 3*(2), 137-157.

Lowe, K. B., Kroeck, K. G. & Sivasubramaniam, N. (1996). Effectiveness correlates of transformational and transactional leadership: A meta-analytic review of the MLQ literature. *The Leadership Quarterly, 7*(3), 385-425.

Maslow, A. (1943). A theory of human motivation. *Psychological Review, 50*, 370-396.

Morecroft, J., Sanchez, R. & Heene, A. (2002). Integrating systems thinking and competence concepts in a new view of resources, capabilities, and management processes. In J. Morecroft, R. Sanchez & A. Heene (Eds.), *Systems perspectives on resources, capabilities, and management processes* (3-16). Amsterdam-New York: Pergamon.

Nanus, B. (1992). *Visionary leadership.* San Francisco: Jossey-Bass.

Northouse, P. G. (2007) *Leadership theory and practice.* Thousand Oaks, CA: Sage

Osborn, R. & Hunt, J. (1975). An adaptive-reactive theory of leadership: The role of macro variables in leadership research. In J. Hunt & L. Larson (Eds.), *Leadership Frontiers* (22-47). Kent, OH: Kent State University.

Parks, J. B., Quarterman, J. & Thibault, L. (2007). *Contemporary sport management* (3rd Ed.). Champaign, IL: Human Kinetics Publishers.

Rafferty, A. E. & Griffin, M. A. (2004). Dimensions of transformational leadership: Conceptual and empirical extensions. *The Leadership Quarterly, 15*(3), 329-354.

Rasmussen, T. (1995). Creating a culture of servant-leadership: A real life story. In L. Spears (Ed.), *Reflections on Leadership* (282-297). New York: John Wiley & Sons.

Riemer, H. (2007). Multidimensional Model of Coach Leadership. In S. Jowett & D. Lavallee (Eds.), *Social Psychology in Sport* (57-73). Champaign, IL: Human Kinetics.

Roberts, W. (1987). *Leadership secrets of Attila the Hun.* New York: Warner Books.

Ross, I. C. & Zander, A. (1957). Need satisfactions and employee turnover. *Personnel Psychology, 10*(3), 327-338.

Sashkin, M. (1988). *The visionary leader.* San Francisco: Jossey-Bass.

Sendjaya, S., Sarros, J. C. & Santora, J. C. (2008). Defining and measuring servant leadership behavior in organizations. *Journal of Management Studies, 45*(2), 402-424.

Stogdill, R. M. (1948). Personal factors associated with leadership: A survey of the literature. *The Journal of Psychology, 25*(1), 35-71.

Stogdill, R. M. (1963). *Manual for the leader behavior description questionnaire-Form XII.* Columbus: Ohio State University, Bureau of Business Research.

Tepper, B. J. & Percy, P. M. (1994). Structural validity of the multifactor leadership questionnaire. *Educational and Psychological Measurement, 54*(3), 734-744.

Thornthwaite, L. (2004). Working time and work-family balance: A review of employees' preferences. *Asia Pacific Journal of Human Resources*, *42*, 166-84.

Trow, D. B. (1957). Autonomy and job satisfaction in task-oriented groups. *The Journal of Abnormal and Social Psychology*, *54*(2), 204-209.

Uhl-Bien, M., Marion, R. & McKelvey, B. (2007). Complexity leadership theory: Shifting leadership from the industrial age to the knowledge era. *The Leadership Quarterly*, *18*(4), 298-318.

Vroom, V. H. (1959). Some personality determinants of the effects of participation. *The Journal of Abnormal and Social Psychology*, *59*(3), 322-327.

Vroom, V. H. (1964). *Work and motivation*. New York: Wiley.

Waring, G. F. (1996). Industry differences in the persistence of firm-specific returns. *The American Economic Review*, *86*(5), 1253-1265.

Whetstone, J. T. (2002). Personalism and moral leadership: The servant leader with a transforming vision. *Business Ethics: A European Review*, *11*(4), 385-392.

Yammarino, F. J., Dubinsky, A. J., Comer, L. B. & Jolson, M. A. (1997). Women and transformational and contingent reward leadership: A multiple-levels-of-analysis perspective. *Academy of Management Journal*, *40*(1), 205-222.

Yammarino, F. J., Salas, E., Serban, A., Shirreffs, K. & Shuffler, M. L. (2012). Collectivistic leadership approaches: Putting the "we" in leadership science and practice. *Industrial and Organizational Psychology*, *5*(4), 382-402.

Yukl, G. (1971). Toward a behavioral theory of leadership. *Organizational Behavior and Human Performance*, *6*, 414-440.

Yukl, G. A. (1981). *Leadership in organizations*. Englewood Cliffs, NJ: Prentice-Hall

Yukl, G. (1999). An evaluation of the conceptual weaknesses in transformational and charismatic leadership theories. *The Leadership Quarterly*, *10*, 285-309.

In: Positive Human Functioning …   ISBN: 978-1-62948-974-2
Editors: A. R. Gomes, R. Resende & A. Albuquerque   © 2014 Nova Science Publishers, Inc.

Chapter 8

LEADERSHIP AND POSITIVE HUMAN FUNCTIONING: A TRIPHASIC PROPOSAL

A. Rui Gomes
Department of Applied Psychology, School of Psychology,
University of Minho, Portugal

ABSTRACT

This chapter addresses the topic of leadership by proposing the Triphasic Model of Leadership Efficacy. The model explains leadership efficacy by suggesting that the best results achieved by the leaders result from a congruent hypothesis that congregates a conceptual cycle of leadership (that includes the elements of leadership philosophy, leadership practice, and leadership criteria) and a practical cycle of leadership (that includes the elements of leadership philosophy, leadership in practice, and leadership criteria). The model also reinforces the importance of considering the antecedent factors of leadership (e.g., situational, leader, and members' characteristics) as possible mediators of the leadership process (which includes the conceptual and practical cycles). The advantages of using the triphasic process of action instead of a tripartite process of leadership that use erratic and non-linear forms of relationships between the leadership philosophy, the leadership in practice, and the leadership criteria are also discussed. Finally, the chapter presents possibilities of testing the triphasic model and discusses implications to the training of leaders according this proposal.

INTRODUCTION

Assuming the role of a leader is a very fascinating and demanding task, not only given the responsibility of influencing other people towards a certain mission and goals but also because this activity is becoming more and more demanding. In the business world, it is common to have several competitors in the same market fighting for the best profit while dealing with scarce resources. In this way, the role of the leaders is a very important one because, depending on their actions, organizations can survive and prosper or may enter a recession and sometimes go out of business.

In this way, it is interesting to know what factors can contribute to the success of leaders. This chapter addresses this topic by proposing the Triphasic Model of Leadership Efficacy that intends to explain the leaders' efficacy by considering a linear relation among three main factors: the ideas/principles/goals of the leader (leadership philosophy), the behaviors assumed by the leader in order to accomplish the valued ideas/principles/goals (leadership practice), and the indicators used by the leaders in order to evaluate the implementation of the leadership philosophy (leadership criteria). This set of factors was selected because they best represent the processes implicated in the leader's actions, establishing a relationship between what is important for them (leadership philosophy), what can be done to concretize the intended ideas/principles/goals (leadership practice), and what sources of evaluation can be defined in order to monitor the acceptation of the ideas/principles/goals by team members (leadership criteria). By acting in an integrated way, the triphasic model assumes that leaders can accomplish their mission in a better way. This will be the main idea defended in this chapter. First, the main principles of the triphasic model are presented. The discussion then progresses into an explanation of the dimensions of the model. In the final part, the differences between the triphasic and tripartite processes of leadership are discussed and implications for the promotion of leaders actuating in a triphasic process are presented.

TRIPHASIC MODEL OF LEADERSHIP EFFICACY

There are some main prepositions of the triphasic model that should be described now because they will be the basis for explaining this proposal later in the chapter.

- The model is called triphasic because it proposes a linear relationship between the leadership philosophy (e.g., ideas, principles, and goals about leadership and being a leader), the leadership practice (e.g., the behaviors assumed by the leader), and the leadership criteria (e.g., indicators used by the leader to evaluate his or her leadership).
- Two interdependent cycles of leadership process are proposed: (a) the conceptual cycle where the leader defines how to act and how to evaluate their actions taking into consideration the ideas/principles/goals about leadership; and (b) the practical cycle where the leader and team members implement the conceptual cycle of leadership.
- From the conceptual cycle to the practical cycle, feedback loops of information and communication between the leader and team members occur that indicate the course of the leadership process. That is, the feedback loops give information to the leader and team members as to how they are progressing in implementing the conceptual cycle in a daily basis of working together.
- The model proposes that linear processes of leadership both at the conceptual and practical cycles correspond to higher leadership efficacy. However, the best results achieved by the leader happen when there is a relationship between the conceptual cycle ("what should be done") and the conceptual cycle ("what really is done"); this

is called the congruence hypothesis. In simple words, the best leadership efficacy occurs when the leader is able to integrate the leadership philosophy into the routines of team members.

- Antecedent factors related to situational characteristics, leader characteristics, and member characteristics can influence the process of leadership of the triphasic model; thus, they should assume the statute of moderator variables between the conceptual cycle of leadership and the practical cycle of leadership.
- The leadership efficacy can be measured by using subjective and objective measures of team members functioning. Both represent useful indicators of the success achieved by the leader in implementing his or her philosophy.

Figure 1 presents these central aspects of the triphasic model that will now be discussed in the chapter.

Antecedent Factors

The most important aspect regarding antecedent factors is that the leader's behavior does not occur in a vacuum. According the triphasic model, three factors can influence the leadership process and the actions assumed by the leader (e.g., situational, leader, and members' characteristics) (see Figure 1). Some conceptual approaches of leadership have addressed these factors, namely, the importance of leader characteristics at the intellectual, psychological, and physical levels (for a review see Vroom & Jago, 2007 and Zaccaro, 2007), the importance of congruence between the leader's styles of action and the characteristics of the subordinates and the work setting (for example see House, 1971), and the importance of the external conditions that leaders have to face by adopting task-motivated or relationship-motivated leadership styles (for example see Fiedler, 1967). In an application to sport contexts, the multidimensional model of leadership (Chelladurai, 2007), the mediational model of leadership (Smith & Smoll, 1996), and the working model of coaching effectiveness (Horn, 2008) have also recognized the importance of these factors. Together, the triphasic model posits the need to consider the situational characteristics (e.g., the organizational goals and expectations regarding the work of the leader, the level and types of demands faced by the organization where the leader operates), the personal characteristics of the leader (e.g., his or her goals, beliefs, and values as an individual, his or her personal resources), and the characteristics of the team members (e.g., sex, age, level of expertise). It is not possible to address each of these factors in this chapter (for a review see Bass, 2008), but the most important point is that they all represent aspects that can influence the leader's behaviors and, as will be explained later, they can moderate the relationship between the conceptual and practical domains of the Triphasic Model of Leadership Efficacy.

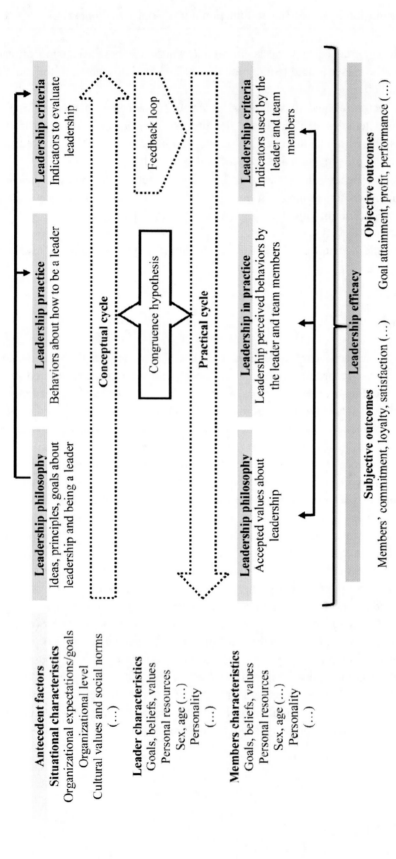

Figure 1. Triphasic model of leadership efficacy.

Conceptual Cycle of Leadership Process

The conceptual cycle of leadership process includes mental representations of the leader in three domains: (a) the leadership philosophy (e.g., the beliefs of the leader regarding what it means be a leader); (b) the leadership practice (e.g., the beliefs of the leader regarding how to assume the role of a leader); and (c) the leadership criteria (e.g., the beliefs of the leader regarding how to evaluate his or her role as a leader) (see Figure 1).

The leadership philosophy includes structural ideas, principles, and goals assumed by the leader regarding what describes his or her leadership practice and role as a leader. Examples of leadership philosophy include, among many others: (a) the need of compromise with hard work and high quality standards by the team members; (b) the need to value the interests of the team above individual interests; and (c) the importance of personal sacrifice in order to achieve the goals of team. The leadership philosophy is characterized by mental representations of the leader and what he or she believes to be the main principles that characterize his or her actions as a leader.

The leadership practice includes all behaviors and actions that the leader thinks can better represent the leadership philosophy. Considering the previous examples of leadership philosophy, the leadership practice could include: (a) being a role model for the team members in aspects related to giving maximum effort in the tasks to be completed; (b) defining and trying to achieve team goals instead of individual goals; and (c) doing what is necessary to accomplish the mission of the team. The leadership practice is characterized by mental representations of the leader regarding how to implement the main ideas and principles about leadership.

The leadership criteria includes the assessment tools used by the leader in order to know if the behaviors assumed to implement the leadership philosophy are indeed producing the desired effects. Considering again the previous examples of leadership philosophy and leadership practice, the leadership criteria could include: (a) the number of tasks performed with high quality standards, (b) the number of team goals achieved by the team; and (c) the number of extra days of work performed by the team members whenever it is necessary to complete an urgent task. The leadership criteria is characterized by mental representations of the leader about the indicators that can be used in order to know if the leadership philosophy is producing the desirable effect on team members. The leadership criteria should not be confounded with the outcomes proposed in the leadership efficacy of the triphasic model; the former relates to each criteria adopted by the leader in order to evaluate the leadership philosophy and subsequent behaviors, while the latter is related to all subjective and objective outcomes observed in team members due to the actions of the leader.

Practical Cycle of Leadership Process

The practical cycle of the leadership process initiates after the conceptual cycle and includes mental representations of the leader and team members in three domains: (a) the leadership philosophy (e.g., the beliefs of the leader and team members regarding what means to be a leader, which can represent accepted values about leadership); (b) the leadership in practice (e.g., the beliefs of the leader and team members regarding how to assume the role of a leader); and (c) the leadership criteria (e.g., the beliefs of the leader and team members regarding how to evaluate the role of the leader) (see Figure 1). The main difference between the conceptual and practical cycles is the fact that the first one is related to the "design" of the processes of leadership by the leader (i.e., what is leadership? How to be a leader? How to evaluate leadership?), while the second one is the "leadership in action" on a daily basis of the leader-team members relationship (i.e., what principles are enunciated by the leader to group members, and how are they perceived by group members? What actions are assumed by the leader in order to implement the principles of leadership, and how are they perceived by group members? What indicators are assumed by the leader in order to evaluate the principles and behaviors of leadership, and how are they perceived by group members?).

In practical terms, the leader enunciates his or her ideas/principles/goals to team members (e.g., leadership philosophy), how to achieve the leadership philosophy (e.g., leadership in practice), and how to evaluate the leadership philosophy (e.g., leadership criteria). This process can be formal (i.e., defined meetings, memos, and other ways to pass the message to the team members) or informal (i.e., on a daily basis by the personal contact between the leader and the members of the team). However, the main aspect is that there is an idea/principle/goal to be achieved, there is a course of action as to how to achieve the idea/principle/goal, and there is at least one indicator to evaluate the achievement of the idea/principle/goal. The practical cycle begins at the moment where both the leader and the team members assume the behaviors in order to achieve the idea/principle/goal that produces a certain result (e.g., leadership criteria). This is why in the practical cycle it is called "leadership *in* practice" while in the conceptual cycle it is called "leadership practice". The final result is a reflection on the leadership philosophy, meaning that if the conceptual cycle was a good one that produced a positive result (e.g., leadership criteria), then there are more chances that the idea/principle/goal will turn into an accepted value regarding how to exert the power of leadership. If this process does not succeed, then there are fewer chances of finishing the leadership cycle by accepting that form of leadership. This interrelation between the conceptual and practical cycles in the triphasic model is called the "feedback loop", meaning that there is a relationship between what the leader thinks should be done (conceptual cycle) and what happens when trying to implement the leadership philosophy on a daily basis (practical cycle) (see Figure 1). Those processes are not totally independent; they influence each other producing feedback loops along the relationship between the leader and the team members. Figure 2 presents an example of a successful feedback loop and of a congruence hypothesis, which will be discussed now.

The Congruence Hypothesis

The triphasic model proposes a linear relationship between the three dimensions of the conceptual cycle: the leadership philosophy will influence the leadership practice and the leadership criteria. Then, in regard to implementing the conceptual cycle, both the leadership in practice and the leadership criteria will produce certain values about leadership through the feedback loops. This is the mechanism that explains the complete process of leadership sustained in the triphasic model.

Conceptual domain		
Leadership philosophy	**Leadership practice**	**Leadership criteria**
Leader: *For me, it is very important that each member of the team be involved in important aspects of our work to do. In fact, involvement is the first condition to compromise toward our mission!*	Leader: *Better compromise with the work to do can be achieved by scheduling weekly meetings in order to hear the opinions of each member of the team about important aspects of the tasks to be done.*	Leader: *In order to know if team members are becoming more involved in the decision-making process, I can make registrations of the type and number of decisions made by the team across time.*

Congruence hypothesis

Feedback loop

Leader: *I felt that the team approved the meeting and liked to participate in the decisions to be made. In fact, involvement resulted in higher compromise toward our mission!* Team members: *We appreciate this decision of the leader to involve all of us in the tasks to be done and in the resolution of the problems that we face as a team.*	Leader and team members: *Every week, we discuss the opinions about important aspects of the tasks to be done. The leader starts by presenting the tasks to be done, hears the opinion of each team member, and then also gives an opinion. We finalized the meeting by taking the decisions about what tasks should be done and anticipating possible problems during task accomplishment.*	Leader: *I make a weekly registration of the type and number of decisions made by the team and I inform every team member each month about the decisions that were made by us. Then, I can compare the results across time.* Team members: *We can consult the registrations of decisions made by us every month, giving a better idea of the decisions we made as a team.*
Leadership philosophy	**Leadership practice**	**Leadership criteria**
Practical domain		

Figure 2. Example of a successful feedback loop and of a congruence hypothesis.

The question is whether this leadership process can be related to different results obtained by the leaders. In this case, the triphasic model advances three main propositions:

- Proposition 1: leaders will achieve higher efficacy when they adopt a conceptual cycle of leadership, connecting their philosophy of leadership TO specific behaviors and TO specific indicators to evaluate leadership. From a empirical point of view,

leaders can increase efficacy when they assume a relationship between the leadership
philosophy, the leadership practice, and the leadership criteria at a conceptual level.

- Proposition 2: leaders will achieve higher efficacy when they adopt a practical cycle
  of leadership, connecting their philosophy of leadership TO specific behaviors and
  TO specific indicators to evaluate leadership. From a empirical point of view, leaders
  can increase efficacy when they assume a relationship between the leadership
  philosophy, the leadership in practice, and the leadership criteria at a practical level.
- Proposition 3: the higher efficacy is achieved when there is a relationship between
  the conceptual and practical cycles of leadership, implying that the leader is
  succeeding in implementing the conceptual cycle of leadership in the practical cycle
  of leadership. If the leader is able to transform the philosophy of leadership into
  practical terms that in turn reinforce the values about leadership, then it has achieved
  the congruence hypothesis (see Figure 1).

Leadership Efficacy

Studies regarding the impact of leadership have generally focused on analyzing the
leaders' impact in subjective measures (e.g., follower satisfaction) and objective measures
(e.g., profit and organization productivity). It is not possible to describe all results about this
topic in this chapter, but it is interesting to note that more studies exist regarding the impact of
leadership using subjective measures than using objective measures (for a review see Kaiser,
Hogan, & Craig, 2008). Despite this aspect, in the triphasic model, the efficacy of leaders can
also be measured by using subjective measures, evaluating, for example, the members'
commitment and loyalty towards the mission and goals of the team/organization and by using
objective measures evaluating, for example, the members' goal attainment and contributions
to the profit and performance of the team/organization (see Figure 1). As discussed in the
congruence hypothesis, it is proposed that the best outcomes both at subjective and objective
levels are achieved when the conceptual and practical cycles are joined together in a unit that
reinforces common values related to leadership.

Testing the Triphasic Model of Leadership Efficacy

Despite the possible interest of the triphasic model, the most important aspect is to
analyze its validity in regard to explaining the efficacy of leadership. It becomes important to
test the proposed propositions by using samples of leaders and team members. This can be
done by using qualitative and quantitative methodologies. For example, by using interview
guides directed for leaders, they can be asked to specify their philosophy as leaders (e.g.,
"Can you describe your most important ideas/principles/goals as a leader?"), their leadership
practice (e.g., "Can you explain to me how do you implement the ideas/principles/goals that
you just described?"), and their leadership criteria ("Can you refer what type of indicators you
use to evaluate the achievement of your ideas/principles/goals?"). Data may then be
compared with the perspective of team members by asking about the philosophy of the leader
("Can you describe the most important ideas/principles/goals of your leader?"), the leadership

in practice (e.g., "Can you explain to me how your leader and team implement the ideas/principles/goals that you just described?"), and the leadership criteria ("Can you refer what type of indicators your leader and team use to evaluate the achievement of the described ideas/principles/goals?").

One last question for both the leaders and team members concerns the accepted values related to the leadership philosophy (e.g., leader: "Do you think this way of action reinforced your leadership? How?"; team members: "Do you think this way of action reinforced the leadership of the leader? How?"). Data can be compared by observing the exercise of leadership in specific contexts and determining whether the feedback loops occur. Finally, subjective and objective measures of leadership efficacy can be used to analyze whether the occurrence of the three proposed propositions (particularly the third one, related to the congruence hypothesis) have an effect on the team members.

Quantitative methodologies can also be used to test the triphasic model; however, the lack of specific measures that evaluate the process of leadership (e.g., leadership philosophy, leadership practice, and leadership criteria) both from the perspective of leaders and team members can prove difficult at this moment to test the propositions of the model. Future research should address this aspect.

Finally, the design of studies can also include measures of the antecedent factors described in the triphasic model. It can be hypothesized that aspects related to organizational expectations/goals (i.e., situational characteristics), the personality of the leader (i.e., leader characteristics), and the sex and age of the team members (i.e., members' characteristics), to name a few, can influence the conceptual and practical cycles of leadership. Thus, they can assume the statute of moderator variables in the study of the triphasic model. For example, a certain leader may have a set of principles related to hard work of team members in order to produce the best products on the market. However, if their organization does not have sufficient resources to accomplish this goal, it may be impossible to compete with other organizations with superior capacity to provide the necessary work conditions. Thus, the leader may have to adapt the leadership philosophy by defining other standards of achievement to the team members.

WHAT ABOUT THE REALITY? THE TRIPARTITE MODEL

At this point, readers may question whether the reality of daily functioning of the leaders and team members is determined by the sequential occurrence of the conceptual and practical cycles. Despite the need of obtaining more data in order to confirm the triphasic model, it is quite possible that, instead of this triphasic process, there is a tripartite process in the leader-team members' relationship. In this latter case, the leadership process does not follow a linear sequence (that it is believed to leave to the best results in terms of leadership efficacy), but assumes an individualistic, erratic, and compartmentalized process between the three dimensions of leadership (e.g., philosophy, practice, and criteria). The relationship between the leadership philosophy and the leadership practice follows a reciprocal influence; it may be that the leadership practice determines the leadership philosophy (while the opposite is true in the triphasic model). The same reciprocal relationship occurs between the leadership philosophy and the leadership criteria. Again, it may be that the results achieved in the leadership criteria determine the leadership philosophy (while the opposite is true in the triphasic model).

One factor that may contribute to this tentative process of assuming leadership in the tripartite model may be related to difficulties of the leaders in reflecting on what it means to be a leader (e.g., formal knowledge) and how to transpose a certain leadership philosophy into practical terms (e.g., formal training). Given these difficulties, leaders tend to rely mainly on "trial and error" strategies of learning and action. This is not to say that leaders who typically engage in the triphasic process of leadership do not use "trial and error" strategies, as they certainly do use such strategies. In fact, we all use these strategies in our relationships with external conditions of living. The major difference may be how much the leader depends on these "trial and error" strategies. Some years ago, I was giving a training session on sport psychology to coaches. The discussion turned to the specific aspects of the coaches' philosophy in regard to training young and adult athletes. My point was to defend a scheme of coaches' actions that could include the described relationship between philosophy-practice-criteria that could be used in both contexts, after doing the necessary adaptations. At this moment, a coach interrupted me and said "well, all of that is interesting, but it's just theory! My philosophy is *if it works I will repeat; if doesn't work I will not repeat again*". For this coach, the leadership philosophy and leadership practice are determined by "trial and error" strategies; more than to discussing how the coach should be a leader and how he should behave, it matters if the result is the intended one. Thus, the leadership criteria constrain both the philosophy and the practice in this case.

In this way, what changes between the triphasic and tripartite models is the sequence and direction of the arrows that link the all process of leadership; thus, in the tripartite model, this relation tends to be bidirectional between the leadership dimensions, as explained below.

Leadership Philosophy ↔ Leadership Practice

The interchange between leadership philosophy and leadership practice is visible when leaders assume that leadership is mainly a process that derives from practice. More important than reflexive processes related to the ideas/principles/goals that sustain the leadership action and formal processes of learning how to lead teams is the long and fruitful contact with the practice of leadership that will sustain and develop the philosophy of leadership. The leadership philosophy is "good" or "bad" if it can or cannot be applied with success to each organizational context. The motto is "Practice makes the leader", meaning that "trial and error" strategies are used in the process of learning the way to exert the leadership action. The consequence is that leaders tend to resist abandoning standardized ways of thinking and acting because they were useful in the past. Sometimes it is habitual to observe in the discourse of these leaders sentences such as "I found the *magic* formula to resolve the problem" or "My feeling says that this should be the correct action"; these statements are difficult to explain and to justify why they are assumed.

Leadership Philosophy ↔ Leadership Criteria

The interchange between leadership philosophy and leadership practice is visible when leaders assume that leadership is "effective" or "ineffective" depending on the final results. Again, more important than reflexive processes related to the ideas/principles/goals that sustain the leadership action and formal processes of learning how to lead teams is the results achieved by the leader and by the team members that will dictate if the leadership philosophy is the right one. The leadership philosophy is "good" or "bad" if it leads to success or failure in each organizational context. The motto is "If it works don't fix it", meaning that leading well or leading poorly is evaluated according to the result obtained. The leader's performance will be evaluated according to the final result and the leadership philosophy can change suddenly as things go well or poorly for the leader and for the team members. The consequence is that leaders have a distanced perspective regarding ethical principles of how the leadership role should be assumed; thus, acceptable behaviors can be sacrificed in order to achieve the desired results.

Overall, the main difference between triphasic and tripartite processes of leadership relates to the way leadership is implemented. The triphasic model proposes that the leadership practice and leadership criteria should be defined by considering the leadership philosophy of each leader, while these processes follow a non-linear relationship in regard to the tripartite model. It is proposed that the best results are achieved in the case of leaders that use triphasic processes of leadership while leaders that use tripartite processes of leadership remain less effective due to their erratic and circumstantial forms of leading individuals and teams.

KEY POINTS TO PROMOTE POSITIVE HUMAN FUNCTIONING

Due to the interest in having leaders with triphasic processes of leadership, it becomes important to discuss the practical implications of their training.

- Leaders have main advantages of comprehending how antecedent factors of leadership can be integrated in the leadership philosophy. Instead of "refusing" the influence of antecedent factors or "changing" the leadership philosophy according external demands, leaders should be encouraged to find ways of integrating both factors in a harmonious way of action.
- The leadership philosophy represents the structural dimension of the leader's action. In this way, leaders should have sufficient knowledge regarding conceptual and technical aspects of the work, knowledge regarding values and norms of being a leader in each specific context, and knowledge regarding what they want and desire as leaders. Instead of presenting to team members sophisticated ideas about leadership philosophy, leaders should present simple, challenging, and acceptable ideas to their team members.
- The leadership (in) practice identifies how the leader behaves in the relationship with others. The biggest challenge to leaders is how to determine specific actions in order to implement the leadership philosophy. Leaders should know how to actuate in regard to implementing each idea/principle/goal among the team members.

- The leadership criteria should be directed at evaluating the specific actions that intend to implement the leadership philosophy. Leaders should know how to define useful and realistic indicators that give each team member the feedback of how he or she is progressing along with the process of performance.
- Leaders should try to achieve the maximum relationship between what they define from a conceptual point of view and what they do from a practical point of view. This will increase the chances of obtaining the congruence hypothesis.
- Finally, leaders should use subjective and objective measures in a parsimonious way to evaluate their efficacy as leaders. Instead of relying on "feelings" of success or failure, leaders should use specific indicators of the impact produced by the leadership activity among team members.

CONCLUSION

Leadership is a very demanding activity, not only because it implies considering a broad set of dimensions that influence the final result (e.g., the situation, the leader, and the team members) but also because leaders operate in increasingly demanding environments; thus, it is important to identify the factors that may contribute to their efficacy. The Triphasic Model of Leadership Efficacy addresses the important topic of leadership efficacy, reinforcing the need of integrating the leader's philosophy, the leader's behaviors, and the leader's indicators of success into a conceptual and practical process of leadership. However, only future research can confirm the interest of this proposal, namely, the advantages that leaders may have by achieving a congruence between what they "intend to do" (conceptual cycle) and what they (and team members) really do (practical cycle).

REFERENCES

Bass, B. M. (2008). Bass handbook of leadership: Theory, research & managerial applications (4th Ed.). New York: The Free Press.

Chelladurai, P. (2007). Leadership in sports. In G. Tenenbaum & R. C. Eklund (eds.), Handbook of sport psychology (3rd ed., pp. 113-135). Hoboken, New Jersey: John Wiley & Sons.

Fiedler, F. E. (1967). *A theory of leadership effectiveness.* New York. McGraw Hill.

Horn, T. S. (2008). Coaching effectiveness in the sport domain. In T. S. Horn (Ed.), *Advances in sport psychology* (3rd ed., pp. 239-267). Champaign, IL: Human Kinetics.

House, R. J. (1971). A path-goal theory of leader effectiveness. *Administrative Science Quarterly,* 16(3), 321-328.

Kaiser, R. B., Hogan, R., & Craig, S. B. (2008). Leadership and the fate of organizations. *American Psychologist,* 63(2), 96-110.

Smith, R. E., & Smoll, F. L. (1996). The coach as a focus of research and interventions in youth sports. In F. L. Smoll & R. E. Smith (Eds.), Children and youth in sport. *A Biopsychosocial perspective* (pp. 125-141). Madison, WI: Brown & Benchmark.

Vroom, V. H., & Jago, A. G. (2007). The role of the situation in leadership. *American Psychologist,* 62(1), 17-24.

Zaccaro, S. J. (2007). Trait-based perspectives of leadership. *American Psychologist*, 62(1), 6-16.

ABOUT THE EDITORS

A. Rui Gomes

Department of Applied Psychology, School of Psychology, University of Minho, Portugal.
rgomes@psi.uminho.pt

Rui Gomes is an Assistant Professor in the School of Psychology at the University of Minho, Portugal. He performs research on two main areas: sport/exercise psychology (e.g., leadership, stress, psychological benefits of exercise, life skills training) and occupational stress (e.g., sources and consequences of stress in high-risk activities, impact of cognitive appraisal on human adaptation to stress). Currently, he leads the research group Adaptation, Performance and Human Development, which was created in 2007 (http://www.ardh-gi.com/). As a sport psychologist, he consults athletes and their families, coaches, and sport managers. Currently, he is the sport psychologist of the Bocce National Team.

Rui Resende

Maia Institute of Higher Education, Portugal.
rresende@ismai.pt

Rui Resende is an Assistant Professor at the Maia Institute of Higher Education. He does research mainly in Coach Education. Presently, he is the Coordinator of the Master's program in Sports Performance and leads the investigative research line "Coaching and Education" in the research group Adaptation, Performance and Human Development. He was a volleyball athlete who won several national titles. He coached teams at the high competition level in Portugal and was also the junior national coach of the Portuguese team.

Alberto Albuquerque
Maia Institute of Higher Education, Portugal.
aalbuquerque@ismai.pt
Alberto Albuquerque is an Assistant Professor at the Maia Institute of Higher Education. His main area of research focuses on the factors involved in the education and training of physical education teachers. Currently, he is the coordinator of the Masters in Teaching Physical Education and the Supervised Teaching Practice.

He is a member of the Research Center in Sports Sciences, Health and Human Development, the Research Center in Sport and Physical Activity, and the research group Adaptation, Performance and Human Development.

He is co-founder and Chairman of the General Assembly of the Scientific Society of Sport Pedagogy. He is a member of the Portuguese Society of Physical Education and the Center for Continuous Education of the Maia Institute of Higher Education.

He collaborates as a reviewer with several international journals in the field of pedagogy.

ABOUT THE CONTRIBUTORS

Preface

Kennon M. Sheldon
Department of Psychology, University of Missouri, Columbia. USA.
SheldonK@missouri.edu

Ken Sheldon is a Professor of Social-Personality Psychology at the University of Missouri-Columbia. His primary research interests concern goals, motivation, creativity, and psychological well-being. He is also active in the "positive psychology" movement, having received a Templeton Prize in 2002 for his contributions to this emerging field. He has written six books, and more than 150 peer-reviewed articles. He pursues backpacking, photography, and tennis in his spare time.

Chapter 1

Mihaly Csikszentmihalyi
School of Behavioral and Organizational Sciences. Claremont Graduate University. USA.

miska@cgu.edu

Mihaly Csikszentmihalyi was born in Fiume, Italy (now Rijeka, Croatia), to Hungarian parents. He left Italy in 1956 to study in the United States. He received a PhD in Human Development from the University of Chicago in 1965, and started teaching at a nearby college. During this time, he developed the basic model of the flow experience.

In 1970 Mihaly was called back to the University of Chicago, where he became Chair of the Department of Psychology.

In 1999 he accepted an offer to teach at the Claremont Graduate University in California, where he started the first doctoral program in Positive Psychology.

Chapter 2

David J. Hancock

School of Kinesiology and Health Studies, Queen's University. Kingston, Ontario. Canada.

David Hancock, PhD, was a Post-Doctoral Fellow at Queen's University and is now an Assistant Professor in Allied Health Sciences at Indiana University Kokomo. David's main research focus is on talent development and expertise in sport, examining athletes, coaches, officials, and parents.

Jean Côté

School of Kinesiology and Health Studies, Queen's University. Kingston, Ontario. Canada.

jc46@queensu.ca

Jean Côté, PhD, is the Director of the School of Kinesiology and Health Studies at Queen's University. Jean is particularly interested in studying how social agents (e.g., coaches and parents) can facilitate positive youth development in sport, both in recreational and elite sport.

Chapter 3

Tripp Driskell

Institute for Simulation and Training. University of Central Florida. USA.
Tripp Driskell is a doctoral candidate in the Applied Experimental and Human Factors program at the University of Central Florida. He received his MS in human factors from Embry-Riddle Aeronautical University.

Eduardo Salas

Institute for Simulation and Training. University of Central Florida. USA.
esalas@ist.ucf.edu
Eduardo Salas is the Pegasus Professor of Psychology and university Trustee Chair at the University of Central Florida where he also holds an appointment as Program Director for the Human Systems Integration Research Department at the Institute for Simulation and Training. Dr. Salas has co-authored over 450 journal articles & book chapters and has co-edited 25 books. He received his PhD in industrial and organizational psychology from Old Dominion University in 1984.

Chapter 4

Robert Weinberg

Department of Kinesiology and Health. Miami University. Oxford, OH. USA.
weinber@muohio.edu

Robert S. Weinberg, PhD is a professor in the department of Kinesiology and Health at Miami University. His peers voted him one of the top 10 sport psychologists in North America. He is past-president of two of the major scholarly and applied sport psychology associations. He has written 8 books, over 140 scholarly articles, over 40 book chapters and has been as a keynote speaker in many countries. He is a certified consultant and has consulted with hundreds of athletes of all ages and abilities.

Chapter 5

Stewart Vella

Educational Research Institute, Faculty of Education. University of Wollongong. Australia.
Dr. Stewart Vella is Postdoctoral Research Fellow in the Interdisciplinary Educational Research Institute at the University of Wollongong, Australia. He completed his PhD by exploring the impact of coach leadership on positive youth development through sport. His research interests span the domains of sports medicine, sports coaching, coach education, and developmental psychology. In recent times, he has worked to apply implicit theories of sporting ability to the coaching domain.

Wade Gilbert

California State University, Fresno. USA.
wgilbert@csufresno.edu
Dr. Wade Gilbert is a Professor in the Department of Kinesiology at California State University, Fresno. He co-edited the Routledge Handbook of Sports Coaching and currently serves as the Co-Editor for the International Sports Coaching Journal and the Journal of Sport Psychology in Action. Dr. Gilbert consults widely with coaches and youth sport organizations, and serves as a scientific advisor for BeLikeCoach, a US-based non-profit dedicated to improving the quality of youth sport settings.

Chapter 6

Gordon A. Bloom

Department of Kinesiology and Physical Education. McGill University. Montreal, Quebec. Canada.

gordon.bloom@mcgill.ca

Dr. Gordon Bloom is an Associate Professor in the Department of Kinesiology & Physical Education at McGill University in Montreal, Canada. His primary area of research examines the knowledge, leadership skills, and behaviors employed by both elite and youth sport coaches that create a positive environment for excellence and participation in sports. This often involves strategies employed by coaches in terms of leadership, coaching style, and team building techniques. Dr. Bloom consults with coaches and sport organizations at the University, Olympic, and professional levels and serves as a youth sport coach in his community.

William R. Falcao

McGill University. Montreal, Quebec. Canada.

Mr. William Falcao is a doctoral student in the Department of Kinesiology & Physical Education at McGill University. The goal of his research is to teach coaches how to promote the psychosocial development of their athletes through sport. This is accomplished through a coach training protocol that fosters the personal development, health, and well-being of young athletes. Will is also the mental training consultant for the McGill men's soccer team, a part-time teacher at a local college, and a college women's basketball coach.

Jeffrey G. Caron

McGill University. Montreal, Quebec. Canada.

Mr. Jeffrey Caron is a doctoral candidate in the Department of Kinesiology & Physical Education at McGill University. Jeff's research is focused on identifying the ways to foster a positive learning environment in sport that encourages people to exercise and remain physically active throughout their lives. Jeff is also the mental training consultant for the McGill men's and women's varsity swim teams, as well as various local high school teams.

Chapter 7

Harold Riemer
Faculty of Kinesiology and Health Studies. University of Regina. Canada.
KHS.Dean@uregina.ca

Harold Riemer is the Dean of the Faculty of Kinesiology and Health Studies at the University of Regina. He received his Ph.D. from the Ohio State University. His research and teaching interests are connected to leadership, motivation, and satisfaction in a sport context. He has been involved in coaching for over 25 years.

Sebastian Harenberg
Faculty of Kinesiology and Health Studies. University of Regina. Canada.

Sebastian Harenberg is a Ph.D. candidate in the Faculty of Kinesiology and Health Studies at the University of Regina. He received his undergraduate and Masters degree from Göttingen University (Germany). His current research focuses on competitive processes within interdependent sport teams and their connection to team dynamics. Sebastian is also an assistant coach for the University of Regina women's soccer team.

INDEX

G

H

I

N

O

P

Q

R

S

T

U